WITHDRAWN

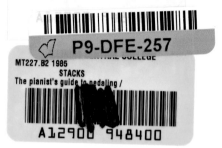

THE PIANIST'S GUIDE TO PEDALING

Contributors

Dean Elder

Mark Hansen

Maurice Hinson

William S. Newman

THE PIANIST'S GUIDE TO
PEDALING

Joseph Banowetz

INDIANA UNIVERSITY PRESS / *Bloomington*

For Alton Chung Ming Chan

Manufactured in the United States of America

Library of Congress Cataloging in Publication Data

Banowetz, Joseph.
  The pianist's guide to pedaling.

  Bibliography: p.
  Includes index.
  1. Piano—Instruction and study—Pedaling. I. Title.
MT227.B2 1984   786.3'5   84–47534
ISBN 0–253–34494–8

1·2 3 4 5 89 88 87 86 85

CONTENTS

Preface

Anyone writing about pedaling takes the proverbial tiger by the tail, for no facet of piano playing is so personal or so much at the mercy of ever-shifting performance conditions—the instrument being played, the acoustics of the hall, and the inevitable moment-by-moment reactions of the performer. And, of course, no aspect of piano playing is so controversial. Pedaling has suffered grossly from both ignorance and neglect. Except for a handful of books in English entirely devoted to the subject, it is generally discussed in a piecemeal fashion—when it is discussed at all.

Often the printed score is of questionable help in solving pedaling difficulties. Even when pedaling indications by the composer are included, they are frequently incomplete, haphazard, or inconsistent, and when followed literally they may lead to puzzling or even chaotic results. Furthermore, well-intentioned editors usually compound the problem.

To achieve artistry in pedaling, the performer must first gain some command of basic pedaling techniques. Just as technical approaches to octaves, scales, trills, and the like should be methodically analyzed and mastered some time during the performer's apprenticeship, so should the uses of the pedals receive similar scrutiny. But to stop with mastery of pedaling technique itself would be crippling, for the art of pedaling should be understood in a wider context, as it applies to different compositional and performance styles. Pedaling, perhaps even more than keyboard technique, is intimately allied to stylistic considerations. An understanding of pedaling technique itself, no matter how comprehensive and thorough, will be of limited use if it is not reinforced with an understanding of the particular composer's idiomatic treatment of the pedals.

With that goal in mind, this volume attempts to give an extensive presentation of pedaling techniques and to relate these techniques to the works of representative composers of the eighteenth, nineteenth, and twentieth centuries. Certain problems are inevitable when attempting a project of this sort. What about earlier composers (such as J. S. Bach, Handel, and D. Scarlatti), whose keyboard music was written for instruments other than the piano? How should we approach the music of composers (such as Haydn and Mozart) who left hardly any pedaling marks or whose pedaling indications (like Beethoven's) are incomplete or highly controversial? And how shall we resolve the question of today's piano versus the piano of an earlier era? Although Haydn, Mozart, and Beethoven wrote a good part of their keyboard scores for the piano, the instruments of their time were rapidly evolving toward today's instrument. How far can the pedaling concepts of their time be applied in our own century?

Even in the piano works of the nineteenth-century Romantic composers, where authentic pedaling indications are more frequent, they are usually inconsistent. Moreover, the present-day player needs to reconcile the old so-called rhythmic form of pedaling notation with today's universally used *legato* pedaling technique. A further problem arises when playing music of the twentieth century. Composers closer to our time tend to "cop-out" in regard to pedaling indications, as is the case with Debussy and Ravel, whose scores are almost bare of directions for pedaling.

No one book can possibly exhaust the subject of pedaling, and it would be foolish to claim such a distinction for the present text. Because of space limitations, only a few representative mainstream composers could be chosen for detailed discussions of pedaling as it relates to their styles. Readers will undoubtedly decry the omission of this or that person—such staples of the piano repertory as Schubert, Mendelssohn, Brahms, Bartók, and Prokofiev, to say nothing of many other nineteenth- and twentieth-century figures of importance. To compensate in part, chapters 2, 3, and 4, on pedaling techniques, contain a wide selection of musical examples taken from the works of many different composers of the eighteenth, nineteenth, and twentieth centuries.

Each composer's own authentic pedaling directions have been used as a foundation for understanding his idiomatic uses of pedal—to the degree that such indications exist. In the cases of J. S. Bach, Haydn, and Mozart, opinions on pedaling are given, always taking into account the problems of performing their compositions on today's vastly different instruments. Beethoven will remain both an enigma and a hot subject of controversy, since some will feel that his surprisingly numerous, often muddy-sounding pedaling indications should be obeyed literally or at least attempted. Others will disagree and opt for a "cleaner" sonority. William Newman's highly illuminating discussion in chapter 7 emphasizes the need to be aware of Beethoven's original pedaling signs and to use them to achieve a better understanding of his style.

Even later nineteenth-century pianist-composers, such as Chopin, Liszt, and Schumann, present grave problems for the performer who will not settle for less than stylistically correct pedaling in their music. Such realizations must take into account all the original pedaling directions left by these composers and use these indications as much as possible in reaching an understanding of their respective styles of pedaling.

In chapter 9, Maurice Hinson goes back to Chopin's manuscripts to examine the composer's own pedaling directions. Some results of this investigation have startling implications for the pianist open to a more imaginative sound concept in Chopin's pedaling. Chapters 10 and 11, devoted to Schumann and Liszt respectively, reveal that both men were extremely innovative in their use of the pedals, indeed much more so than altered later editions of their music would often indicate. As with Hinson's conclusions in the case of Chopin, it is hoped that the performer will find these personalized usages of value both as applied to the specific examples cited and as a stylistic guide to performing similar passages for which the composers have left no pedaling marks.

Performers seeking to arrive at pedaling solely through the printed page will encounter insurmountable problems in the music of Debussy and Ravel. Their scores are almost devoid of pedaling indications, and the few that exist are often sketchy and vague. For this reason, chapter 13 takes a new approach and attempts to understand pedaling in Debussy and Ravel through an examination of the way a master pianist performed and taught their music. There has been no greater interpreter of the piano music of these two composers than the late Walter Gieseking. His pedaling of the Impressionistic style, as analyzed by Dean Elder, who was himself a Gieseking pupil, comes as close as possible to an artistic fulfillment of the complex and highly individualistic pedaling demanded in this music.

The Spanish school of pedaling is touched upon in chapter 12, with Mark Hansen's examination of two relatively obscure pedagogical treatises on pedaling by Granados and his pupil Frank Marshall—the latter, in turn, having taught the great Spanish pianist Alicia de Larrocha. These texts give fascinating glimpses into the teaching methods of these eminent musicians and are further illuminated by de Larrocha's own comments.

Indications for pedaling in printed scores are numerous in form. Those chosen for use in chapters 2, 3, and 4, on the techniques of each of the three pedals are explained early in chapter 2, which is devoted to the damper pedal. In the chapters on individual composers, however, the original pedaling signs of the day for taking the pedal and its release, namely the venerable 𝄢 and ✳, are retained. Although these signs can be hopelessly imprecise at times, any "interpretation" or "clarification" is best left to the performer's judgment rather than to the editor's.

Unless otherwise stated, all musical examples show only the composer's own indications, whether they be marks of expression, dynamics, articulation, phrasing, or tempo. Directions for dynamics or tempi given earlier, but still in force during the excerpt, are shown in parentheses. Time signatures in effect are always added, except in those rare instances when the composer himself omits them.

A word of caution about testing the pedaling techniques: Pianos and acoustics differ radically. The suggestions for pedaling are best tried on a grand piano, preferably seven to nine feet in length. It is always assumed that the example will be played at concert tempo, with the proper articulation, voicing, and dynamics. An alteration of any of these elements will almost invariably render the most carefully chosen pedaling invalid.

All discussion of the *una corda* pedal applies only to a genuine shifting mechanism, not to the left pedal found on spinets and uprights, which merely brings the hammers closer to the strings so as to decrease the striking distance. The middle, or *sostenuto*, pedal is found with consistency only on American-made grands. Many European instruments still do not have this mechanism. Correct regulation is always assumed. Most uprights do not have a true *sostenuto* pedal. Only on some Steinway uprights and on a few of the newer Japanese uprights, does the middle pedal function as a true selective *sostenuto* mechanism available for any of the dampers.

The bibliography is restricted to sources in the English language. Although the number of entries may give the impression that references on pedaling are plentiful, that is somewhat misleading, for many entries are very brief or elementary in content. Only a comparative few show real depth or comprehensiveness, and hardly any relate pedaling to specific musical styles. No attempt has been made to evaluate the references, for what may be virtually self-evident to the experienced performer might prove of great value to the less advanced player.

Pedaling has rightfully been termed "the soul of the piano." Its misuse, either from a technical or a stylistic standpoint, can seriously flaw even the most polished performance. The author fervently hopes that the present text will help to foster a better awareness of both of these elements.

ACKNOWLEDGMENTS

I would like to convey my warm thanks to Messrs. Elder, Hansen, Hinson, and Newman for their invaluable contributions. Their expertise in their respective areas has immeasurably aided in making this project both far richer and more complete. My good friend Maurice Hinson is owed a double debt of gratitude, for without his steady encouragement—and at times prodding and insistent urging—this book would undoubtedly still be in the "planning" stage. Thanks must also go to Morris Martin and Robert Follet of the North Texas State University Music Library. Their help, plus the extensive treasure trove of reference material in this superb library, has enormously facilitated what at first seemed like an endless task. Special gratitude is also due Douglas Taylor, who on several occasions called my attention to obscure materials from his own astonishingly extensive library. I am grateful for the careful reading of the first draft of the early chapters by the eminent concert pianist and member of the Indiana University music faculty James Tocco. His suggestions were of the greatest benefit and help. Also warmly appreciated is the work of my copyist, Robert Keefe, whose artistic hand created the wonderfully clear musical examples. Last, but certainly not least, thanks also should go to my pupils, during whose lessons many of the ideas for this book were conceived. On many occasions they have waited patiently in the midst of a lesson while I jotted down a reference to a passage they had just played, in order to use it as an example.

JOSEPH BANOWETZ
Hong Kong, March 1984

1

The History
of the Piano's Pedals

The historical development of the pedals, which eventually culminated in the three found on most present-day grand pianos, was a complex evolution that spanned more than a 150 years. This aspect of the piano's growth is important not only for its historical interest but also for the performance-practice insights it affords the pianist who wishes to play the music of earlier composers at a high artistic level.

When the first *gravicembalo col piano e forte* was built in Florence by Bartolommeo Cristofori in 1709, in many respects its sound still resembled that of the clavichord and harpsichord. But now, in place of producing the sound with the jacks and quills of the harpsichord or the metal tangents of the clavichord, hammers covered in deer leather were used to strike the strings. By 1726 Cristofori had built about twenty of these instruments. To help withstand the blows from the newly invented hammer action, stronger and larger strings and sounding boards soon began to be installed. Other early pianoforte builders, such as Gottfried Silbermann and Johann Zumpe, quickly expanded and modified Cristofori's original concept. As a result the tone of the early fortepiano began to grow in sonority, and in a few decades the new instrument bore faint resemblance to its earlier identification as a harpsichord with hammers. The fortepiano's phenomenally rapid growth in popularity all over the Continent quickly made both the clavichord and the harpsichord obsolete.

The Damper Activating Mechanisms

The earliest pianos were equipped with hand stops for controlling the dampers. They allowed for some degree of selective dampening, for the performer could raise the dampers at will from either the bass or the treble areas. But hand stops soon proved too cumbersome, since to operate them the player was required to lift his hands from the keyboard momentarily; so knee levers were introduced around 1765 on the pianos made in Germany. Selective divisions of damper activation into both treble and bass groups remained a common feature and were to be found on pianos made until at least 1820. A further refinement of the damper mechanism was introduced in 1777 by Adam Beyer in London. His pianos were equipped with a pedal having a cleft foot, which controlled the treble and bass damper groups individually.

Other refinements of the early foot-controlled pedaling mechanism were quickly adapted in 1783 by John Broadwood in London and the Erard brothers in Paris, then by Johann Stein in Augsburg in 1789. On Broadwood's instruments, Beyer's original concept of divided control over the dampers was retained. By depressing the appropriate half of the cleft pedal, the player could lift all the bass dampers or all the treble dampers (with middle C the dividing line); and by depressing both halves of the pedal simultaneously, he could lift the entire set of dampers off the strings. The Erard instruments of this time could raise the entire set of dampers or the treble dampers alone, but not the bass alone. Split pedals of these general types continued to be built until around 1830; they were then supplanted by the single damper pedal common to today's instruments.

An interesting offshoot of the divided damper mechanism came in the nineteenth century in the form of the *Kunstpedal*. This short-lived mechanism divided the dampers into eight sections controlled by four cleft-footed pedals. Although this expansion into a more refined selective pedaling mechanism would logically seem to have led to the invention of the modern middle *sostenuto* pedal, there is no direct evidence that this was the case.

The damper mechanism itself took various forms during its growth. On the early pianos built in London by Zumpe during the mid-1760s, the dampers consisted of wooden levers that were hinged to the back of the case and placed above the strings. Each damper had a piece of soft leather, which was pressed down on the strings by a spring made of whalebone. When a key was depressed, a rod fitted to the end of the key raised the damper to allow the string to vibrate. Broadwood's instruments, however, utilized an improved dampening mechanism that placed the dampers under the strings. A similar device was later built by the Erard firm in France, which even as late as the end of the nineteenth century continued to choose this form of construction for its damper mechanism. The dampers of the Erard pianos rapidly stopped the sounds of the fundamental and lower partials, yet left a residue of upper harmonics. This effect resembled the dampening found on the early English pianos but was radically different from the rapid dampening effect achieved on the Viennese and German instruments. With the exception of Erard, by the end of the nineteenth century, most piano builders chose to keep the dampers mounted above the strings in their grands, thereby utilizing gravity to help achieve rapid dampening.

The Sound of the Early Piano
Because of differences in both size and material, the sound of the early piano was quite different from that of today's instrument. Construction of the hammer was an important element contributing to this difference. The evolution of the hammer can be roughly divided into three stages. On the earliest instruments through to Mozart's time, the hammers had an inner wood core with a soft, resilient leather covering, usually of deerskin. By the first part of the nineteenth century, hammers were being made entirely of leather layers and were becoming larger. Felt came into use after the 1830s, and although leather continued to be used on some instruments until around 1850, after that time hammers made entirely of felt became the rule.

Alpheus Babcock's invention in 1825 of the continuous cast iron ring piano frame made possible a greater support of tension for the strings. Pianos before this time, with their wooden frames, lighter stringing, and smaller hammers, naturally had much less resonance than today's powerful instruments. But the sound of the early piano had an edge and clarity that are decidedly missing from the more-rounded, less-sharply defined tone of modern instruments. These basic differences in sound must be considered when choosing pedaling for works written during the eighteenth and early nineteenth centuries.

The Pedal Piano
A significant early device was the pedal piano. An independent pedal board added to the piano could produce and sustain an independent line of bass notes and thus bore a relationship to selective dampening. The compass of the early pianos was restricted, and this mechanism provided a tempting means of expanding the number of bass notes. It could double tones played with the fingers, thereby strengthening the relatively weak bass sonority found on the pianos of the day; and notes played by the feet on the pedal board could be held indefinitely, irrespective of what the hands might be playing at the moment. At first, this mechanism required a second set of strings, but in 1815 the Viennese piano builder Josef Brodmann began constructing a self-contained pedal board. Soon the

Erard firm started producing pedal board instruments in which extra strings were no longer necessary. Yet in spite of these refinements, the pedal board was eventually phased out as the modern piano evolved.

Several major composers were associated to some degree with the pedal piano. Mozart had one built around 1784, by either Johann Stein or Anton Walter. The instrument is now lost, and as far as is known, Mozart wrote nothing specifically for it. Both Mendelssohn and Schumann had pedal pianos built in 1843. Although Mendelssohn wrote no specific works for the pedal piano, Schumann composed six Studies, Op. 56, four Sketches, Op. 58, and six Fugues on B-A-C-H, Op. 60, for this instrument. Liszt at one time owned a piano to which a two-manual harmonium and a pedal keyboard had been added. One of the last important nineteenth-century pianists to write extensively for the pedal keyboard was Charles Henri Valentin Morhange (better known as Alkan), who wrote a number of works for it in the early 1870s. Charles Gounod wrote *Fantaisie sur l'hymne national russe* for pedal piano and orchestra in 1886 and a Concertante for the same combination of instruments in 1888.

The Sostenuto *Pedal*

A number of the damper activating mechanisms described above, as well as the pedal piano itself, are related at least in spirit to the *sostenuto* pedal. A true *sostenuto* pedal mechanism, which enabled the player to sustain specific tones without affecting other notes, was first shown at the Paris Exhibition of 1844 by the Marseille firm of Boisselot and Sons. Another *sostenuto* pedal mechanism was built by Alexandre François Debain of Paris in 1860, and a similar invention was brought out by Claude Montal in 1862. But none of these efforts attracted much notice. Finally, Albert Steinway of the American Steinway firm took out a United States patent on the *sostenuto* pedal in 1874. After two subsequent patents covering further details for its use in both grand and upright instruments, the *sostenuto* pedal was given its first public advertisement in 1876. At this time it was called a tone-sustaining pedal. A similar mechanism was patented in France by A. M. Wolff in 1875. Soon the American Steinway firm began to install the new device on its grands and better uprights. Steinway's example was quickly imitated by other American piano builders, but not all piano makers in other countries followed suit. Few European firms added the *sostenuto* pedal to their instruments, regardless of the size of the grand. Even the German-made Steinway instruments, constructed at the firm's Hamburg factory, lacked this pedal on all but the nine-foot concert grands. To this day, in most cases, this pedal is standard equipment only on instruments built in the United States; and in all countries uprights rarely have a true *sostenuto* pedal mechanism.

The Una Corda *Pedal*

As the early pianos grew in volume, builders turned their attention to ways of modifying the tone. Two basic methods were first used to reduce the volume of sound. Probably the earlier was the *pianozug,* or *feu celeste,* which consisted of a thin strip of leather or felt interspersed between the hammers and the strings. The resulting sound had a muted, sweet quality. The second type of pedal mechanism, the *Verschiebung,* was closely related to the so-called soft or *una corda* pedal of today's grand piano. It functioned by shifting the keyboard and hammers to the right so that only one string, instead of two or three, would be struck. Initially introduced by Cristofori in 1726, this mechanism was soon taken up by other piano builders and was quickly incorporated as a standard piece of equipment. On the pianos of the late eighteenth to early nineteenth centuries, the pianist could shift from the normal three-string *(tre corde)* position to one in which either two strings *(due corde)* or only one *(una corda)* would be struck, depending on the depth to which the pedal was pressed. This subtle but important choice does not exist on modern pianos, but was readily available on the earlier instruments. Beethoven refers to this selective degree of shifting in a number of his piano works. In the second movement of Concerto No. 4, he specifies that distinctions of *una corda, due corde,* and *tre corde* be made. Also in the third movement of the Sonata, Op. 106, he asks first for use of the *una corda,* then later requests *poco a poco due ed allora tutte le corde* (gradually two and then all the strings). On today's instruments, such a differentiation is possible only between *due corde* and *tre corde,* not between *una corda* and *due corde.*

Other Pedals on the Early Piano

A large number of early pedal devices for modifying the sound passed in and out of vogue, most of them designed to imitate other instruments. At their worst, these modifications threatened to make the piano into a vulgar musical toy. Turkish music was the rage during the late eighteenth century, and composers attempted to imitate the exotic musical sounds of the Janizary, the military bodyguard attached to Turkish rulers. The Janizary pedal, one of the best known of the early pedal devices, added all kinds of rattling noises to the normal piano performance. It could cause a drumstick to strike the underside of the soundboard, ring bells, shake a rattle, and even create the effect of a cymbal crash by hitting several bass strings with a strip of brass foil. Mozart imitated Turkish Janizary music in the *Allegretto alla turca* movement of his Sonata, K. 331, and in his opera *Die Entführung aus dem Serail,* as did Beethoven in his incidental music to *Die Ruinen von Athen* and the Symphony No. 9.

Another common pedaling device of the day was the so-called bassoon pedal. This mechanism laid a roll of paper and silk over the bass strings, thereby creating a buzzing noise that listeners of the day felt resembled the sound of the bassoon. Yet another mechanism, the so-called *cembalo* stop, pressed leather weights on the strings and modified the sound to make it resemble that of the harpsichord. Even *crescendo* and *decrescendo* pedals, which altered the tone by raising or lowering the lid of the piano or by opening and closing slots in the sides of the case, were constructed to modify the quantity of sound in somewhat the same manner as on the organ. Another short-lived and equally bizarre device forced air across the strings in an attempt to amplify the tone after the hammers had struck them. These and a good number of other novelty pedal mechanisms eventually faded from existence as the piano grew to maturity in the latter part of the nineteenth century, finally leaving as survivors of this tortuous evolution only today's basic three pedals.

PART ONE

Pedaling Techniques

2

The Right Pedal

Pedaling, admittedly, is one of the most difficult aspects of piano playing to discuss from the printed page alone; and few would deny that, to paraphrase an old expression, one performance is worth a thousand words. The pedal is a highly personal part of any piano performance, and no two players will use exactly the same pedaling, nor will the same performer use identical pedaling from performance to performance. Often two artists will use totally different pedalings for the same passage, yet each may succeed in being convincing at the moment. Many factors explain this flexibility. Such diverse and variable elements as tempo, dynamics, tone, articulation, balance of parts, the style and period of a work, the hall, the instrument, and even the very mood of the performer constantly influence the choice of pedaling. Written indications for pedaling, no matter how carefully notated, and even when given by the composer, often demand modification by the performer. The ear alone, rather than a set of printed directions, must always be the final guide for an artistic performance.

Written Directions for Pedaling
Notation and terms for the right pedal can take a bewildering variety of guises, and all too often the composer can be incredibly imprecise or incomplete in his directions. The most common sign for depressing the right pedal is the cumbersome 𝄁𝄁, with the ✱ being used for its release. These signs were used almost exclusively from the late eighteenth century to the early twentieth. Not only are they too large, but too often they are imprecisely placed. In the composer's manuscript, for instance, crowding and space considerations, ledger lines, and haste in writing often result in

these signs being pushed to one side or the other. The situation is then compounded as the music suffers the vagaries of the copyist and imprecise engravers and printers. Even after ascertaining exactly what the composer wrote, the interpreter's task is just beginning, for as will be seen later in this text, different composers use pedal indications in a variety of personalized ways. The task of unraveling what their pedal indications mean as well as deducing what is omitted from the score is a formidable one.

Moreover, during the nineteenth century the majority of pianists evidently did not use what is now termed "*legato* pedaling" until well into the second half of the century. Instead, a pedaling technique termed "rhythmic pedaling" was far more commonly practiced. In this now archaic technique, the pedal was simultaneously depressed *with* a harmony, released an instant *before* the next change of harmony, then again depressed *simultaneously* with the sounding of the following new harmony. In other words, the player kept time with the pedal. Such a method demanded that the performer maintain as much of a *legato* as possible with the fingers. Its advantage, especially in slow *cantabile* passages, was that as each harmony was caught in a new change of pedal it received the maximum amount of sympathetic partials, since the dampers were raised at the moment of hammer impact. In "*legato* pedaling" as it is practiced today, the pedal is released *with,* then re-depressed immediately *after,* each new harmony. The older "rhythmic pedaling" is reflected in much of the original pedaling notation of the nineteenth century. (See Chapter 11 for further discussion of this older style of pedaling.)

The following are some of the common terms indicating the use of the right pedal:

English: damper pedal, loud pedal, open pedal, sustaining pedal, amplifying pedal
French: *avec pédale, la pédale forte, pédale grande, gardez la pédale*
German: *Aushaltepedal, Das Dämpferpedal, Das Dämpfungspedal, Fortezug, Grosses Pedal, mit Pedalgebrauch*
Italian: *col pedale, con pedale, il primo pedale, pedale, pedale del forte, sempre pedale, senza sordini, ped. simile*

Editors and composers are increasingly adopting more precise forms of pedal notation, most of which are virtually self-explanatory. The signs shown in Example 1 are some of the most common. They will be used in this text in musical examples where pedaling is added. In the examples given in the sections devoted to pedaling styles relating to specific composers, the original notation of the period is retained.

Ex. i

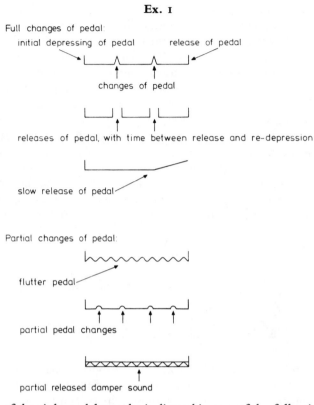

Release of the right pedal may be indicated in any of the following ways:

French: *sec, sans pédale*
German: *kein Pedal, ohne Pedal*
Italian: *con sordini, senza pedale, secco, non ped.*

The Role of the Right Pedal
The right pedal has two primary roles—to prolong and connect tones that
cannot be held by the fingers alone, and to color them. Far too many
pianists regard the first function, that of holding and connecting notes, as
the dominant one. Its second function, that of coloring tones, is at least
of equal significance. All use of the right pedal must be a constant inter-
play of these two elements. In addition to being called the "sustaining"
pedal or "damper" pedal, the right pedal is frequently termed the "loud"
pedal or *forte* pedal, since a note or chord played with the dampers raised
from surrounding strings will actually sound a bit louder than the same

notes played with the dampers in place. But the term "loud" pedal is misleading and decidedly does not describe accurately the real role of the right pedal. For that reason, only the terms "right" pedal and "damper" pedal will be used in this text. Of much greater importance than any slight increase in volume when the dampers are raised is the immediately apparent richer quality of tone. Both result from sympathetic vibrations of partials that are created in the strings surrounding those actually struck by the hammers.

Each tone has an ascending column of partials, and what the ear perceives as a single fundamental note is actually a sum total of many other tones, just as certain colors may be a combination of several other colors. The fundamental tone C, for instance, has the sequence of partials shown in Example 2. The filled-in notes do not exactly correspond to the present-day tempered system of tuning and notation.

Ex. 2

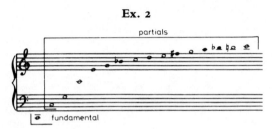

The fundamental C has a frequency of 64 vibrations per second. The frequency of each succeeding upper partial is a multiple of the first partial, in the sequence 2, 3, 4, 5, etc. Therefore, the second C has a frequency of 128 vibrations per second, the G above 192 vibrations per second, and so on (see Example 3). Because of the loudness of the primary sound, the partials cannot be heard clearly. It was only in the mid-nineteenth century that the existence of these additional sounds surrounding a single tone was scientifically demonstrated by the German physicist Hermann von Helmholtz (1821–1894).

Ex. 3

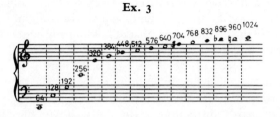

Two simple experiments at the piano will demonstrate the existence of the partials. Slowly depress and hold the second from the lowest C in

Example 3, keeping the damper raised but not letting the hammer strike the string. Then loudly strike the fundamental C (an octave below) and immediately release it. The C that remains silently depressed will be heard vibrating faintly. In the second experiment, strike with a sharp *staccato* middle C and the E, G, and B flat each a third above, while silently holding down the C below middle C. The C that remains held will be heard to vibrate. Even when playing high notes whose strings are not equipped with dampers (approximately the top octave and a half), a use of pedal will allow sympathetic partials to vibrate in the open strings that lie below.

The pedal's role in enriching the tone quality by permitting the activation of a rich conflicting mixture of sympathetic partials is of the greatest importance. It is not too extreme to regard this role of the pedal as equivalent to the vibrato of the singer or the string player. Too many pianists misunderstand and all too often ignore this wonderful tool for achieving an enriched tone color and sonority.

Positioning the Foot

Split-second coordination is often necessary, especially when using quarter-, half-, or three-quarter or vibrato pedaling techniques, or when utilizing partially released damper levels of sound. An incorrect position of the foot will therefore impede the sensitive interaction between foot and hands. Unfortunately for pianists, feet—like hands—come in different sizes, and fashion dictates radically different shoe shapes for men and women. This matter is especially significant when two pedals must be used at the same time by the same foot, as is sometimes done with the middle and left pedals.

For a person with a moderate to large foot, when working the damper pedal, the foot should be placed so that the greatest point of pressure is applied from the juncture point of the toes and foot. Women wearing high heels will need to apply pressure from a point slightly more toward the ball of the foot. If the pedal is depressed with pressure from the full ball of the foot, as is often recommended, there will be more strain and considerably less flexibility because of the higher position of the ankle.

In developing the delicate rapport that must exist between the pedal and the lower part of the foot, the player should have the feeling of using the toes almost as much as the foot itself when using the damper pedal. There must always be a feeling of resistance being applied against the resistance of the pedal itself. Particular care should be taken that the dampers do not slap the strings as the pedal is changed. The heel should never leave the floor. A good exercise is to depress the pedal rapidly and release it slowly, then reverse the procedure. Some pianists find it beneficial to practice in stocking feet, to gain a better sense of rapport between the lower part of the foot and the pedal. One should do so with great caution, particularly if the pedal is stiff or in a high position. Possible strain on the muscles, or even nerve damage, can result. Soft-soled slippers might be a good compromise.

The Downward Journey of the Pedal

An understanding of what happens during the downward journey of the pedal is extremely important to achieving artistic pedaling. During the following discussion, reference will be made only to the use of the damper pedal on a grand piano. On most spinet and upright instruments, the operation and sound modification are of a fairly crude nature, and they render many of the pedaling techniques that are to be discussed fairly meaningless.

The full downward ride of the damper pedal may be divided into four areas, each of which has its own particular significance (see Example 4). Only two of these areas are functionally useful to the pianist. As the pedal is first depressed, it travels a small distance before the dampers begin to rise from the strings. Although this area of free play by the pedal should ideally extend for only about an eighth of an inch of distance, the adjustments on different instruments can vary drastically. On some pianos the dampers instantly begin to lift once the slightest pressure is applied to the pedal. On others the pedal must be depressed halfway or even more before the dampers begin to leave the strings. This last situation is particularly disconcerting to a performer who is used to playing on an instrument with a properly regulated pedal mechanism. Full awareness of the amount of free play in the pedal is vital in the use of many subtle pedal techniques. The pianist must at all times sense exactly when the dampers first begin to move upward.

As the pedal continues to be depressed beyond the area of free play, the dampers begin to rise from the strings. From this point until the moment when they just clear the surface of all the strings is the next area of the pedal's downward trip. Within this area the pianist will employ such differing pedaling techniques as quarter-, half-, or three-quarter pedaling; flutter pedaling; and partial released damper levels of sound. It is especially important that the instrument be properly regulated so that all the dampers rise at the same rate of speed. This area of the pedal's downward journey is one that is relatively unexplored by most performers.

The next area begins when the dampers finally clear the strings, allowing a full release of tone. At this point all notes may be fully held over and will receive their maximum richness of tone quality, now that the surrounding strings are allowed to vibrate freely with sympathetic partials.

The final area of the pedal's downward journey begins just beyond the point at which the dampers fully leave the strings. In this phase the dampers continue to rise even further from the strings. Like the initial area of free play, this last area is not of use to the performer, except in the negative sense of being able to recognize its boundaries when using subtle and often rapid pedaling.

Ex. 4

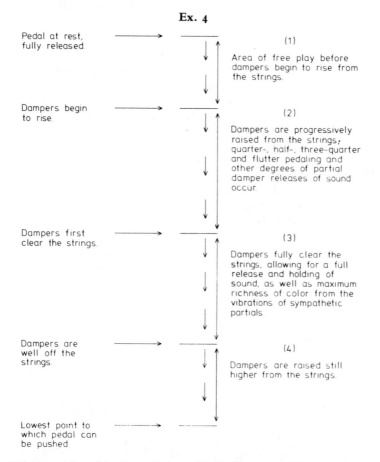

Pedal at rest, fully released

(1)
Area of free play before dampers begin to rise from the strings.

Dampers begin to rise

(2)
Dampers are progressively raised from the strings; quarter-, half-, three-quarter and flutter pedaling and other degrees of partial damper releases of sound occur.

Dampers first clear the strings

(3)
Dampers fully clear the strings, allowing for a full release and holding of sound, as well as maximum richness of color from the vibrations of sympathetic partials.

Dampers are well off the strings

(4)
Dampers are raised still higher from the strings.

Lowest point to which pedal can be pushed

To get an idea of the boundaries of these four areas, slowly depress the damper pedal while standing, so you can watch the action of the dampers. Test chords with the pedal, seeing (and hearing!) at what point tones initially begin to be caught by the pedal, then begin to be released, etc. With increased experience a player develops a sixth sense that quickly locates the exact boundaries of the four pedaling areas on an unfamiliar instrument. The pedal need not be brought all the way to the top to achieve a clear change of sound. Allowing it to rise fully may cause an annoying thud when the pedal hits the wooden framework supporting the pedals. Some pianists have the habit of jerking the foot to the right when a clean change of pedal is required, in a sort of twisting motion from the heel. This ugly gesture is completely unnecessary and should not be used even as a crutch in teaching, no matter how desperate a teacher may become with a pupil whose pedaling is muddy.

LEGATO PEDALING

Legato pedaling is also called "syncopated" pedaling or, infrequently, "following" pedaling. It is the most commonly used pedal technique. Its simplest application occurs when two tones or chords are to be connected with a seamless, unblurred *legato*. When a clean change of pedal is desired, with no carry-over from the old harmony and no hole in the sound, the following steps are necessary:

1. Play, then catch the first chord with the pedal.
2. As the next chord is then played, lift the pedal.
3. Listen to the sound of the new chord. The dampers should have stopped the sound of the old harmony at the instant the hammers again struck the strings.
4. As the fingers continue to hold the keys, re-depress the pedal. Listen again, to be certain none of the old harmony is carried over in the new change of pedal.
5. Repeat the procedure for each new chord.

These five steps may be tested in the first movement of Beethoven's Sonata, Op. 53, shown in Example 5.

Ex. 5

The amount of time between the lifting and re-depressing of the pedal in *legato* pedaling allows for a great variety of coloring. Identical *legato* connections of chords may be obtained if the pedal is changed in any of the following approximate rhythms, but the richness of surrounding partials will be progressively cut down as the pedal is released for longer periods between each pedal change. A decision on the pedaling will depend on the performer's own desire for color in a given passage. In Example 6, from Beethoven's *Variations on a Waltz Theme by Diabelli,* the changes of pedal could take the form of any of the approximate rhythms shown or anything between.

Ex. 6

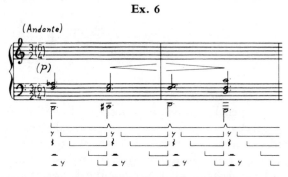

During passages having slightly faster chord changes and overlapping repeated notes that demand a smooth *legato* sound, it is particularly important that as much connection as possible be done with the fingers themselves. In Example 7, *legato* pedaling not only serves as an aid in connecting the notes themselves but also enriches the tone quality. This passage from Beethoven's Sonata, Op. 10, No. 1, will pitilessly expose either bad pedaling or a faulty *legato.*

Ex. 7

Legatissimo *Pedaling*

Legatissimo pedaling effects are often needed in passages requiring a special color or atmospheric sonority. Used properly, *legatissimo* pedaling can create the effect of one harmony growing from another and will minimize sharp attacks and breaks in the sound. In Example 8, a *legatissimo* pedaling technique used properly in the fourth movement of Scriabin's Sonata No. 1, Op. 6, helps create the illusion of a hushed choir of voices. Changes

of pedal should come just after each new harmony. The resulting brief
atmospheric blur and haze of sound should never be permitted to become
extreme.

Ex. 8

Legato *Pedaling in a Low Register*

Legato changes of pedal with low bass notes are frequently mishandled,
and muddy pedal changes occur, even on commercial recordings of inter-
nationally recognized artists. Part of a low bass harmony is sometimes
accidentally held over into the following harmony and clashes with it. To
ensure that such pedal changes will be clean, the dampers must be allowed
to rest on the strings long enough to stop completely the ringing of the
preceding harmony. This is especially important when playing on a
seven-foot or full concert grand piano, where the more powerful lower
strings require a significant amount of time to be fully dampened. To test
this, play an octave or a single note within the lowest two octaves of the
keyboard with a *fortissimo staccato* touch without pedal and wait to hear
how long it takes for the sound to stop. Now depress the pedal, immediately play the same note or octave with a *fortissimo staccato* touch, and
quickly release the pedal. The time needed for the dampers to stop both
the actual notes played and to dampen the ringing of sympathetic partials
will be even longer than in the first instance.

When pedaling a low bass change, the pedal must not be re-depressed
until the ear plainly hears a clear sonority after the new bass tone or
harmony has been sounded. Training the ear to listen for this clarity of
sound is of the greatest importance, for the time it takes for the dampers
to achieve a clean change will vary from instrument to instrument. It is
never enough simply to leave the pedal up for an approximate length of
time and then re-depress it, hoping for a clean pedal change. In Example
9, from the Brahms Scherzo, Op. 4, delayed pedal changes are necessary
if clarity is to be achieved.

Achieving similar clear *legato* pedal changes becomes more difficult
the faster the tempo and the more rapidly the hand must move to the next

Ex. 9

group of notes. In the passage from the Chopin Ballade, Op. 23, shown in Example 10, the speed is such that it is just possible for the performer to hold on to each bass downbeat octave long enough to achieve a clear pedal change. A slight lapse between the release and re-depression of the pedal is necessary, so that the dampers can rest on the strings long enough to stop all the sound of the preceding harmony. During this brief time without pedal, the left hand must hold the downbeat bass octave until the re-depression of the pedal takes place; then it must move rapidly to the next chord to maintain the rhythm.

Ex. 10

Lifting the Pedal Early in Legato *Pedaling*
When it is impossible to hold each new change of bass long enough to ensure a clear change of pedal, a new pedaling approach must be used. In Example 11, from the Chopin Nocturne, Op. 27, No. 1, the pedal must be released a split second before each new change of harmony, then caught again at exactly the moment the new harmony is played. When done properly in tempo, no break in the sound will be evident, since time is needed for the dampers to stop the sound from the old harmony. The ringing from the preceding harmony fills up the slight gap between the pedal release and the new simultaneous key and pedal attack, yet thins out sufficiently to make possible a clear new pedal change. In this example, the pedaling is given by the composer and will create the correct effect if obeyed exactly.

Ex. 11

Similar problems may be seen in Example 12, where even more-rapid changes of pedal are required, both to connect and to color the chords. In this passage, from Chopin's Polonaise, Op. 53, it is especially important to sense at what point the pressure of the foot begins to lift the dampers, as well as to gauge exactly how much further the foot must be pressed before the dampers just clear the strings. Here, pushing the pedal all the way to the bottom and then releasing it completely takes too much time.

Ex. 12

Large Rolled Chords in the Left Hand
When playing large rolled chords in the bass it is often difficult to achieve clarity at each pedal change and to catch the lowest notes of each roll clearly. In Example 13, from Schumann's Phantasie, Op. 17, the rolls should be played rapidly before each right-hand chord, with the right hand being released just as the bottom note of each roll is played. A similar effect of large broken chords occurs later in the same movement (see Example 14). In the notorious skips in the coda, the pedal must be depressed with each sixteenth note, then raised on each rest, so that the sound of the full harmony is retained in each new pedal change.

If all the notes of a left-hand roll can be held until the new pedal change is made, it is usually better to roll the chord before the beat. In Liszt's Etude in F minor (from *Etudes d'exécution transcendante*), shown in

Ex. 13

Ex. 14

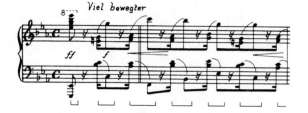

Ex. 15

Example 15, this common type of passage may be seen. The change of pedal should occur on the very top note of each roll.

There may be passages in which it is impractical to release the right hand at the instant the pedal catches the bottom notes of a large rolled left-hand chord. A release of the right hand before each left-hand roll in Example 16, from Schumann's "Eusebius" (from *Carnaval*, Op. 9), would result in a disjointed non-*legato* effect. Here the left hand may be

Ex. 16

rolled *on* the beat. Under no circumstances should the top notes of each left-hand roll be accented, since they fall after the strong pulse formed by each beat.

The rhythm of each left-hand rolled chord could be played approximately as either: or: . The right-hand melody should remain flexible and free. Some performers use this approach of rolling the chords *on* the beat in the opening of the second movement of the Schumann Phantasie, Op. 17, illustrated in Example 13. This solution does not seem totally satisfactory, since it weakens the rhythm by having the top notes of the rolls fall on an extremely weak part of the beat. The slight breaks in the right hand, when played in tempo and with the correct dynamics, will not be noticeable.

Large Rolled Chords in the Right Hand
Large rolled chords may also occur in the right hand. If all the notes in the roll can be held until the new pedal change, as was seen in Example 15, it is usually better to play the roll *before* the beat, with the pedal change coming on the top note of the roll. In Example 17, from the first movement of Brahms's Sonata in F-sharp minor, Op. 2, playing the roll *on* the beat would unnecessarily delay the top C-natural half note and therefore break the rhythmic flow of the melody.

Ex. 17

If all the notes of a broken chord cannot be held until the new change
of pedal on the final note, then beginning the roll *on* the beat may prove
a practical solution. But the player should not follow the often quoted old
rule of subtracting the time value of the rolled notes below from that of
the top melody note. Most listeners invariably hear the emphasized top
melody note as falling on the beat, even when its actual arrival is slightly
delayed. Subtracting the time value of the preceding roll will make the
melody note seem too short. In Example 18, from the Chopin Barcarolle,
Op. 60, begin the large rolled chord *on* the beat, playing the right hand
D sharp simultaneously with the F-sharp octave in the left hand, then
rapidly continue the roll to the top. Under no circumstances take a new
change of pedal on the top G sharp, but rather make certain a clear new
pedaling is begun as the F-sharp octave and D sharp are played. Here a
slight stretching of the rhythm is necessary, to accommodate the rolled
notes and to allow the top G sharp its full eighth-note value.

Ex. 18

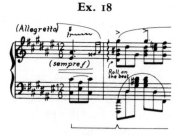

A similar passage occurs in Example 19, from the Chopin Prélude,
Op. 28, No. 13. Each chord should be played unaccented and simultaneously with the low bass notes that fall on each half of the bar; then each
melody note should be played immediately afterward. The small curved
lines between the top two notes of each chord are Chopin's manner of
indicating that a slight break should occur at this point.

Ex. 19

In Menotti's *Ricercare and Toccata on a Theme from "The Old Maid and the Thief,"* shown in Example 20, the right-hand rolled chords must be played *on* the beat, since the melody lies in the lowest note of each roll.

Ex. 20

FINGER PEDALING

One of the most useful aids to conventional *legato* pedaling is a technique commonly termed "finger" pedaling. Notes are held through with the fingers during a period when no pedal is used or when the pedal must be changed frequently. With such holding-over of notes, the player can give the illusion of having utilized longer stretches of unbroken pedaling.

Maintaining an Unbroken Accompanimental Texture
Finger pedaling is commonly used to avoid breaks in the overall sonority of an accompanimental figuration as the pedal is changed at frequent places in the melody. It is often needed at the resolution of a dissonance over an unchanging harmony, as may be seen in Example 21, from "Un sospiro" (from Liszt's *Trois Etudes de concert*).

Ex. 21

In Example 22 there may be seen a more extended, complex use of finger pedaling. Here, in Chopin's Nocturne, Op. 27, No. 1, a careful holding-over of notes in the left hand prevents gaps in the sound fabric of the accompaniment yet permits necessary changes of pedal in the

melodic material above. The low C sharps act as an important harmonically supportive pedal point during the first five and a half bars.
Each C sharp should be held with the finger until the next change of
pedal.

Ex. 22

Finger Pedaling by Silently Re-depressing Notes

Notes in a supporting harmony that cannot be reached by the hand may
still need to be held by finger pedaling. In such cases, notes can be
re-depressed silently after they are first played, then caught in a new
change of pedal. In doing this variety of finger pedaling, care should
always be taken that the keys are not re-depressed too rapidly, to avoid
a second sounding of the notes. When silently re-depressing a note, it is
not necessary to push the key all the way to the key bed. Depress it only
until a slight resistence is felt. This resistence occurs about an eighth of an
inch before the key reaches the bottom. Pushing the key to this point
allows the damper to be fully raised and held, yet avoids an unwelcome
faint restriking of the hammer. An excellent opportunity for this pedaling
technique occurs in the first movement of Brahms's Sonata, Op. 5, as
shown in Example 23.

Ex. 23

Another illustration of this technique may be seen in Example 24, from Schumann's "Eusebius" (from *Carnaval*, Op. 9). Although half-pedaling can be used here, both the slowing of the tempo and the downward direction of the melody make a use of finger pedaling more feasible for controlling the balance of bass and melody.

Ex. 24

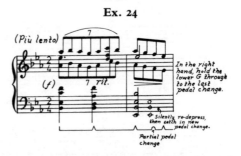

In Example 25, from Debussy's "La cathédrale engloutie," the rests at the end of each bar may be pointed out by silently re-depressing the downbeat chords. The pedal should be changed on the final quarter beat, thereby allowing each re-held downbeat chord to be heard alone again at the end of the bar. There does not have to be a change of pedal on each downbeat once this pattern is begun, since all the dotted whole-note chords are the same.

Ex. 25

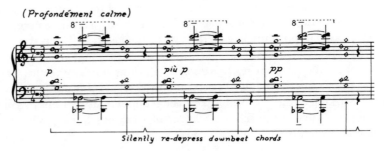

Silently re-depress downbeat chords

Finger Pedaling Indicated by the Composer
A composer may indicate finger pedaling by writing longer-valued notes, as in Example 26, from the Chopin Nocturne, Op. 48, No. 2.

Longer-valued notes in an accompanimental figuration may denote not only that finger pedaling is to be used but also that these notes should receive greater dynamic emphasis. In Example 27, from the second movement of Chopin's Concerto, Op. 11, the half notes in the left hand

Ex. 26

Ex. 27

should be held for their full duration and lightly emphasized for harmonic
support.

Finger Pedaling in Alberti Bass Figurations
So-called Alberti bass and other broken-chord figurations can often
benefit from finger pedaling. The degree to which the notes are held over
will depend on the character of the passage itself, as well as on the style
of the composition. The lively tempo, vivacious mood, and classical
flavor would probably preclude the use of finger pedaling in the passage
in Example 28, from the first movement of Beethoven's Sonata, Op. 31,
No. 3.

Ex. 28

In a passage of more moderate tempo, with a melodic line that has
some variety of articulation, some degree of finger pedaling may be
desirable, as in Example 29, from the first movement of Haydn's Sonata
in D major, Hob. XVI/51.

A slow, lyrical passage may demand a full *legatissimo* touch to give the
desired effect of full pedal. In Example 30, from the second movement of
Mozart's Sonata in F major, K. 300k, little, if any, pedaling can be used

Ex. 29

Ex. 30

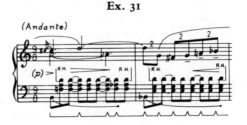

in the melodic material. Finger pedaling is necessary for the Alberti figuration in the left hand in order to avoid excessive dryness in this warmly expressive lyrical passage.

Redistributing Notes between the Hands

A redistribution of notes between the hands may in some instances facilitate an effective use of finger pedaling, as in Example 31, from Grieg's Notturno, Op. 54, No. 4. Here, taking the D's with the right hand makes it possible for the left hand to hold the downbeat bass notes through the entire bar.

Ex. 31

Harmonic Outline

In making use of finger pedaling techniques, it is always necessary for the player to understand the function of the harmony. In Example 32, an improper analysis of the harmony could lead to a bad choice of finger pedaling, with a resulting improper blending of harmonies. In this passage from Chopin's Ballade in G minor, Op. 23, the left-hand quarter note on the third beat of each measure must not be carried over into the next part of the bar.

Ex. 32

Finger Pedaling to Sound Sympathetic Partials

Some twentieth-century composers utilize the sounding of sympathetic partials for special effects. This interesting technique may be seen in Example 33, from the *Klavierstück,* Op. 11, No. 1, by Schoenberg, where the composer asks the player to keep the right-hand chord silently depressed. Note that Schoenberg also asks for this passage to be played *ohne Ped.* (without pedal). Example 34, from Copland's *Piano Variations,* also uses this technique.

Ex. 33

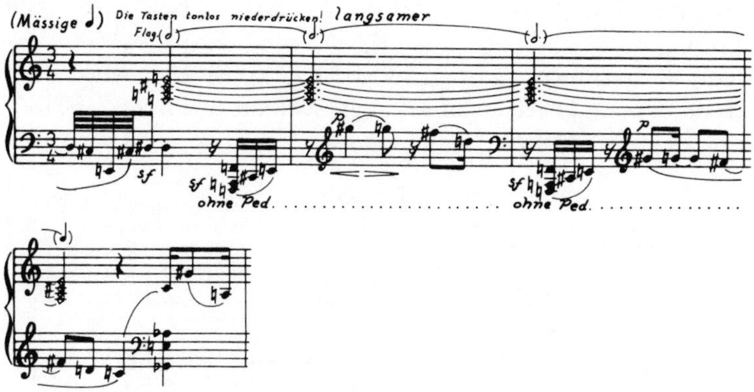

Ex. 34

PEDALING MELODIC MATERIAL

Melodic direction, tempo, dynamic level, surrounding accompanimental figuration, harmony, articulation, phrasing, and style are all factors that influence the choice of a pedaling for a particular melody. Often one element may be in momentary conflict with another, so that a decision must be made as to which one deserves the stronger consideration. Although there are many exceptions to any "rules" that can be formulated regarding pedaling in melodic material, some general guidelines may be useful.

Pedaling an Unaccompanied Melody
When a single-note *legato* melody in a passage of slow-to-moderate tempo stands alone, without surrounding accompaniment, it is usually desirable to pedal at least the longer notes for color, to keep the sound from being too dry. In Example 35, from Liszt's "Les jeux d'eaux à la Villa d'Este" (from *Troisième Année de Pèlerinage*), the desired *legato* touch can be produced by the fingers alone, but the tone will not have the richness that the pedal can provide. In this passage, a sudden change of color to a dry sound from the previously heavily pedaled bars would not be appropriate.

Tempo, dynamics, and register must be considered when deciding which notes in an unaccompanied *legato* melodic line have to be individually pedaled. In Example 35, the sonority of the register is fairly rich and

Ex. 35

the tempo is slow enough to permit pedaling on each different note. But melodic material that moves more rapidly may sound well with longer stretches of pedal, especially if the register is not too low or the dynamic level is not too great. In Example 36, from the Chopin Mazurka, Op. 67, No. 2, the speed, dynamic level, and register allow a change of pedal only once per beat. The *Cantabile* indication implies a moderate tempo.

Ex. 36

Pedaling a Melody with Accompaniment

When a melody has an accompanimental figuration, the choice of a suitable pedaling is more complex, and one element must be weighed against another. Many times a trade-off may have to be made; for instance, some clarity in the melodic line may have to be sacrificed to maintain harmonic support through use of pedal. Voicing and balance of all elements of the musical fabric are important, and only the broadest of guidelines can be given in this area of pedaling. The pianist must learn to rely on his own (cultivated) instincts and, above all, on his ears.

Upward-Moving Melodies with Accompaniment

An upward-moving melody that lies in a middle-to-high register can as a general rule take longer stretches of pedal than can a downward-moving melody. This, of course, assumes that the overall harmony of the melody and the accompaniment will blend. In Example 37, all these conditions are satisfactorily met in a passage from Schubert's Impromptu, Op. 90, No. 3. This upward-moving passage sounds well with longer pedaling because of the *crescendo*.

Ex. 37

But a change of register in otherwise similar melodic material may require more frequent pedal changes, to make clear separate chord inversions and to keep the sound from accumulating excessively. Such a passage may be seen in Example 38, from the fourth movement of Beethoven's Sonata, Op. 2, No. 3.

Ex. 38

In Example 39, a later passage from the same movement, a thicker texture and a lower register still make frequent pedal changes necessary, even though the melodic material continues to move in an upward direction.

Ex. 39

A *decrescendo* in an upward-moving melody also may necessitate a lighter use of the pedal, as in Example 40, from Chopin's Barcarolle, Op. 60.

Ex. 40

Downward-Moving Melodies with Accompaniment
A slow melody moving downward usually requires changes of pedal on every note, especially if the notes of the accompaniment are fairly static

and can be held with the fingers. In the excerpt from Schumann's *Etudes symphoniques* shown in Example 41, a separate pedal must be taken with each melody note to avoid having them sound as though they are part of the harmony.

Ex. 41

In Example 42, from the second movement of Beethoven's Sonata, Op. 2, No. 2, the composer carefully thins the texture beneath the melody by removing part of the left-hand chord on the second beat.

Ex. 42

The direction of the writing often makes it necessary for the performer to treat the pedaling of melodic material quite differently from bar to bar, as in Example 43, from Schumann's "Abschied" (from *Waldszenen,* Op. 82).

Ex. 43

There are exceptions to pedaling each note of a downward-moving melody. In Example 44, a strong bass support must be furnished by the accompaniment, with the lowest B flats acting as a pedal point. It is therefore necessary to maintain a relatively unbroken fabric of sound

throughout each change of harmony in the left hand. Since the tempo in
Chopin's Nocturne, Op. 9, No. 1, is moderate and the register of the
right hand is fairly high, there will be only slight blurring of the
downward-moving parts of the melody.

Ex. 44

Diatonically Moving Melodies with Accompaniment
Even in a melody moving diatonically in an upward or downward direction, a strong supporting accompaniment figuration will often allow a
liberal use of pedal, as long as major changes of harmony are clearly
delineated and supported by the pedal. Chopin's Nocturne, Op. 48, No.
2, as shown in Example 45, has many examples of this type of pedaling.

Ex. 45

To the listener, the actual amount of dissonance involved in a longer
stretch of pedal may not be as important as the time it is given to be
absorbed into the listener's consciousness. If Example 46, from the second movement of the Brahms Concerto No. 1, were to be played *allegretto*, the pedal would only need to be changed on each beat, rather than
with each eighth note of the melody. The correct pedaling is shown here.

Ex. 46

Nonharmonic Tones in a Melody

When rapid nonharmonic tones come before a longer note in a melodic line, usually they should not be held in the same pedal. This particular problem occurs in much of Chopin's music, since most of his *appoggiaturas* should be played *on* the beat. In Example 47, the *appoggiatura* (written as ♪) in his Ballade, Op. 38, should not be retained in the following change of pedal.

Ex. 47

Longer groups of nonharmonic tones present the same problem, as seen in Chopin's Nocturne, Op. 37, No. 1, in Example 48. Here, the player should avoid catching the small notes in the change of pedal on the third beat.

Ex. 48

Ornaments in a Melody

Starts of trills that contain notes other than the two in the trill itself must be carefully pedaled to avoid catching these unwanted tones. In the Chopin Ballade, Op. 47, as shown in Example 49, F and G flat represent the opening notes of the trill and are played on the beat. The player should

Ex. 49

avoid catching the F in the pedal. Chopin assumes that the trill starts on
the upper note, A flat, and therefore the G flat should not be repeated.

Rapid, unmeasured trills, as in Example 49, usually benefit from a
plentiful use of pedal. But a transparent, lighter-textured trill may demand little or no pedal, to keep the sound from accumulating too rapidly
or becoming muddy. Example 50, from the first movement of Mozart's
Sonata, K. 570, should not receive an extended use of pedal.

Ex. 50

Inverted mordents, indicated by a sign or written-out in small notes,
should be pedaled so that only the last note of the ornament is caught by
the pedal. Many of these occur in the music of Chopin. A typical instance
may be seen in Example 51, from his Etude, Op. 25, No. 10.

Ex. 51

A turn, whether written as a sign or in small notes, may often be held
through in a longer pedal, provided the notes of the turn are not played
loudly and that they come on a weak, unaccented part of the beat. This
ornament also appears frequently in Chopin, and may be seen in Example
52, from the Nocturne, Op. 48, No. 2.

Ex. 52

Underplaying Nonharmonic Tones to Minimize Blurring
A nonharmonic tone may have to receive less emphasis, so that in a long
pedal it can blend more smoothly into the prevailing harmony. In Example 53, from the third movement of Brahms's Sonata, Op. 2, all notes not
belonging to the basic D–F sharp–A harmony should be slightly underplayed. The pedaling is the composer's.

Ex. 53

In Example 54, from the Chopin Prélude, Op. 28, No. 17, the D flat
should not be emphasized. The pedaling is Chopin's own.

Ex. 54

Avoiding Breaks in a Legato *Melody*
Frequently it is better to connect a pair of repeated notes in a melody with
the pedal than with the fingers. To achieve an unpedaled one-note *legato*
connection, one would not let the key come completely to the surface
before re-depressing it. In Example 55, from the first movement of
Sonata in B-flat major, Op. Posth., of Schubert, the pedal is needed both
for connecting the repeated notes and for color.

Ex. 55

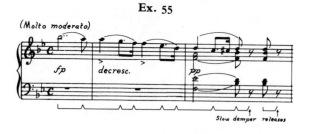

Connecting a Technically Awkward Passage

The pedal may be used to connect a technically awkward passage in a
melody, as in Example 56. In this excerpt from the second movement of
Beethoven's Sonata, Op. 2, No. 3, it would be extremely difficult to
achieve a perfect *legato* without use of the pedal, unless the player has a
large span. The fingering has been added.

Ex. 56

Connecting a Melody Played over a Large Roll

Special effort must often be taken to prevent breaking the melodic line
when pedaling a roll that comes before the beat. In Example 57, from
Schumann's "Träumerei" (from *Kinderszenen*), the first right-hand F in
the second bar must be held and not repeated until the left-hand B flat is
played and caught in the pedal.

Ex. 57

Many cadence points have rolled chords underneath a *legato* repeated
note in the melody and require this same care in maintaining a finger
legato until the new pedal is caught. In Example 58, from Liszt's "Sonetto
104 del Petrarca" (from *Deuxième Année de Pèlerinage*), each top G sharp
of the right hand must be held with the fifth finger until the pedal is
changed with the lowest note of each roll. The dynamic level at this point
should be around *piano*.

In other situations, it may be necessary to release the underlying
harmony a fraction of a second early, while still holding on to the melody
until it is caught in the new pedal. In Example 59, from the Etude, Op.
4, No. 3, of Szymanowski, the melody notes must be caught in the same
pedals as the grace-note octaves in the left hand, in order to avoid no-

Ex. 58

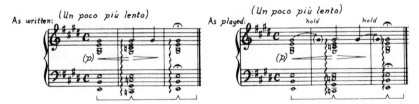

Ex. 59

ticeable breaks in the melodic line. Hold each right-hand octave outlining the melody as each left-hand grace-note octave is played. Release the chordal notes in the middle of the melody octaves just as the pedal catches each left-hand grace note octave. That will minimize blurring. (The right-hand notes to be held over into the new pedal change are marked with small curved lines.)

When it is impractical to connect a melodic line that has a roll beneath it, the pedal should be changed as late as possible during the roll, both to connect the melody and to avoid creating a hole in the sound fabric of the harmony below. In the passage from Schumann's *Papillons* No. 5, Op. 2, shown in Example 60, it is important to catch the lowest of the grace notes in each new pedal. To do so, some small amount of finger pedaling will have to be used while changing the pedal at about the second note of each roll. Schumann gives no dynamic indication. A *piano* would seem appropriate here.

Ex. 60

In other passages it may be necessary to roll a large chord rapidly *on* the beat, to prevent a hole in the melodic line and to ensure as well that all the notes of the chord are clearly caught by each new pedal. Liszt's "Chapelle de Guillaume Tell" (from *Première Année de Pèlerinage*) has a clear example of this type of passage, shown in Example 61. Liszt's own fingering is given. Also see Example 16.

Ex. 61

PEDALING ACCOMPANIMENTAL FIGURATIONS

In properly pedaling a melody, the performer must understand the various components that make up the accompanimental figuration. Relating, integrating, and balancing the melodic and accompanimental elements are vital to achieving artistic pedaling.

The Relationship of Melody, Accompaniment, and Bass Line
Most nineteenth-century piano music has a characteristic keyboard distribution: The melody is usually placed in the treble and played by the right hand, and the accompaniment is given to the left hand. The accompanimental figuration is always supported by some sort of fundamental bass line. Although every pianist knows that primary melodic material should be given dynamic stress, many performers do not clearly separate the accompaniment into distinct areas of emphasis. As a general rule, the underlying bass line should receive more dynamic stress than the accompanimental figuration. A sensitivity to the correct dynamic proportions of these three elements is essential for achieving correct pedaling. Example 62, from Schubert's Impromptu, Op. 142, No. 3, illustrates a typical layout.

In Example 63, from the Prelude and Fugue, Op. 35, No. 1, Mendelssohn places the melody in the middle of the accompaniment. The low E's provide a fundamental bass pedal point and should be lightly stressed, even though they are not marked in longer-valued notes.

Ex. 62

Ex. 63

In Schumann's *Kreisleriana,* shown in Example 64, the melody is placed in the left hand. This time the grace notes provide the supporting bass line and must be clearly caught in the pedals the composer has indicated in the first two bars.

Ex. 64

Example 65, from Variation 9 of Schumann's *Etudes symphoniques,* Op. 13, demonstrates how a bass line must support a rapidly moving accompanimental figuration and two different melodic parts. The low

Ex. 65

32nd notes on each half of the bar must be stressed so they can support
the heavily pedaled haze of accompanimental figuration and diatonically
shifting melodic material above.

Pedaling with Chord Inversions

Within a harmony that remains the same, there must usually be a change
of pedal when the fundamental bass line changes from root position to an
inversion, as in Example 66, from Schubert's Impromptu, Op. 90,
No. 1.

Ex. 66

Stressing the Fundamental Bass Part

A composer will often indicate that a supporting bass line must be
stressed, either by double-stemming notes having the same time values or
by writing notes with longer values. The degree to which such a bass
line is emphasized will affect the choice of pedaling. Example 67, from
the Chopin Scherzo, Op. 31, shows double-stemming of notes with the
same time values; while in Example 68, in the fourth movement of Sonata
in A, Op. Posth., Schubert asks for emphasis in the bass line by writing
notes of longer value.

Ex. 67

Ex. 68

In some instances *staccatos* may indicate light accents in a fundamental
bass line, as in Example 69, from Chopin's Ballade, Op. 52.

Ex. 69

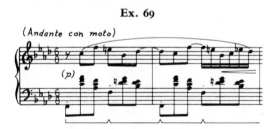

Unbroken Sonority in Accompanimental Figuration
Evenness in touch and color in accompanimental patterns is often dis-
rupted by carelessness in pedaling. A common error is to change the pedal
on the first note of a melody when the harmony in the accompanimental
figuration remains the same. For example, in the Chopin Nocturne, Op.
27, No. 2, shown in Example 70, under no circumstances should the
pedal be changed on the downbeat of the second bar.

Ex. 70

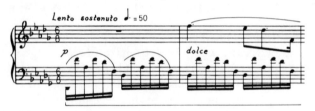

In the Chopin Prélude, Op. 28, No. 4, shown in Example 71, no
break in the sound should occur between any of the left-hand chords as
the pedal is changed to accommodate the melody notes. Nor should there
be a change of tone color when moving from a fully pedaled to a briefly
nonpedaled chord. To avoid such breaks in the sound, the player should
maintain a *legatissimo* touch in the left hand, never letting the fingers leave
the keys or permitting the keys to come all the way to the surface when
they are repeated.

Ex. 71

Example 72 shows the problem of maintaining evenness of texture in a two-against-three rhythm. In this excerpt, from the second movement of Schumann's Sonata, Op. 22, the fingers must carefully hold the chords while the pedal is changed on each octave.

Ex. 72

PEDALING AS AN AID TO PHRASING AND ARTICULATION

Using the pedal imaginatively and artistically when dealing with matters of phrasing and articulation is greatly neglected by many pianists. Here the pedal can be a great help or an extreme hindrance. When handled correctly, it can underline, project, and color a phrase or a slur.

Using the Pedal when Phrasing
Although no performer would wish to make a break in the sound at the conclusion of every phrase, occasional slight breaths in a melodic line can lend variety and musical emphasis to overall phrasing. In Example 73, Schumann's own written phrasing in this excerpt from "Pierrot" (from *Carnaval,* Op. 9) calls for such a breath in the right hand, while the left hand holds the octave until the change of pedal and then moves to the next octave.

Ex. 73

In Example 74, from the third movement of Schumann's Sonata, Op. 14, the changes of both register and harmony justify the use of a slight phrase breath at the end of the first four bars. A breath would not be justified after every eight bars of the entire theme, for that would soon grow stale in its effect.

Ex. 74

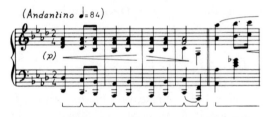

In Example 75, taken from Mendelssohn's *Variations sérieuses,* Op. 54, a breath will sound well at the end of the first four-bar phrase. Another may also be added in the following bar, to set off the unexpected harmonic shift to a C-major chord.

Ex. 75

Clarifying a Tied Note

The last note of a phrase is sometimes tied over to the first note of the next phrase, making necessary a slightly early release of the pedal in the other parts, before the start of the new phrase. Such a break will help to clarify the melody. In Example 76, from the third movement of Schubert's Sonata, Op. 164, there must be a slight break in the sound in the lower parts to enable the tied F to carry through clearly. Since the first four bars are played *forte,* the lower repeated F on the downbeat of the bar after the

Ex. 76

as written: (Allegro vivace)

as played: (Allegro vivace)

fermata will be too loud in relation to the top (tied) F, unless the sound
carrying over from the previous F is lessened by a brief lifting of the
pedal.

Releasing the Pedal Slowly at the End of a Phrase

The slow release of the damper pedal is often desirable when rounding off
the final note or chord of a phrase, or when tapering off the sound of a
chord before a silence. In these instances it is usually helpful to think of
a string player, who permits the sound of a final held note to diminish
gradually as the end of a bow is reached. To accomplish this effect on the
piano, a note or chord can be released slowly by the fingers alone or by
the pedal. The latter allows the dampers to stop the ringing of the strings
gradually, rather than let them fall rapidly so that an abrupt choking of
the sound results. The opening of the Chopin Ballade, Op. 23, provides
opportunities for this kind of shaping of phrase endings, as shown in
Example 77.

Ex. 77

When the final chord of a phrase comes before a silence and must be
colored with the pedal, the sound may be gradually diminished by a slow
release of the pedal. But the fingers must first release the keys. In Example 78, the closing bars of Beethoven's Sonata, Op. 109, the composer
gives an indication for pedal on the third beat. Additional pedaling would
seem necessary for color.

Ex. 78

When the dampers are worn and hardened, there may be an annoying buzzing sound when a slow pedal release is used to round off a phrase. If, for instance, that were the case in Example 78, the following could be done to help minimize this trouble.

1. Play the final chord as before, catching it in the pedal.
2. Keep the keys held down with the fingers.
3. Quickly release the pedal at about the time a slow lifting of pedal would ordinarily take place.
4. Slowly release the notes with the fingers after the pedal has been released.

This procedure cuts out the sympathetic partials immediately before the release of the chord and minimizes any buzzing that will occur as the keys are released slowly by the fingers. It is admittedly a troublesome procedure and at best only a stopgap measure for what is actually the fault of the instrument.

Many of the above pedaling techniques have been used for holding over notes that cannot be held by the fingers or to achieve a *legato*. But in other instances the pedal has been used only for sonority. In some respects this use of the pedal when playing melodic material—to enrich and color the tone quality—remains the most important role of the damper pedal. It is an ever-present possible usage that should never be ignored or taken for granted.

Pedaling Slurs
Pedaling on the first stressed note of a slur can be an effective use of the damper pedal, as shown in Example 79 from *Vision fugitive,* Op. 22, No. 4, of Prokofiev.

Ex. 79

Use of the pedal is especially necessary in Example 80, since the slur in this excerpt from the fourth movement of Beethoven's Sonata, Op. 2, No. 2, cannot be connected by the fingers alone.

Ex. 80

In Example 81, from the second movement of Beethoven's Sonata, Op. 27, No. 1, the pedal should be raised slowly over each three-note slur in order to avoid blocks of sound and to help retain a sense of one single melodic line.

Ex. 81

A lifting of the pedal can be used in Example 82 to help shape and define each slur ending, shown in these bars from Schumann's *Introduzione ed Allegro appassionato,* Op. 92.

Ex. 82

A slow, gradual release of the pedal before a slur ending that comes before a silence can be an especially effective way of helping to shape the sound with the pedal. In Example 83, from Schumann's "Vogel als Prophet" (from *Waldszenen,* Op. 82), a smooth *decrescendo* and a gradual cessation of the sound on the final D will be obtained more easily with a slow lifting of the pedal.

Pedaling a Portato *Touch*
A passage with *portato* articulation indications demands a special use of the pedal. If at all possible, the raised dampers should be released gradu-

Ex. 83

ally at the end of each note to avoid stopping the sound in an abrupt, chopped manner. Done correctly, the effect should be similar to that of a string player tapering off the last note of a phrase as the end of the bow is reached. It is important to release the keys with the fingers just before raising the pedal over the notes demanding this *portato* pedaling. This type of pedaling is especially effective when the *portato* notes occur before rests, as in Example 84, from the first movement of Beethoven's Sonata, Op. 2, No. 2.

Ex. 84

Although there are no rests following the *portato* chords and notes in Example 85, from Beethoven's Variations, Op. 34, the tempo is still slow enough to permit a tapering off of the sound with both the fingers and the pedal.

Ex. 85

Pedaling a Non-legato Touch

Some passages demanding a heavy, slightly detached, non-*legato* touch can benefit from brief touches of pedal. Since there will be an unpedaled area before each key attack, the pedal may be depressed simultaneously with each note or chord. An excellent opportunity to use non-*legato* pedaling occurs in Debussy's Arabesque No. 1, as shown in Example 86.

Ex. 86

Pedaling a Staccato *Touch*

Some loud notes marked with *staccato* signs may need a brief touch of pedal for sonority and color. The *staccato* chords in Example 87, from the third movement of Beethoven's Sonata, Op. 27, No. 2, lend themselves well to this use of the pedal, since there is ample time between the chords.

Ex. 87

Passages with Contrasting *Articulations*

When there are contrasting articulation indications occurring simultaneously, one articulation should not be altered at the expense of another by careless pedaling. This concept is particularly important when playing music from the classic era. Beethoven's piano works, for instance, are filled with passages having many kinds of articulation markings. Example 88, from the second movement of his Sonata, Op. 110, has great complexity in the articulation. Although some pedal is needed to accent slurs, it should be kept to a minimum.

In Example 89, from the second movement of Beethoven's Sonata, Op. 10, No. 2, the contrasting sets of articulation in the two melodic parts in the right hand preclude using the pedal.

When a series of notes without articulation indications are found in a piece that is otherwise carefully supplied with markings, a non-*legato*

Ex. 88

Ex. 89

Ex. 90

touch is usually implied. In example 90, from the first movement of Beethoven's Sonata, Op. 14, No. 1, the repeated eighth notes must not be pedaled. A common error in this passage is to depress the pedal with the last eighth note of the left hand, thereby creating an unintended slur.

In the excerpt from Schumann's *Papillons* No. 1, Op. 2, shown in Example 91, the left-hand downbeats can be given a full *legato* pedal effect if they are held by the finger until just after the pedal is depressed. Then move the hand to the chord on the second beat. That will enable the *staccato* octaves in the right hand to be clearly detached.

Ex. 91

Pedaling through Articulation Indications and Rests

There are many instances when the performer must hold the pedal through *portato, leggiero, staccato,* slur, or rest indications. Many pianists do not realize that a pedaled passage played with a *legato* touch will have a different tone quality from one in which other touches are used, even though the pedal connects the notes equally in all cases. The difference will be in the form of subtle degrees of shading and *rubato* resulting from the variety of touches being used. It cannot be stressed too strongly that the player must obey the articulation indications written by the composer, regardless of the amount of pedaling used. An example of this type of passage is found in Chopin's Nocturne, Op. 9, No. 2, as shown in Example 92. The pedaling, articulation, and fingering are all by the composer. Chopin's markings should probably be interpreted as regular *legato* pedaling taking place at each new change of harmony in the left hand.

Ex. 92

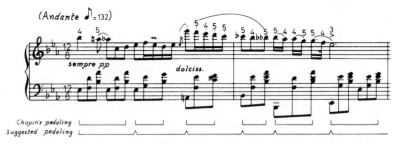

Some works that have many short slurs and rests within the melodic line may still demand fairly long stretches of pedal because of the style and need for extended harmonic support. In these instances the articulation indications must be made apparent by using slight *rubati* and subtle shadings. In Example 93, from Chopin's Nocturne, Op. 27, No. 2, the composer's original pedaling is given, along with a suggested *legato* pedaling.

Ex. 93

Many other composers write passages requiring varying contrasts of articulation within stretches of extended pedal. Example 94 shows how Debussy, in his "Soirée dans Grenade" (from *Estampes*) uses slurs and *staccato, portato,* and *tenuto* indications to show subtle degrees of stress and lightness, all within stretches of pedal that follow the pedal points on each downbeat.

Ex. 94

A careful adherence to articulation indications in a pedaled area will often give a subtle shift to the rhythm, as in Example 95, where Brahms, in a passage from the first movement of his Concerto No. 2, uses slurs to project a hemiola rhythm in the right-hand triplets.

Ex. 95

Carefully following Brahms's articulation indications in the excerpt from the first movement of his Concerto No. 1, shown in Example 96, will give the melody notes marked *staccato* and *portato* a distinctive tone quality and ensure that their phrasing will be unrushed.

Ex. 96

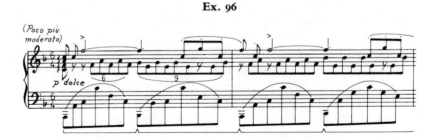

Staccatos may be used to indicate a lightness of touch in accompanimental figurations as a contrast to a rich *cantabile* sound in the melodic material. In Example 97, from Chopin's Nocturne, Op. 55, No. 1, the composer's original pedaling is given. It probably should be interpreted as regular *legato* pedaling, with each change coming on, not before, each half bar.

Ex. 97

USING THE PEDAL TO PROJECT RHYTHM

When handled intelligently and with imagination, the pedal can be a valuable ally when projecting both written and unwritten rhythms. This use is yet another of the varied roles the pedal can play as a coloring tool.

Pedaling Written Accents

The pedal often may be used to color and emphasize a written accent, so long as it does not alter the articulation in another part of the writing. In Example 98, from the first movement of the Beethoven Sonata, Op. 31, No. 2, the pedal does not need to be used to connect but only to accent the *sforzando* chords.

In Example 99, from the first movement of Beethoven's Sonata, Op. 111, the rapid tempo will allow the performer to use only the briefest possible touches of pedal on each *sforzando* accent.

Ex. 98

Ex. 99

In Variation 12 of Mendelssohn's *Variations sérieuses,* shown in Example 100, the pedal acts as a technical aid, for it is understandably difficult for many pianists to produce the additional force necessary to emphasize the *sforzando* accents throughout this difficult variation.

Ex. 100

Pedaling to Accent a Staccato *Sign*
Occasionally a *staccato* sign may be used to indicate an accent. This usage was common in the eighteenth and early nineteenth centuries. The performer must judge from the musical context whether a dot or a wedge-shaped marking signifies a shortening of the note or an accent, or perhaps both at the same time. In Example 101, touches of pedal could be used on each eighth note marked with a *staccato* (accent) indication, even though use of the pedal, in this excerpt from the first movement of Beethoven's Sonata, Op. 13, is not absolutely necessary.

A similar instance occurs in Example 102, from the third movement of Beethoven's Sonata, Op. 14, No. 1. Since this passage calls for a considerably higher dynamic level than in the preceding example, small, exceedingly brief touches of pedal are completely justified.

Ex. 101

Ex. 102

Accent Pedaling

A kind of accent pedaling may be used in passages having an accented, heavy non-*legato* touch. In Example 103, from Schumann's *Papillons* No. 3, Op. 2, the lifting of the dampers should be simultaneous with the sounding of each octave. Then, as the hand is lifted to move on to the next octave, the pedal should also be lifted. There should be an audible break in the sound of about a sixteenth note of time. But caution is advised, for as the player now has the rare luxury of "keeping time" with the pedal, there will be a strong temptation to stamp the foot audibly.

Ex. 103

Pedaling Unwritten Accents

Even when accents are not written by the composer, the pedal can be used to emphasize an appropriate beat or rhythmic pulse. Pieces related to dance forms lend themselves particularly well to this pedaling treatment. In Example 104, Schumann indicates the character of his Novellette in D Major as *Ballmässig* ("dancelike"). The single pedaling indication at the very beginning of the piece is his way of telling the performer to use some pedal.

Ex. 104

The typical mazurka rhythm of Example 105, from Chopin's Mazurka in D Major, Op. 33, No. 2, demands a characteristic accent on the first and third beats.

Ex. 105

Pedal Release as a Form of Accent

A rhythm may be projected not only with an accent on a note but also by a precise, sudden pedal release of a note or chord before a rest. The rest then becomes a kind of "attack" of its own. Loud passages demand special care, for the pedal may actually have to be released a fraction of an instant early, in order to stop the sound precisely on the rest. This type of passage may be clearly seen in Example 106, from the second movement of Beethoven's Sonata, Op. 110.

Ex. 106

A frequent error is to hold the pedal longer on a chord occurring before a long rest, thereby giving it a kind of accent. In the excerpt from

the second movement of the Beethoven Sonata, Op. 109, shown in
Example 107, the sound of each chord must be of exactly the same
duration, yet colored by a quick touch of pedal.

Ex. 107

Pedaling to Project a Syncopated Rhythm

In passages where a syncopated rhythm is difficult to project over an
extended period, the pedal may be used to maintain the feeling of a
regular pulse. In the first movement of Schumann's *Faschingsschwank aus
Wien,* Op. 26, the identical syncopated pattern keeps going for 40 bars.
Although the rhythm remains clear on the printed page, to the listener it
sounds as though each bar line comes one beat earlier. The pedaling
shown in Example 108 will help to project the actual rhythm by giving
a slight swell and change of color in the sound, resulting from the release
of sympathetic partials as the dampers are raised on each downbeat.

Ex. 108

Avoiding Negative Pedaling Accents

Just as a touch of pedal can project an accent, so a sudden absence of pedal
can result in a negative accent. An excellent instance occurs in Example
109, from Chopin's famous Fantaisie-Impromptu, Op. Posth. 66. Here,
the natural temptation is to lift the pedal on the second half of each bar,
to correspond with the change of position of the broken chord in the bass
from root position to first inversion. Changing the pedal a sixteenth note
later tends to minimize the rather heavy effect that would result from
underlining the D sharp if the pedal were changed exactly at the middle
of the bar.

Ex. 109

PEDALING AND DYNAMICS

An artistic use of the damper pedal is closely tied to its relationship to dynamics. This area has been left relatively unexplored by performers, yet it is one in which the opportunities for imaginative uses of the pedal are well-nigh limitless. A systematic introduction to these pedaling techniques is absolutely essential for even the moderately advanced pianist.

Swell Effects on a Single Note or Chord

The damper pedal can in a limited manner be used to make a *crescendo* or *decrescendo* on one note or chord. Although it is impossible to make individual tones louder by means of touch once they have been played, the volume can be increased a little bit with the pedal. This effect is more evident in a recording studio or small recital hall than from the stage of a large concert hall, where many subtle details are often lost.

The next two examples contain original indications by the composers for a swelling of sound on one note. Although both composers were experienced pianists, intimately acquainted with both the capabilities and the limitations of the keyboard, performers may be tempted to attribute these markings to the composers' wishes for orchestral or vocal effects. But that would seem an easy way to avoid the issue. In passages marked with a *crescendo-decrescendo* over one note, a slight swelling of tone can be obtained if the pedal is depressed immediately after playing the note or chord having the swell indication. When the dampers are raised at the instant the pedal is depressed, there will be enough sound left to activate vibrations of partials from surrounding strings, thereby producing a small amplification of the overall sound.

Example 110, from Debussy's "Hommage à Rameau" (from *Images* I), contains an instance of this unusual notation. When the chord having the swell is first played, the dampers should not be raised. Then, about a sixteenth note of time later, the pedal should be depressed quickly.

Ex. 110

In Example 111, from the second movement of Beethoven's Sonata, Op. 14, No. 1, a swelling of tone is even more difficult to achieve, both because of the high register of the writing and because only a single note is to be played. Beethoven evidently intends to convey the idea of an expressive *portamento* slide, as might be done by a singer or a violinist. To help give the desired effect, play the E with a bit more tone than the *pianissimo* dynamic level indicated in the previous bar.

Ex. 111

A well-known indication for a swell on one chord occurs in Schumann's "Paganini," from his *Carnaval*, Op. 9. The treatment of this controversial passage is fully discussed in Chapter 9.

Forte-piano *Effects*

A *forte-piano* indication written for a single long note or chord is usually interpreted as a *forte* attack, with the sound then gradually dying away to a *piano* without further aid from the performer. But this interpretation, especially when heard on a resonant concert instrument, may not allow sufficient time for the sound to decay to a desired lower dynamic level. Several solutions enlisting the aid of the damper pedal are possible. The opening chord of Beethoven's Sonata, Op. 13, can be handled in the following three ways:

1. Play the downbeat tied quarter note chord *forte* and catch it with the fully depressed pedal. Immediately release the keys, but hold the sound with the pedal. Then using the pedal, permit the dampers to touch the strings lightly several times, progressively dampening the sound until the

Ex. 112

desired degree of softness is reached (see Example 112). This brushing of
the dampers on the strings has to be done in an exceedingly careful
manner, in order to avoid an excessive choking of the sound at any given
moment.

2. Play the downbeat tied quarter note chord *forte* and catch it with the
fully depressed pedal. At the instant the chord is played, release the pedal
and raise the fingers from the keys. Now quickly re-depress the notes of
the chord, being careful to depress the keys only far enough to raise the
dampers but not let the hammers audibly strike the strings (see Example
113). This second method creates a much sharper initial accent than the
first one, but it is very risky. It is all too easy to miscalculate these rapid
motions and create a break in the sound between the raising of the pedal
and the re-depressing of the notes with the fingers. As the chord is
retaken, an unwanted repetition of sound will also occur if the keys are
re-depressed a fraction too far.

3. Do not play the chord as a full *forte,* but give considerably less
emphasis to the more full-bodied lower notes. (An identical *forte-piano*
marking is also used over long notes in the orchestra part of Mozart's

Ex. 113

Concerto in D minor, K. 466.[1] It is also mentioned in contemporary pedagogical writings by Johann Quantz[2] and Leopold Mozart,[3] although always in relation to orchestral instruments, not the piano.)

It is not known whether Beethoven actually wished the sudden lessening of sound that can be obtained by either of the first two methods. Certainly at the time the Sonata, Op. 13, was written (1797–98?, first published 1799), this pedaling effect would have been extremely difficult, if not impossible, on most instruments of the day. But at least one major pianist has taken this marking quite literally. Edwin Fischer (1886–1960), who was one of the great Beethoven players of the twentieth century, used this effect on a pre-World War II recording of this work. Since it was made on 78rpm discs, there was no possibility in the recording session of electronic tampering or splicing, as can be done with present-day recordings.[4] Listening to the recording, one cannot tell which of the two methods Fischer used to create the sudden *forte-piano* effect on the opening chord. He wrote later that the orchestral effect of a *forte-piano* should be attempted, since "it is more in accord with the idea of *pathétique*,"[5] but he does not explain how to achieve it on the piano. A later recording by Fischer of the same sonata does not utilize this effect.[6]

Another example of Beethoven's use of a *forte-piano* effect over one note is found in the second movement of his Sonata, Op. 2, No. 3, shown in Example 114. This time the dynamic drop is from a *forte* to a *pianissimo*.

Ex. 114

Schubert also occasionally uses this type of indication, as shown in Example 115, from the fourth movement of his Sonata in B-flat major, Op. Posth.

Ex. 115

Bartók specifically asks for a cutting of the sound on one note in his Sonata for piano, as shown in Example 116. In a footnote he asks the performer to "Muffle the sound suddenly on pedal and key." To do so, the performer must carry out the following two steps: 1. After playing the last beat of the 7/4 bar, immediately release both notes with the fingers; then let the pedal briefly slap the strings to cut the sound down to a *piano*. 2. Re-depress the D without sound, at the same time playing the right-hand *piano* chord on the downbeat of the 6/4 bar; then catch both it and the left-hand D in the pedal.

Ex. 116

Dampening the Sound after a Loud Chord
Even if a composer does not write a *diminuendo* after a strongly accented chord, there are instances where a sudden dampening of the sound may be necessary. In Example 117, from Chopin's Ballade in F major, Op. 38, the composer's own pedaling is given. At the time this work was written (1836–39), most pianos did not have the full resonance of today's concert instruments. If Chopin's original pedaling is used, the first few *pianissimo* repeated notes will be covered. Therefore, it may be necessary to make a half-pedal change as the first A is played.

Ex. 117

Pedaling a Long Crescendo
The pedal can often be of aid in making a large *crescendo* when the same harmony is outlined in rapid figuration, as in Example 118, from the *Klavierstück* in E-flat minor, D. 946, by Schubert.

Ex. 118

Even when a single note is repeated, the pedal can aid greatly in building a *crescendo,* as in Example 119, from Chopin's Ballade in F minor, Op. 52.

Ex. 119

In Example 120, from Schumann's "Hasche-Mann" (from *Kinder-szenen*), a long pedal can help to build the indicated *crescendo.* Since the chromatic scale moves in an upward direction, an unpleasant blur should not result if both rapidity and a steady *crescendo* are maintained.

Ex. 120

Another striking instance of a long pedaling through a *crescendo* and partial chromatic scale figurations occurs in Example 121, from Messiaen's *Vingt Regards sur l'Enfant-Jésus.* The pedaling is by the composer. No time signature is given in the original.

In Example 122, from Schumann's "Florestan" (from *Carnaval,* Op. 9), the harmonic clash of the melody against the prevailing harmony in the left hand will not be unpleasant if a large, steady *crescendo* is maintained. The pedaling is by the composer. Although the entire piece is in 3/4 time, these last bars appear to be shifted to 2/4.

Ex. 121

Ex. 122

Pedaling a Crescendo in a Tremolo

Tremolo passages having *crescendos* are usually aided by a full pedal, as in Example 123, from Liszt's *Hungarian Rhapsody* No. 12. But not all tremolo passages should be pedaled, especially when the tremolo is measured and has a strong motivic, even melodic, significance. The passage from the first movement of Beethoven's Sonata, Op. 53, shown in Example 124 is a good instance of this feature.

Ex. 123

Ex. 124

Pedaling Glissandos with Crescendos

Brilliant upward-moving glissandos almost always benefit from a use of pedal, as shown in Example 125, from Debussy's Prélude from *Pour le Piano*.

Ex. 125

In Example 126, from Stravinsky's piano transcription of three movements of his ballet *Petrouchka*, an unbroken pedal should be used to enhance the brilliance of both the rapid alternating chords and the final glissando. The previous dynamic indication was a *crescendo* starting fourteen bars earlier.

Ex. 126

Scale Passages with Crescendos

Many rapid scale passages need pedaling for color. Scales that move rapidly upward, particularly if they are played with a *crescendo,* can often be heavily pedaled, as in Example 127, from the third movement of Chopin's Concerto No. 1.

Ex. 127

In Example 128, from Liszt's "Funérailles" (from *Harmonies poétiques et religieuses*), the top chromatic line receives strong harmonic support from the underlying repeated rolled chords. With the help of the *crescendo,* this layout permits a generous use of pedal.

Ex. 128

Short bursts of pedal may help when reinforcing a *crescendo,* as in Example 129, from Liszt's "Mazeppa" (from *Etudes d'exécution transcendante*).

Ex. 129

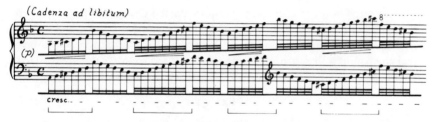

When running scale figurations move in a downward direction, it usually is impossible to hold the pedal for as long a time as in an upward-moving passage. Other important pedaling factors that must be considered are the register of the writing and its dynamic level. In Example 130, from Chopin's Nocturne, Op. 62, No. 1, the entire downward run played without a change of pedal sounds well only if a steady, large *crescendo* is made to the downbeat of the following bar.

Ex. 130

(Andante)

Chopin's pedaling

Pedaling a Long Decrescendo

The pedal can aid in making longer *decrescendos*. In Example 131, from Chopin's Ballade in G minor, Op. 23, the sound may not die away rapidly enough to merge smoothly into the *pianissimo* at the beginning of the *meno mosso*. Therefore a series of half-pedal changes are necessary. Only the performer's ear can determine the exact number and degree of such partial changes of pedal that will be needed on a particular instrument to lower the accumulated sonority smoothly to a *pianissimo*.

Ex. 131

Repeated notes or chords may require partial changes of pedal to keep the sonority from building too quickly, as in Example 132, from the third movement of Beethoven's Sonata, Op. 27, No. 1. Here, there is a danger that the sound will accumulate into an unwanted *crescendo* during the first two beats if the pedal is kept fully depressed during this time.

Ex. 132

In Example 133, from Chopin's Nocturne, Op. 48, No. 1, a *decrescendo* beginning in the second half of the bar and leading to the *pianissimo* in the following bar is strongly implied. The pedaling is Chopin's own, but additional partial changes of pedal following the *piano* and *accelerando* indications may be required in the second half of the bar.

Example 134, taken from Debussy's "Mouvement" (from *Images I*), shows where the pedal must be changed quickly several times following the initial strong *sforzando* accent in order to show the abrupt *decrescendo* clearly. In making these quick partial pedal changes, be certain not to lose

Ex. 133

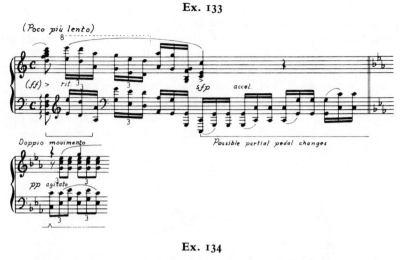

Ex. 134

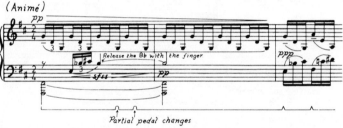

the low F-sharp octave. The B flat will have to be released by the finger
while the dampers brush the strings during the partial changes of pedal.

In Example 135, from the third movement of Schubert's Sonata, Op.
164, the bar after the *sforzando* at the conclusion of the *crescendo* contains
a *decrescendo,* which would imply a delayed slow lifting of the pedal.

Ex. 135

Anticipatory Pedaling after a Silence

Maximum richness of sound may be wished when a note or chord is
played following a silence, either at the start of a work or movement or

within the piece itself. Depressing the pedal before starting to play will produce a richer sound than will striking the note or chord first and depressing the pedal a split second later, since with the dampers already raised, the sympathetic partials will vibrate fully. Anticipatory pedaling is also on occasion termed "acoustical" or "timbre" pedaling. Example 136, from the opening of the first movement of Beethoven's Concerto No. 5, Op. 73, contains an instance of this kind of pedaling. With the immediately preceding *fortissimo* E-flat chord played by the orchestra, the open strings of the piano will pick up sympathetic partials even before the pianist begins to play!

Ex. 136

In Example 137, the two chords in the opening bars of Chopin's Scherzo, Op. 20, require the fullest possible sonority. Anticipatory pedaling can be used not only for the first chord but in a sense for the second one as well. Hold the pedal through both chords without a change. The chords are similar enough in harmonic content, and the opening one dies away sufficiently before the playing of the second, so that undesirable blurring should not occur.

Ex. 137

Anticipatory pedaling can be used even for soft beginnings of works, where maximum beauty of sound is needed. No finer instance is to be

found than in the opening of the Beethoven Concerto No. 4, as shown
in Example 138.

Ex. 138

Anticipatory pedaling may be used within a piece, as in Example 139,
from Chopin's Prélude, Op. 28, No. 18. Since the final two chords come
after a fairly long rest, there is ample time to depress the pedal before the
penultimate chord.

Ex. 139

Example 140, from the second movement of Beethoven's Sonata, Op.
10, No. 1, contains another instance of anticipatory pedaling used within
the course of a piece.

Ex. 140

Anticipatory Pedaling for Unbroken Sonority
Anticipatory pedaling may even be used in some passages that are not
preceded by silence. If the first harmony is played at a considerably lower
dynamic level or has had sufficient time to fade away completely, anticipatory pedaling will not result in an unpleasant clash of opposing so-

norities. This technique may be seen in Example 141, from Chopin's
Fantaisie, Op. 49. The composer's own pedaling is given.

Ex. 141

Simultaneous Pedaling for Richness of Tone

When anticipatory pedaling is impractical, depressing the pedal simultaneously with the new note or chord will achieve the maximum amount
of richness of tone color. In Example 142, from "The Great Gate of Kiev,"
from Mussorgsky's *Pictures at an Exhibition,* the left-hand grace notes
allow the pedal to be lifted a split second early, so it can then be re-
depressed at the moment the following chord is played. The dampers
should rise as the chords are played, not afterward.

Ex. 142

Sudden Drops in Dynamic Level

An abrupt change to a soft dynamic level following a loud passage will
demand special care with the pedal. In Example 143, from the first
movement of Beethoven's Sonata, Op. 106, there must be a small break
in the sound at the end of the *forte* area so that the first few notes in the
piano are not covered. The pedaling is by the composer.

In the first movement of Beethoven's Sonata, Op. 57, some pianists
use the first pedaling shown in Example 144 to obtain a clear emergence
of the *piano* melody notes following the preceding *fortissimo* chords. In
my opinion, this solution results in a very un-Beethovenian sound; I
prefer the second scheme. As in Example 143, an early lifting of the pedal
right before the *pianissimo* will better accomplish the desired clarity of
texture.

Ex. 143

Ex. 144

Echo Pedaling

An example of echo pedaling, incorrectly used from a stylistic standpoint, was given in Example 144. But this technique does have valid uses,
particularly in twentieth-century music. Echo pedaling is executed by
silently re-depressing or holding notes from a pedaled area, then releasing
the pedal to permit these notes to stand out alone. In Example 145, from
Britten's *Night-Piece (Notturno)*, the composer says, "These [notes] should
be silently pressed down before the pedal is released" in the final bar.

Ex. 145

BLURRING FOR COLOR AND
SPECIAL EFFECTS

The pedal can be used for deliberate blurring of certain kinds of scales, cadenza-like figurations, and ostinato patterns. It also may be used by the composer for blurring rapid figurations as a kind of special effect. Often such blurring will take place over some kind of pedal point, which serves as a harmonically stabilizing support. The examples below are but a very few in which the pedal is used in this general manner.

Pedaling Whole-Tone and Pentatonic Scales

The whole-tone scale can often be heavily pedaled, for its equidistanced intervals tend to blend more smoothly than do the irregular intervals found in other scales. In Example 146, from Debussy's *L'isle joyeuse,* the long A pedal point helps support the long pedal in the upper parts.

Ex. 146

On occasion, the pentatonic scale can also sound well when heavily pedaled. In Example 147, from Debussy's *Masques,* directions for pedaling are given by the composer.

Ex. 147

Pedaling Cadenza Figurations

Long pedaling effects can be used effectively in cadenza passages that lie in a high register and have a strong harmonic support in the bass. The pedaling shown in Example 148, from Chopin's Nocturne, Op. 9, No. 3, is original.

Ex. 148

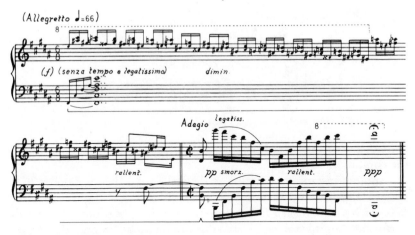

Blurring in Ostinato Figures

In several works based on Hungarian folk material, Bartók is fond of using long pedals as a support for ostinato, dronelike figurations. Example 149, taken from No. 15 of the *15 Hungarian Peasant Songs,* has a long unbroken pedal extending from bar 1 through bar 40. To keep such a passage from sounding excessively blurred, the player must make certain to give the bass a firm support, paying special attention to the downbeat accents.

Ex. 149

Blurring for Special Mood Effects

A light blurring of the pedal can create an atmosphere of mystery. In Example 150, from Grieg's "Wedding Day at Troldhaugen" (from *Lyrische*

Ex. 150

Stücke), the damper pedal may be held for four bars. The pedaling is by the composer.

Another instance of blurring of the pedal for a special mood is to be seen in Example 151, from Messiaen's "Regard de l'Eglise d'amour" (from *Vingt regards sur l'Enfant Jésus*). Here the composer asks that the performer "jumble the pedal" and that the sound be "confused and menacing." No time signature is given in the original.

Ex. 151

PARTIAL CHANGES OF PEDAL

Many pianists do not seem to realize that when the pedal is changed, a sudden full dampening of the sound may not always be desirable. At times the player may wish to carry over part of the sound from the preceding note or notes. In accomplishing a partial change of pedal, the dampers must be allowed to touch the strings for only an instant before again being raised. On concert grands, the dampers must rest fully on the strings for a significant length of time to stop all vibrations completely, so lifting them again quickly still allows a good amount of the sound to be carried through. Experimentation should be made on isolated notes or chords to see how long the dampers must remain in contact with the strings before all sound is stopped. With practice it should be possible to eliminate varying amounts of the sound by a rapid brushing of the dampers on the strings immediately following the sounding of a loud sonority. In specific works, only the player's individual taste and sensitivity of ear can determine the fine line between a partial change of pedal that produces some degree of desired blurring and one that is too dry and loses too much of an intentional carry-over of sonority. The term "half" pedaling is commonly used for a partial change of pedal, but it is somewhat misleading, since in many cases more than half of the old sonority must be carried over, and in others much less. Patient experimentation on a good instrument, when a passage is playable in concert tempo with all the dynamics in place, is the best teacher.

Partial Changes with a Bass Line or Pedal Point

A partial change of pedal is most often needed when a bass sonority that cannot be held with the fingers must be carried over as a pedal point into the next harmony. Debussy's music for piano is particularly full of such places, as in Example 152, from his "Jardins sous la pluie" (from *Estampes*).

Ex. 152

In Example 153, from Chopin's Polonaise, Op. 44, a complete change of pedal on the second beats of the bars where the melody moves downward would rob the sonority of the A pedal point. A partial change of pedal is therefore necessary.

Ex. 153

There are instances when an upper melodic part must be carried through by the pedal, as in Example 154, from Franck's *Prélude, choral et*

Ex. 154

Partial pedal change

fugue. In earlier bars of this section, the composer indicates that all the chords are to be rolled, with the left hand crossing over to take the highest note.

Many problem spots in which long pedal points must be held can be solved by using the *sostenuto* pedal (see chapter 3).

FLUTTER OR VIBRATO PEDALING

Flutter pedaling, or "vibrato" pedaling, as it is also commonly termed, may best be described as a rapid, fairly shallow movement of the pedal that permits the dampers to brush the strings so that neither an entire choking of the sound nor a full vibration of the strings will take place. The fluttering motion of the dampers should be as rapid as possible, in order to avoid audible blocks or chops in the sound. At no time should the pedal hit as it is raised or be depressed completely (see Example 155).

Ex. 155

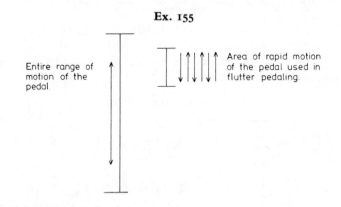

Using Flutter Pedaling for Color

One classic instance of the use of flutter pedaling is the entire last movement of Chopin's Sonata, Op. 35. In the excerpt shown in Example 156, its light, irregular blurring produces the macabre "wind over the grave" effect.

Ex. 156

A similar use of flutter pedaling may be found in the Chopin Nocturne, Op. 15, No. 1, as shown in Example 157. To change the pedal at every pair of sixteenth notes would create slurs, and to play the passage without pedal would create a sound that would be too dry in any but the most resonant hall. A rapid flutter pedaling will give needed resonance and color, without creating lumps of pedaled sound.

Ex. 157

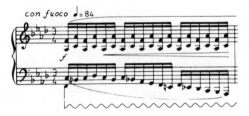

Occasionally a composer will specifically indicate flutter pedaling, as in Example 158, from the first movement of Barber's *Piano Concerto*.

Ex. 158

Flutter Pedaling to Reduce Sonority

There are instances when a texture must be reduced in sonority more rapidly than is normal. The trill shown in Example 159, from Chopin's *Barcarolle*, Op. 60, must receive a rapid *decrescendo*.

Ex. 159

In Example 160, from the first movement of Beethoven's Sonata, Op. 109, as the *decrescendo* is made, flutter pedaling can reduce the sound so that when the *piano* is reached, the full change of pedal will not result in an abrupt drop-off of the dynamic level. The long pedaling indication from the *forte* to the *piano* is Beethoven's own, but because of the greater resonance of today's instruments, it must be slightly modified with flutter pedaling.

Ex. 160

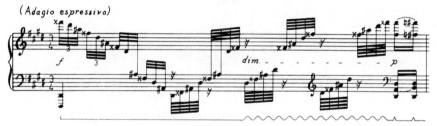

Combining Finger and Flutter Pedaling

Finger and flutter pedaling used together can be effective on occasion. Pianists deal with Chopin's Etude, Op. 25, No. 2, shown in Example 161, in various ways. Some performers use no pedal, and others use only quarter- to half-released dampers. A combination of finger and flutter pedaling is a third possibility, if the performer has a fairly large span in the left hand. A final choice in this piece rests with the player's own taste, the hall, instrument, etc.

Ex. 161

PARTIAL RELEASES OF DAMPER SOUND

A generally ignored aspect of pedaling is that which involves partial releases of damper sound. Although in most changes of pedal, anything from a full resting to some degree of brushing of the dampers on the strings is necessary, in other situations different quantities of the sound can be retained by delaying the moment when the dampers come in full contact with the strings. Four different levels of sound release, all measured by the listener's ear, are convenient approximate guidelines. The boundaries of each will depend on how far above the strings the dampers are kept:

1. A total release of sound is accomplished when the dampers are fully raised from the strings. This change may also be termed "full" pedal.
2. A 75 percent release of pedaled sound occurs when the dampers barely touch the strings. To test for this, play a loud chord, then immediately release the notes with the fingers. Keep the pedal depressed to the point at which the dampers almost leave the strings, so that approximately 75 percent of the initial sound is carried over.
3. A 50 percent release of pedaled sound occurs when the dampers are allowed to rest lightly on the strings. To test for this, play a loud chord as above. Less sound should carry over than with the 75 percent released damper. Another test is to play a scale at a moderate speed with the pedal partially depressed. There should be some muddiness, but not as much as in a rapid scale played with full pedal. *Staccato* notes or chords will not cut off immediately, yet the sound will decay much more quickly than if played with full pedal.
4. A 25 percent release of pedaled sound occurs when the dampers rest almost completely on the strings. There should be only a slight amount of foot pressure on the pedal. When playing a rapid scale passage, no perceptible blurring should occur. Scales or chords played with 25 percent released sound will have a distinctly richer tone quality than those played with no pedal. In passages of medium-to-rapid tempo and a dynamic level between *pianissimo* and *mezzo forte,* a 25 percent release of damper sound can counteract an overly dry sound resulting from a dead room or a small instrument.

The above percentages refer to the amount of released damper sound, *not* to the distance the pedal must be depressed. In dealing with this pedaling, it is of paramount importance to have a properly regulated instrument, on which the dampers rise from and lower onto the strings at a uniform speed.

Releasing 25 Percent of Damper Sound

Some passages may demand an ethereal, otherworldly atmosphere. In Example 162, from the second movement of Beethoven's Sonata, Op. 111, a full pedal change on each sixteenth note will give a slurred, lumpy effect. Also, the tempo is too rapid to permit a change of pedal on every 32nd note, and flutter pedaling on larger instruments will usually produce an overly heavy sonority. A released damper sound of roughly 25 percent gives just the correct blend of color and clarity of texture.

Ex. 162

In Example 163, use of 25 percent released damper sound should not be used to cover a faulty *legato* in this passage from Chopin's Nocturne, Op. 62, No. 2, but should only be used to give the left-hand sixteenth notes a slightly richer color. Full pedaling on each pair of sixteenths would create slurs, and pedaling on individual sixteenths is virtually impossible at concert tempo.

Ex. 163

The excerpt from Debussy's Prélude "Feux d'artifice" shown in Example 164 needs a 25 percent release of damper sound to avoid dryness yet maintain transparency and sparkle.

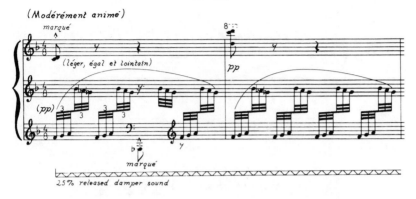

Ex. 164

Releasing 50 Percent of Damper Sound

Release of 50 percent of damper sound is particularly useful in passages where the harmony between pedal changes remains the same, but when a full buildup of resonance is not desired, as in Example 165, from the third movement of Beethoven's Sonata, Op. 7.

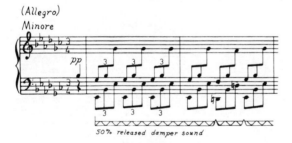

Ex. 165

In the second movement of Ginastera's Sonata No. 1, as shown in Example 166, the composer requests that both the damper and left pedals be used. A 50 percent release of damper sound will ensure that the rapid shifts of harmony do not become too muddy but will allow there to be an atmospheric haze of sound.

Staccato chords in slow passages must often be lengthened slightly to avoid excessive dryness, as if played by a full orchestra in a large concert hall. A released damper sound of 50 percent can be an effective way of achieving this effect, as in Example 167, from the second movement of Beethoven's Sonata, Op. 7.

Ex. 166

Ex. 167

In Example 168, from the second movement of Beethoven's Sonata, Op. 31, No. 1, a 50 percent release of damper sound will make the left hand *staccato* triplets sound more like light cello *pizzicati*.

Ex. 168

Released damper sound of 50 percent is needed in Example 169, from the second movement of Beethoven's Sonata, Op. 57, to prevent the right-hand material from sounding merely like broken-chord figurations and to help retain its true identity as a melody.

The light blurring that results from a 50 percent release of damper sound can suggest the sound of another instrument. In the excerpt from Debussy's "Soirée dans Grenade" (from *Estampes*), shown in Example 170, such blurring will add atmosphere to the writing, which imitates the sound of a guitar heard from the distance; and in Example 171, we have the famous "music box" variation of Brahms's *Variations and Fugue on a Theme by Handel*. No tempo indication is given by the composer.

Ex. 169

Ex. 170

Ex. 171

Releasing 75 Percent of Damper Sound

A 75 percent release of damper sound will produce nearly full resonance yet allow rapid passagework to remain transparent, as in Example 172, from Schubert's Impromptu, Op. 90, No. 4, and Example 173, from the third movement of Beethoven's Sonata, Op. 2, No. 3.

Ex. 172

Ex. 173

75% released damper sound

PASSAGES WITHOUT PEDAL

Just as the damper pedal may be used for sonority or even blurring, so its absence on occasion may be an effective coloring tool. Example 174, from the Brahms Ballade, Op. 118, No. 3; Example 175, from Debussy's Prélude "General Lavine—eccentric"; and Example 176, from Copland's *Piano Fantasy,* contain passages in which the composers themselves request temporary abstinence from the pedal. The *una corda* indication is by Brahms.

Ex. 174

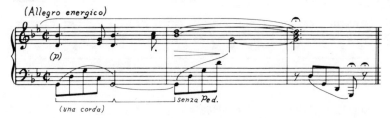

(una corda)

Ex. 175

Ex. 176

ACHIEVING VARIETY IN REPETITIONS

Slight variation of identical musical material that is heard several times is a well-known nineteenth-century musical tradition. Such pianists as Josef Hofmann (1876–1957) and Ignaz Friedman (1882–1948) raised this interpretive device to an incredibly imaginative and personalized level of artistry.

An excellent instance of using the pedal to create variety in repetitions may be seen in the middle section of the famous *Marche funèbre* movement of Chopin's Sonata, Op. 35. If one follows all the repeats given by the composer, the first eight bars of the middle section will be heard a total of four times. These repetitions occur in a fairly brief space of time and can become monotonous if played in a sterile, "place-the-needle-back-on-the-record" manner. Although Chopin marks each statement of this section with a uniform *pianissimo* indication, most performers use some artistic imagination and present each one with a slight change of color, voicing, and dynamics and even with rubato. If the first four bars of this material are presented successively at four different dynamic levels, the pedalings shown in Example 177 could be used. Chopin himself recommends pedaling once each bar when playing *pianissimo,* presumably without using the left pedal. It is up to the performer to decide which of the other three solutions to use and in what order, following the initial presentation at Chopin's requested *pianissimo* level without left pedal.

Ex. 177

THE PEDAL AS AN *ATTACCA* DEVICE

The pedal is sometimes used by a composer to join separate movements of a work, as in Example 178, from Beethoven's Sonata, Op. 109, and Example 179, from his Sonata, Op. 27, No. 1. In each case, the pedaling is by the composer and joins the first and second movements of the sonata.

Ex. 178

Ex. 179

3

The Middle Pedal

The middle pedal is most frequently termed the *sostenuto* pedal, and may as well be called the "tonal" pedal, "sustaining" pedal, or "organ point" pedal. It is *terra incognita* to most pianists, who regrettably do not recognize it as one of the most valuable tools for coloring and clarifying musical texture. But once the initial mystery surrounding its use is stripped away, the perceptive performer will soon grasp the enormous possibilities for its application. Even with a little practice, it can soon become an indispensable part of the performer's pedaling technique.

On a grand piano, the mechanism of the *sostenuto* pedal is controlled by a long bar running along the base of the dampers; its cross section is shaped something like a question mark or a comma (see Example 1). Protruding from the base of each damper is a tapered hinged tab of wood covered with felt. When the *sostenuto* pedal is depressed, the bar rotates slightly so that its tail can catch the tabs of any dampers that are raised. They will remain locked until the *sostenuto* pedal is released. Dampers slightly off the strings will not be caught by the *sostenuto* pedal mechanism; the dampers must be raised to a certain height before the tabs will be engaged. (This point is important for the technique described on pp. 105–107.)

The following are common names for the middle pedal:

English: prolonging pedal, sostenuto pedal, Steinway pedal, sustaining pedal, S. P., tonal pedal, Ped. 3
French: *Prolongement, Pédale de prolongation, Prol. Ped.*
German: *Tonhaltepedal*
Italian: *Il pedale tonale*

Briefly stated, the middle pedal does only one thing when it is depressed: it will catch and hold any dampers that are already fully raised from the strings. Three conditions must be met:

Ex. 1

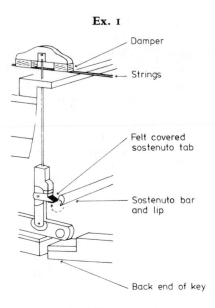

1. The note or notes to be caught by the *sostenuto* pedal must be played and held by the fingers until the *sostenuto* pedal is fully depressed. On all grand pianos, the *sostenuto* pedal will catch the raised dampers from any strings equipped with them. On most grands the dampers stop at the second highest F or F sharp, since the limited resonances of the higher strings do not create an offensive blur when mixed. If a note or chord once caught and held by the *sostenuto* pedal is repeated, it is not necessary to re-catch it with a renewed change of the pedal.

2. The right pedal must not be depressed at the same moment the *sostenuto* pedal catches the notes to be held, for then *all* the dampers will be caught by the *sostenuto* pedal. However, once the *sostenuto* pedal has been depressed, the player is free to use the damper pedal as much as necessary. The note or notes caught with the *sostenuto* pedal will continue to be held through any changes made by the right pedal.

3. The *sostenuto* pedal must be kept completely depressed during its use, since even a slight amount of release will immediately result in the catching of other unwanted tones.

The pianist who is unaccustomed to using the middle pedal should learn to manipulate it rapidly. The time for the three-part sequence of playing the note or notes, making certain that the damper pedal is fully released, and then depressing the middle pedal should be held to the bare minimum. In most of the pedal techniques to be discussed, split-second timing is crucial, and these steps must become almost a single action, rather than a staggered three-state chain of events.

Use the right foot for the damper pedal and the left foot for both the *sostenuto* and left pedals, except when no right pedal is used at all. Then the right foot can manipulate the middle pedal, while the left foot works the left one. Occasions when all three pedals must be used are discussed on pp. 118–21.

Since the middle pedal was not in general use in Europe for decades after its patenting in 1874 by Steinway, there are relatively few written indications for it until well into the twentieth century. Therefore the performer must decide when its use is effective and appropriate. As with the damper pedal, even written indications by the composer or by an editor for use of the *sostenuto* pedal may require some modification. In deciding whether to use the middle pedal, first play the passage with the damper pedal alone, perhaps holding long notes with a series of partial pedal changes. Then make certain that the use of the middle pedal will not alter the composer's original musical idea but will merely clarify it and bring it to a fuller realization. Such major twentieth-century composers as Barber, Bartók, Carter, Copland, Harris, and Sessions, to name a few, specify the use of the middle pedal in several of their compositions. In these cases one should not consider any other pedaling, except in an emergency, when the piano has a malfunctioning *sostenuto* pedal or none at all. Unfortunately, on many instruments, even in concert halls, the middle pedal is not properly regulated. Moreover, to this day, some European concert instruments are not equipped with a middle pedal. It is therefore imperative to have an alternative pedaling solution for any passage in which the middle pedal is used, even though the substitute is inferior. Such compromise solutions should be rehearsed enough so that the player can shift to them on short notice at a performance.

Holding Bass Pedal Points
When pedal points are to be sustained beneath shifting harmonies, the composer may write them as notes of long value that cannot be held by the fingers themselves. In many instances a pedal point may be of extremely long duration and impossible to sustain beyond a fairly short period of time when an extended series of partial changes of the damper pedal must be made. In these situations the middle pedal becomes an invaluable tool for accomplishing a fuller realization of the composer's written intentions. Example 2, from Franck's *Prélude, choral et fugue*, has such a pedal point. The dynamic level is roughly *fortissimo,* having been reached by a *crescendo* starting from a *forte* two and a half bars earlier. This dynamic level, in combination with the *molto ritardando* that begins a bar

earlier and the relatively low register of the writing, precludes using either one long pedaling for the bar with the pedal point or the clear retention of the pedal point by means of half-pedaling alone. Only the F-sharp whole notes should be caught by the middle pedal.

Ex. 2

The excerpt from Nielsen's *Theme and Variations,* Op. 40, shown in Example 3 contains another pedal point that will benefit from use of the middle pedal.

Ex. 3

The catching of the G pedal point in Example 4, from Shostakovich's Prelude and Fugue in D-flat major, necessitates depressing the middle pedal rapidly between the first and second beats of the second measure shown. Since the touch throughout is a *marcatissimo* non-*legato,* this solution is perfectly feasible and may be done strictly in tempo.

In Examples 2, 3, and 4 there would seem to be no reason for unclear blurring of the right pedal, assuming the middle pedal is being used for the pedal points. But in Example 5, from Albeniz's "El Albaicin" (from *Iberia*), an atmospheric blurring with the damper pedal will be appropriate so as to maintain the original effect of keeping the B-flat pedal point by means of partial pedal changes, as the composer would have done on most of the instruments of the day. The amount of damper pedal used will vary from instrument to instrument.

Because of its near Impressionistic style, this particular excerpt is perhaps a borderline case for using the middle pedal, as are so many passages in the music of both Debussy and Ravel. Many pianists, to be

Ex. 4

sure, will wish to hold the B-flat pedal point in Example 5 as long as possible by means of partial changes of pedal alone. On some instruments that can be readily accomplished, but on other, less-resonant ones, the middle pedal may prove a welcome asset. The resourceful performer will have both means at his disposal.

Ex. 5

Avoiding Breaks in the Melody

Catching a pedal point with the middle pedal may be a valuable aid in avoiding unwanted breaks in a *legato* melodic line above. In Example 6, from Brahms's *Variations and Fugue on a Theme by Handel,* the composer calls for the damper pedal to be held unbroken through bars 1 and 2, then changed and held through bars 3 and 4. There should be some carry-over of damper pedal from one harmony to the next, but the blurring should not be excessive. Using the middle pedal as well maintains the pedal points clearly, but without the breaks in the melody that would result if the damper pedal had to be changed for the low bass notes.

Ex. 6

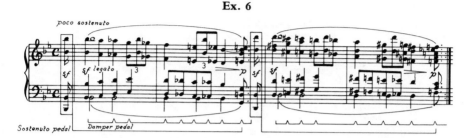

A further instance of using the *sostenuto* pedal both to hold a bass pedal point and to avoid breaks in the melody occurs in Example 7, from Schumann's *Etudes symphoniques,* Op. 13. It should be recalled that once a pedal point is caught by the middle pedal, there is no need to re-catch it as it is repeated. The G-sharp half note should be played first, then rapidly caught by the *sostenuto* pedal.

Ex. 7

At times it may be impossible to catch a bass pedal point with the middle pedal without catching another note being sounded at the same time. In these situations, the performer must decide if an overly large blur will result from catching additional notes. In Example 8, from the Intermezzo from Schumann's *Faschingsschwank aus Wien,* the downbeat F in the right hand will not create an offensive muddiness, since it is in a fairly high register, is not immediately repeated, and is the unaccented end of the preceding phrase. Although Schumann indicates that the damper pedal is to be held without break for the entire two bars, the resulting

Ex. 8

muddle of sonority is too great. Although Schumann gives no dynamic indication, the music would seem to demand a *forte*.

Contrasting Touches during a Pedal Point

Often a pedal point must be held while the articulation of other parts demands clarity of pedal or even dryness. Much of Rachmaninoff's music contains long bass pedal points. Although most of them need to be carried through with the damper pedal for sonority and color, there are occasions when assistance from the middle pedal is definitely needed. In Example 9, from Rachmaninoff's *Etude-Tableau,* Op. 33, No. 5, there is no way to make the *pianissimo* chords sound *staccato* if the rolled chord before them is held with the damper pedal. Since this sixteenth-note motif has occurred throughout the piece and has usually been played with an unpedaled *staccato* touch, there seems no musical reason to change the sound to a pedaled blur. Here the middle pedal is unquestionably useful.

In Example 10, from Schumann's Phantasie, Op. 17, the pedal point A flat must be caught during the rest after the F in the right hand. Here is a good instance of the way the middle pedal can be used to clarify articulation and texture. Although Schumann's original score calls for the

Ex. 9

damper pedal to be depressed on the A-flat pedal point, no release is given. There should undoubtedly be a release on the third beat of the following bar. Schumann's request for pedal makes it possible to hold the A-flat octave while the left hand moves away. Here there would seem to be no musical reason for blurring with the damper pedal the recurring pattern of eighth note, sixteenth rest, sixteenth note.

Ex. 10

Catching Notes within Chords

When a single note or perhaps an octave within a chord must be caught with the middle pedal, the other notes of the chord must be released early. Then the note to be held is caught by the middle pedal between the release of the old notes and the striking of the next notes to be played. Extremely rapid reflexes and practice on a responsive instrument are necessary for the successful management of this difficult technique. In Example 11, from the first movement of Prokofiev's Sonata No. 7, all the eighth notes are to be played *staccato*. The G octave pedal point in the left hand must be caught by the middle pedal between the C–E in the right hand and the following A flat. Once caught on the downbeat, the G octave does not have to be re-caught in successive repetitions. This rapid and difficult catching of the G octave must be accomplished without break in the rhythm.

In Example 12, from the fifth movement of Brahms's Sonata, Op. 5, the composer's indication for the right pedal is an apparent makeshift solution for holding the longer notes in the right hand. The dotted half

Ex. 11

Ex. 12

notes in the right hand should be caught by the middle pedal during the rest following each downbeat chord. Brahms gives damper pedal indications for the downbeats of bars 90, 92, and 94, but they should not be observed if the middle pedal is used.

Breaking the Hands to Catch a Pedal Point

There are times when the performer may wish to catch a bass pedal point with the middle pedal, but doing so would also catch an unwanted note. In Example 13, from Debussy's "Jardins sous la pluie" (from *Estampes*), the G octave pedal point extends from bar 100 through bar 115. If an extremely small break is made between the G octave and the downbeat B in the right hand in bar 100, the G octave can be caught alone in the *sostenuto* pedal. But the octave must be caught very quickly so that the breaking of the hands is as inconspicuous as possible. As in the Albeniz excerpt from "El Albaicin," shown in Example 5, a great deal of sonority should be maintained with the damper pedal, even though the *sostenuto* pedal is also used. To the listener, the G pedal point should appear to be held by partial changes of pedal. As in Example 5, the instrument will have much to do with how this passage is handled.

Ex. 13

←bars 102-113→

Holding Implied Pedal Points

The pedal points in all the foregoing examples were indicated with notes of longer value. But even when a composer does not write bass pedal points in long notes, the performer may decide that certain implied pedal points should be caught with the middle pedal. Catching them in Example 14, from Chopin's Etude, Op. 10, No. 12, gives the performer better control of the pedaling during the following two beats. A use of flutter pedal in this example will give color without grouping the left-hand sixteenths into blocks of pedaled sound.

Ex. 14

Anticipatory Use of the Sostenuto *Pedal*

When the player wishes to catch a note with the middle pedal but cannot do so because of other notes being played at the same time, it may be

possible to catch the note silently with the *sostenuto* pedal before it is
actually to be sounded. An excellent example of this use of the middle
pedal occurs in one of Liszt's transcriptions of Bach's organ works. As
seen in Example 15, from the Prelude and Fugue in A minor, the A pedal
point beginning in bar 10 is held through the next 13 bars. If the *sostenuto*
pedal is depressed when the A is first sounded in bar 10, it will also catch
the C an octave above; and breaking the hands to catch the pedal point,
as described above, would result in a noticeable gap in the flowing
sixteenth-note pattern. The solution is to catch the A before starting the
piece. Silently depress it, then depress the middle pedal and hold it
through bar 23, releasing it finally on the downbeat of bar 24. Neither
Bach's nor Liszt's score gives either a dynamics or a tempo indication.

Ex. 15

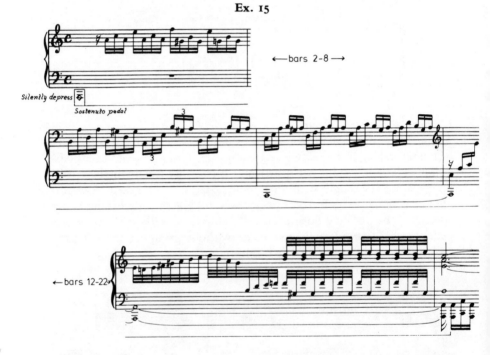

A similar application of this pedaling technique occurs in Example 16,
from Liszt's "Funérailles" (from *Harmonies poétiques et religieuses*). The
low C, which is first sounded in the first bar, remains as a much-needed
pedal point for the first seventeen bars of the piece. There is no way to
catch it alone in bar 1 or later because of the overlapping notes being
sounded above, and as the intervals get wider in the left hand, it is

impossible to hold it without some sort of break occurring in either the pedal or the hand. Using a similar *sostenuto* pedal technique as in the preceding example, silently depress both the low C of bar 1 and the C above, since the latter will be used starting in bar 9, then catch and hold these notes with the middle pedal. Release the middle pedal and the damper pedal a split second early before playing the first of the *fortississimo* D flats, to make certain none of the old harmony carries over.

Ex. 16

If the middle pedal is used in Liszt's "Funérailles," it is important to have something of the same heavily pedaled sound that would have resulted from using the damper pedal alone to hold the bass C pedal points. Liszt himself indicates that there are to be long, unbroken stretches of the damper pedal during the first seventeen bars. But on a modern-day concert instrument, they will create an overly muddy texture. Nonetheless, there should be some blurring of sonorities by the damper pedal, even when the middle pedal is also used, in order to convey Liszt's intended effect of tolling funeral bells. A crystal-clear delineation of harmonies by the damper pedal would be just as incorrect as an excessive mass of blurred sonorities through overly heavy pedaling. The performer should try out Liszt's original pedaling, then match its broad outlines to a use of the *sostenuto* pedal.

Using the Middle Pedal to Achieve a Clear Damper Pedal Change
The middle pedal can be used not only to hold notes through a series of
shifting harmonies but also to ensure a clear change of the damper pedal.
Clear damper pedal changes are often difficult when the harmonies lie in
a low register and when the hand must immediately leave the new harmony that is being caught in the pedal. In these situations the time the
dampers have to rest on the strings between pedalings may not be enough
to ensure that a clear change is made and that all the vibrations from the
old harmony have been silenced. At these times the middle pedal may
prove valuable, as in Example 17, from Liszt's "Sonetto 47 del Petrarca"
(from *Deuxième Année de Pèlerinage*). Here the finger must release the low
A on the downbeat of bar 4 rapidly so that the hand can move up to the
E and C sharp on the second beat. Achieving a clean change of the damper
pedal here is not easy. As a safeguard the *sostenuto* pedal can catch the A;
then the damper pedal can be changed once or even twice afterward to
eliminate all unwanted harmonies from bar 3. The rest on the downbeat
in the treble part must be carefully observed as the low A is caught by the
sostenuto pedal.

Ex. 17

Example 18, from the first movement of Brahms's Sonata, Op. 5,
contains another difficult change of pedal that can be helped by using the
middle pedal. As in Example 17, it solves the problem of eliminating all

Ex. 18

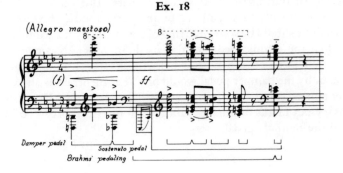

the sonorities from the previous bar. Brahms's own pedaling implies that the low C's should act as pedal points until the second beat of the next bar.

Clarifying a Melodic Line
A melodic line may benefit from more frequent damper pedal changes at the same time as the underlying harmony must be held with the middle pedal. In Example 19, bars 72–76 of Brahms's Intermezzo, Op. 117, No. 2, the *appoggiatura* at the beginning of each group of right-hand sixteenth notes demands to be followed immediately by a pedal change. Brahms gives damper pedal indications for the second beats of bars 73 and 75.

Ex. 19

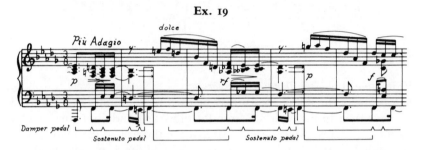

As a Form of Finger Pedaling
As has been seen in the discussion of the damper pedal, finger pedaling can often be used to hold over a part of the basic underlying harmony while a part of the melody shifts and receives appropriate changes of damper pedal. This technique works only when the notes can all be covered by the hand. As shown in Example 20, from Liszt's "Sonetto 47 del Petrarca," the middle pedal may be used to retain the primary harmony while the damper pedal is used for clear changes required by the melody.

Ex. 20

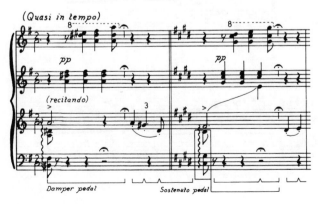

In Example 21, from Liszt's "Sonetto 123 del Petrarca," more frequent pedaling in the melody is desirable because of the frequent downward motion of the melody and because of the several nonharmonic tones, which do not blend with the prevailing harmony.

Ex. 21

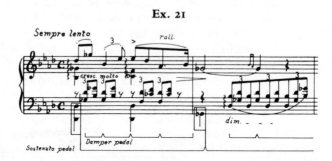

Facilitating Awkward Technical Passages

Occasionally the middle pedal may be used to hold notes that the hand cannot reach. In Example 22, from Beethoven's Rondo in G major, Op. 51, No. 2, many players cannot stretch the interval of the tenth that is demanded if the G tied half notes are to be held for their full time. Here a silent depressing of the G, then catching it with the middle pedal before beginning the piece, will solve the problem. Later, when the same material recurs, in Example 23, the problem may be solved by playing the bottom left-hand G a split second before the G and B above, and catching it quickly with the middle pedal.

Ex. 22

Ex. 23

In Example 24, from the first movement of the Bartók Piano Sonata, the middle pedal can be used to facilitate an enormously awkward passage, in which holding the long notes with the fingers requires an extraordinary amount of strength. Catch the right-hand F-sharp octave with the *sostenuto* pedal as soon as the left-hand *staccato* D is released.

Ex. 24

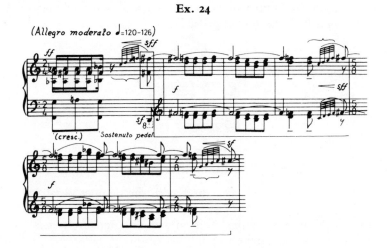

Catching and Releasing Notes by Key Level

Until now, we have assumed that only those notes to be caught by the middle pedal would be depressed at the moment this pedal is activated, and that the damper pedal would not be in use at the precise instant that notes are initially caught by the *sostenuto* pedal. But it is possible to catch notes with the *sostenuto* pedal at the same time other notes are sounding and while the damper pedal is being used. This technique is only for the very advanced pianist, since it demands the most sensitive of reflexes and an instrument that is perfectly regulated. Nonetheless, it should be included in any comprehensive reference to pedaling technique involving the *sostenuto* pedal, no matter how difficult, involved, or delicate the procedure.

To gain an idea of this pedaling technique, two exercises should be mastered. For the first one, play Example 25 slowly, carefully following these steps:

1. Play the first two C's.
2. Continue to hold the left-hand C with the finger and play the D in the right hand. Then, let the D rise slowly, just to the point at which the damper first touches the strings.
3. Fully depress the *sostenuto* pedal.

4. Play the E in the right hand, while releasing the finger on the C in the left hand. Finally let go of the E.

If the exercise has been done correctly, the C alone will remain caught by the *sostenuto* pedal, and no interruption will be apparent between the three notes of the right hand. This pedaling technique is possible, as explained earlier, because the dampers must be raised to a certain height before they can be caught by the *sostenuto* pedal.

Ex. 25

The second exercise uses Example 26:

1. Play both hands on the first beat with the damper pedal fully depressed.
2. While holding the C in the left hand with the finger, release the chord in the right hand. Continue to hold the damper pedal.
3. Slowly lift the damper pedal until the right-hand chord fades slightly. Hold the pedal at this point.
4. Depress the *sostenuto* pedal, then release the left-hand C.
5. Play the next two chords, now using a fully depressed change of damper pedal on each chord, and continue to hold the *sostenuto* pedal.

If these steps have been followed carefully, only the left-hand C will have been caught by the *sostenuto* pedal, and there will be no interruption in the sound carried over from one chord to the next.

Ex. 26

Eventually, the player should be able to bypass the step of first depressing the finger or pedal before releasing it to the correct height and go directly to the correct level. Example 27, from the second movement

Ex. 27

Ex. 28

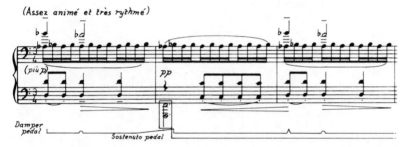

of Brahms's Sonata, Op. 2, and Example 28, from Debussy's Prélude from *Pour le Piano,* are instances in which this highly specialized pedaling technique for the middle pedal might be used.

Sounding Sympathetic Partials

Some twentieth-century composers use the middle pedal to create special effects through the sounding of sympathetic partials. In Example 29, from the first movement of the Carter Piano Sonata, a footnote by the composer reads, "Omit the notes in brackets if harmonics are audible."

Ex. 29

For the correct effect in this passage, a resonant instrument is necessary. No time signature is given.

Special Acoustical Effects
Some pieces demand a slight haze of pedal resonance or even the faint sounding of a pedal point. Sometimes these effects can be accomplished better with the middle pedal than with conventional partial changes or releases of the damper pedal. In some instances, a note or group of notes not actually sounded in the piece can be silently depressed, then caught by the middle pedal. If these notes form the fundamentals of the notes actually being sounded above, a faint haze of sympathetic partials will be heard. To set the partials of the note C in vibration, one can use any of the fundamentals below it.

Ex. 30

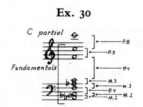

As an experiment, silently depress each of the notes below the high C in Example 30, catching each one with the middle pedal, then striking and releasing the high C. The high C will continue to vibrate softly. As the lower, more distant notes are struck, the vibration will grow fainter. If several or all of the fundamentals are caught by the *sostenuto* pedal, the ringing of the top C will be much stronger. This experiment can be done for any note, provided the same intervallic relationship of notes below is kept. The intensity of partials to be set up will be determined by the number and physical closeness of the notes that are silently caught with the middle pedal.

A wonderful opportunity for applying this use of the middle pedal occurs in Debussy's Prélude "Voiles." Since much of the piece is based on the whole-tone scale, many pianists try to pedal it with virtually one extended wash of damper pedal. Unless the pianist has the control of a Gieseking, the results may become hopelessly muddled. Using the middle pedal may be a good compromise solution.

The following procedure will produce an atmospheric haze of music but not a dirty smog of sound. Naturally, some use of the damper pedal can also be made. Before starting to play the piece, silently depress any combination of notes shown at the head of Example 31 (none of which are used anywhere in the work itself) and catch then with the *sostenuto* pedal.

Ex. 31

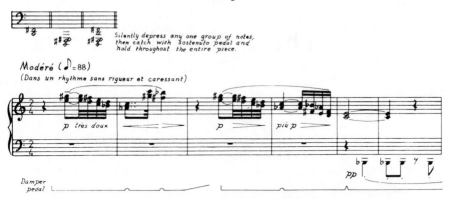

The first group of notes will create a slightly louder series of partials than will the second. The third will of course add the greatest haze. For a final touch, the B-flat pedal point found throughout the piece can be silently depressed along with the other fundamental tones, and the left pedal can be held throughout most of the piece if the instrument being played demands it. The damper pedal should also be used.

Another work which lends itself well to this pedal technique is Chopin's *Berceuse,* Op. 57. Since the opening D flat remains as an implied pedal point throughout but must not become overly prominent, the use of the middle pedal shown in Example 32 is one possible solution. Partial changes of the damper pedal, as well as some use of the left pedal, will also be needed.

Ex. 32

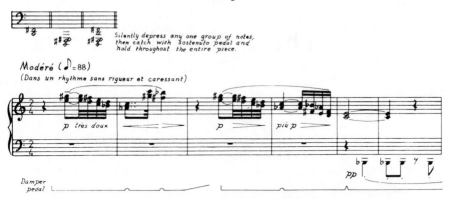

4

The Left Pedal

The left pedal is often termed the *una corda,* the *sordino,* or the "muting" pedal. Its function is not merely to help the performer to play more softly but also to enhance the mellowness of the sound and eliminate any percussiveness in the tone quality. The left pedal is often compared to the string player's mute, although this over-used analogy is not completely accurate. Yet if we always think of the left pedal as a device for coloring and changing tone quality, rather than a crutch for playing more softly, we will come much closer to an artistic use of this valuable pianistic tool.

The left pedal could much more appropriately be termed the "shifting" pedal, for that is exactly what it does on grand pianos. As the left pedal is depressed, the entire set of hammers shifts slightly to the right, so that on the majority of notes, two instead of three strings are struck (see Example 1). The quantity of sound is certainly reduced, but of much greater significance is the alteration of tone quality that results from the hammer's striking with a less-impacted, softer part of its surface. Also of great importance is the setting up of a light vibration in the unused string, as the hammer strikes the other two strings. This creation of partials lends a veiled tone to the overall sonority.

With use, the head of the hammer will show some grooving from repeatedly striking the strings in the same place. On hammers that have received heavy, constant use, the grooves often look like deep gashes; and age may destroy the resilience of the felt even further. With ideal regulation, the hammers should move just far enough to the right to strike in the softer, relatively unworn part of the felt between the impacted grooves. The Bösendorfer firm, in fact, takes care that the hammers operate in this manner. Although on its instruments the third string is still struck to some degree, the advantage of having the hammer hit consistently in a softer area is well worth the slight additional volume.

On most grands, a full depression of the left pedal will send the hammers far enough to the right that, although two instead of three strings are struck on the majority of notes, the hammers still strike in or at the edge of the impacted grooves. Especially in the upper register, a rather tinny, wheezy sound may result. Many performers who are sensitive to the uses of the left pedal feel that, short of a regulation of the pedal itself by a technician, the best solution is to depress the left pedal only part way, so that the hammers will strike in a less-impacted area.

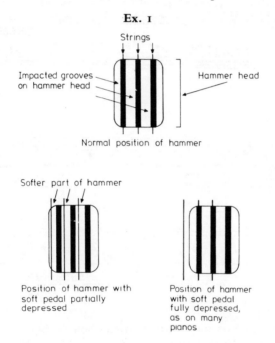

Ex. 1

Strings

Impacted grooves on hammer head

Hammer head

Normal position of hammer

Softer part of hammer

Position of hammer with soft pedal partially depressed

Position of hammer with soft pedal fully depressed, as on many pianos

Operating the left pedal in this manner will naturally vary from instrument to instrument. Pianos with relatively unworn hammer surfaces may work well with a full depression of the left pedal, while those with deeply grooved hammer surfaces may require meticulous control so that a particular part of the hammer surface will strike the strings and make for a maximum mellowing of the tone. The ear rather than the eye must be the performer's guide. The performer should determine if the left pedal is properly regulated and if the hammers are voiced so that no unevenness or wheeziness of tone will result when the pedal is used. Everyone has a favorite passage for testing the left pedal. Example 2,

Ex. 2

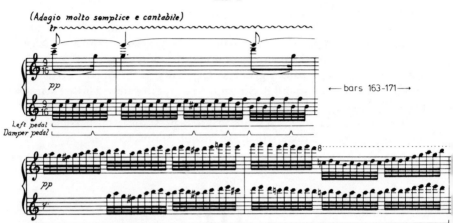

Ex. 3

from the second movement of Beethoven's Sonata, Op. 111, and Example 3, from Schubert's Impromptu, Op. 90, No. 3, are two possible choices.

Passages with a relatively high dynamic level may still demand use of the left pedal, as in Example 4, from Liszt's "Bénédiction de Dieu dans la Solitude" (from *Harmonies poétiques et religieuses*), where the indication for the left pedal is by the composer. This passage is also a good one for testing the left pedal.

Positioning the Left Foot

Many teachers tell their students that the left foot should be kept on the left pedal at all times, ready to depress it when needed. And to be sure,

Ex. 4

there is nothing more annoying than seeing a performer suddenly lunge forward just at the moment the left pedal is needed. Many pianists, especially those who play with energetic, often distracting, bodily motions, may engage in extraneous actions with the left foot—shuffling, keeping time, or stamping. Too often their "expressiveness" comes out in these spastic motions, not in the sound of the playing itself! But there are times when keeping the left foot glued in readiness on the left pedal is not wise, for when there are passages for both hands at either end of the keyboard, the left foot may be needed for balance.

If both hands are at the upper end of the piano, place the left foot to the left of the pedals. If both hands are playing in the low register, shift the left foot to the right, behind the right foot. In very loud passages the left foot may be placed back underneath the bench for balance, as the player thrusts forward into the keys with full shoulder weight. Even when the left pedal is in use, the heel can be angled to the left or the right, depending on which end of the keyboard the two hands are playing. A small shift of position can do wonders toward maintaining a comfortable sense of balance.

Written Directions for the Left Pedal

Although the term *una corda* was used in Beethoven's time, the actual physical construction and consequent effect on the tone of this pedal was vastly different than in our own day (see chapter 1). But the antiquated term *una corda* has remained in use to indicate the left pedal, along with various other terms:

English: soft pedal, shift pedal, muting pedal
French: *une corde, sourdine, la pédale sourde, petite pédale*
German: *mit Verschiebung, mit einer Saite, mit Dämpfung*
Italian: *sordino, una corda, u.c., sul una corda, poco a poco una corda*

A release for the left pedal may be indicated by *tre corde, 3 cordes, ohne Verschiebung, tutte le corde, t. c., poco a poco tre corde, poco a poco tutte le corde, or due corde.* Use of both the left and the right pedals at the same time may be indicated by Ped. 1 and 2, *con 2 Pedale,* 2 ped., *Les deux pédales, Mit beiden Pedalen, Beide Pedale, I due pedali, Très enveloppé de pédales,* 2 Ped., *due Ped., or con sord e Ped.*

Composers' Indications for the Left Pedal
When a composer gives indications for the use of the left pedal, these directions must of course be carefully followed. In Example 5, from the second movement of Schubert's Sonata, Op. 53, the indication *mit Verschiebung* literally means "with shifting," or in other words, play with the left pedal. But Schubert gives no indication for releasing it.

Ex. 5

Beethoven gives a number of indications for the left pedal, most frequently in the last piano sonatas. In Example 6, from the third movement of his Sonata, Op. 106, the pedaling directions for both the use of the left pedal *(una corda)* and its release *(tutte le corde)* are extremely precise.

In some instances when the left pedal is released, the performer may have to continue playing softly. At such times it is often necessary to reduce the dynamic level slightly, in order to compensate for the release of the left pedal. In Example 7, from the fourth movement of Beethoven's Sonata, Op. 106, the composer's own indications for the use and release of the left pedal are given.

When use of the left pedal seems appropriate but is not specifically requested by the composer, the performer must use his sense of musical style, but should not rely on the left pedal as a lazy way of playing more softly.

Ex. 6

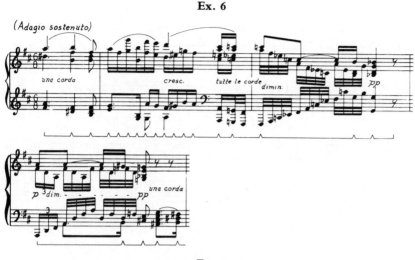

Ex. 7

Echo Effects

Echo effects in particular may lend themselves well to a use of the left pedal, as in Example 8, from the first movement of Schubert's Sonata, Op. 164, where an entire four bar-phrase is repeated *pianississimo*.

However, a *piano,* or even a *pianissimo,* does not always necessitate use of the left pedal. In many instances a composer will imply its use within an already extremely quiet dynamic area. In Example 9, from Debussy's *Masques,* the indications *sourd* ("muffled," "muted") and *en s'éloignant* ("fading away") would seem to call for the left pedal. The *pianissimo* indication is probably precautionary, since this indication is the last given in previous bars.

The Left Pedal in the Middle of a Phrase

An often-quoted guideline for the use of the left pedal is that it should not be depressed in the middle of a phrase, even when there is a *diminuendo.* There is a large element of truth in it, since employing the left pedal

Ex. 8

Ex. 9

Ex. 10

midway in a phrase may cause a noticeable change of tone quality. In Example 10, from Chopin's Barcarolle, Op. 60, the left pedal should probably not be depressed during the *diminuendo*.

There are a number of exceptions to this broad "rule"; for example, a passage that has a striking color change suggested by the harmony or by the composer's own dynamic indications. Chopin's Nocturne, Op. 9, No. 1., shown in Example 11, has a number of such color changes.

Ex. 11

Shaping Slurs or Phrase Endings

In many situations the left pedal may be used within a phrase to taper slur endings or final parts of the phrase itself. This usage works especially well on instruments whose tone quality is excessively hard and bright, and where the pianist must use every conceivable means to control dynamics and tone quality. No inflexible rules can be made in this regard, for on some pianos the left pedal will alter the tone quality in such an abrupt manner as to preclude its use in softening the quantity of sound within a phrase. As with so much of pedal technique, the player must constantly experiment and above all listen critically to his own playing. Example 12, from Chopin's Fantaisie, Op. 49, and Example 13, from Schubert's Impromptu, Op. 142, No. 3, show how the left pedal might be used in shaping slurs and phrases, assuming that the change in tone quality is not too extreme on the instrument being played at the moment.

Ex. 12

Ex. 13

In Accompanimental Figuration

The left pedal may be used to soften accompanimental figuration, thereby giving it a different tone quality from the primary melodic material. It must again be emphasized that the instrument being played must be carefully evaluated, to see if its tone quality lends itself to this pedal technique. In Example 14, from Schubert's Impromptu, Op. 90, No. 3, and Example 15, from Chopin's Etude, Op. 25, No. 7, the left pedal should be lifted briefly as each note of the melody is played.

Ex. 14

Ex. 15

For Intensity of Tone

Composers may ask for use of the left pedal in passages where great tonal intensity is required, as in Example 16, from Liszt's *Recueillement*. The indications for both the damper and the left pedal are original.

Use of the left pedal, even when not specifically requested by the composer, may be desirable in a *cantabile* passage where a great deal of emotional intensity demands an equal intensity of tone, but where the

Ex. 16

Ex. 17

Second time use left pedal.

volume itself must not be too great. In Example 17, from Schumann's Romanze, Op. 28, No. 2, the performer may wish to use the left pedal only when the repeat of the first eight bars is taken.

In Transcriptions

In transcriptions of organ works, the left pedal may be used not only when the volume of a given passage must be lessened but also to alter the tone quality when the writing imitates a different stop of the organ. Such a passage occurs in Example 18, from the Busoni piano transcription of the Prelude of Bach's Toccata in C major for organ.

Using All Three Pedals Simultaneously

Occasionally all three pedals are to be used simultaneously, with the left foot manipulating the left and the middle pedals. This technique is not easy, but it can be done with sufficient practice. Percy Grainger, whose ideas on pedaling still prove to be extremely advanced, says of this technique:

> The player must be freely able to take and release the soft pedal while holding the sustaining pedal, to take and release the sustaining pedal while holding the soft pedal. Players with small feet, new to this problem, are apt to think it an impossibility, but experience shows that all sizes of feet can master this

double-pedal-technic with sufficient practice. It is an *absolute necessity* to modern pianism.[1]

To position the left foot over the left and middle pedals:

1. Place the heel of the foot slightly to the left of the left pedal. The toes should face in the direction of the damper pedal, the heel away from the damper pedal.
2. First press the left pedal down with the left side of the foot, the pressure being applied on the ball of the foot.
3. Apply pressure to the *sostenuto* pedal with the right side of the foot from the toes, still keeping the left pedal firmly depressed.

The exercises in Example 19 may be used to practice shifting the left foot from one pedal to the other.

Ex. 19

Example 20, from Liszt's Sonata in B minor, and Example 21, from Ravel's "Ondine" (from *Gaspard de la Nuit*), show passages in which all three pedals may be used at the same time.

Ex. 20

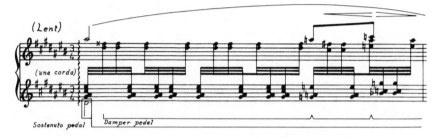

Ex. 21

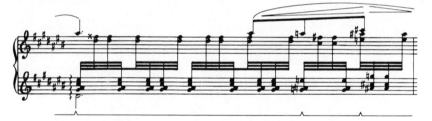

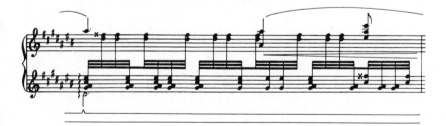

PART TWO

*Pedaling Works of
Selected Composers
and Styles*

5

Using the Pedals
When Playing Bach

The Right Pedal

Many performers insist that because the right pedal did not exist on the instruments for which Bach wrote his keyboard music, it should not be used when playing his music on the piano. This reasoning, to be consistent, should perhaps be then extended to conclude that Bach's music should not be heard at all on the piano, since none of his keyboard works, so far as is known, were written for Cristofori's newly invented *Gravicembalo col piano e forte*. Each musician must settle this issue for himself. But assuming that one does not wish to be deprived of the modern piano and its rich color and sonority when playing Bach, how then should the use of pedal be approached? Can pedaling be done in a manner that will not corrupt and compromise Bach's music?

A great deal of the mischief regarding Bach's keyboard music and the damper pedal has resulted from confusing a nineteenth-century sound concept—which favored using the pedal primarily for massed sonorities, figurational blending, and sustaining long bass pedal points—with a Baroque ideal of contrapuntal clarity of parts, each set off by contrasting articulation. When Bach's keyboard music is played on the piano, the right pedal is rarely needed to sustain larger groups of notes. What then should be its role?

For today's performer of Bach, perhaps the most important role of the damper pedal is the achieving of a seamless *legato,* when desired. Although harpsichordists, clavichordists, and organists of Bach's day had to achieve a *legato* with the fingers alone, they did not have the added concerns of greater key depth, weight, and even size that face the pianist of today. Key weight and depth of depression are special problems when repeated notes or chords must be played *legato*. In using the pedal for this type of *legato* connection, the player should try to re-depress the pedal between, rather than immediately after, each repeated note or chord, therefore minimizing the time the dampers are actually raised. The shorter the time the dampers remain away from the strings the less chance there is of an audible change in the tone quality. Of course, the player must achieve as much *legato* as possible with the fingers. Example 1, from the Prelude in B-flat minor, *WTC* I, and Example 2, from the Fugue in F minor, *WTC* I, contain typical instances of the right pedal helping to make a *legato* connection between repeated notes.

Ex. 1

Ex. 2

Example 3, from the Fugue in C minor, *WTC* II, and Example 4, from the Fugue in F minor, *WTC* I, show awkward skips and large intervals that must be connected with the right pedal.

Ex. 3

The right pedal can also be used as an enrichment of tone quality, especially in melodic passages that have notes of long value. Bach himself preferred a *cantabile* manner of playing, as set forth in the dedication preface to his Inventions.[1] Moreover, since none of the keyboard instruments of the early eighteenth century dampened the sound as quickly as does a modern grand, their sound cannot be regarded as dry. The key-

Ex. 4

board works of Bach that were conceived for the less-brilliant, expressive style of the clavichord generally require a greater degree of *cantabile* and *legato*. Bach's Prelude in E-flat minor, *WTC* I, shown in Example 5, is clearly written in this style.

Ex. 5

Passages in which the player is expected to arpeggiate large chords freely, as in the Fantasie in A minor, BWV 944, in Example 6, may call for some use of the right pedal.

Ex. 6

Throughout the Fantasie in C minor, BWV 906, light touches of the right pedal may be used to accent short ornaments or slurs in bright, energetic passages that are strongly rhythmic in nature. In Example 7, the short slurs are found in Bach's original text.

Ex. 7

The Left Pedal

Although a general avoidance of the left pedal should be regarded as the norm in Bach's music, there are occasions when it can be a valuable tool for coloring. Repetitions of sections, which on the harpsichord might have been varied by a change of registration, can be colored by using the left pedal. But the performer should never permit this kind of echo device to become overused or predictable. Although the left pedal will sometimes prove valuable in the third of the *Variations in the Italian Manner,* BWV 989, shown in Example 8, as a means of achieving variety, its use should not become automatic as every repeat is taken.

Ex. 8

Use left pedal during repeat.

The Middle Pedal

There are a few passages in Bach's music in which the imaginative player can use the middle pedal to hold long pedal points that cannot be held by either the fingers or the right pedal. Most of them are found in works that seem to have been composed with the pedal keyboard in mind. In Bach's day the pedal keyboard could be attached to the clavichord or the harpsichord, so that the same strings could be activated by the pedals as well as by the hands. This device was particularly useful for organ students who had to do some practicing at home. James Grassineau, in his *Musical Dictionary* of 1740, writes that when the pedal keyboard is attached to a clavichord, it "cannot be heard at any considerable distance; hence some call it the dumb spinet; whence it comes to be particularly used among the nuns, who learn to play, and are unwilling to disturb the dormitory."[2] According to a description of Bach's estate at his death, there was in his possession one set of such pedals.[3]

One instance of Bach's writing that seems to utilize a pedal keyboard is found in Example 9, bars 79–87 of the Fugue in A minor, *WTC* I. Here it is impossible to hold the extended A pedal point starting in bar 83 for its full duration with either the finger or the right pedal. Two solutions utilizing the middle pedal are possible. Perhaps the better one is to depress the A silently during the rest in bar 80 and catch it quickly with the middle pedal. When the A is actually sounded three bars later, it will already be caught and will hold. The other possibility, shown in Example 10, is to use the middle pedal to catch both the low A and the A an octave higher on the fourth beat of bar 83. Although that will result in an extra A being held in the pedal, the harmonic idea of an overall A pedal point will remain the same. According to Carl Philipp Emanuel Bach, long tied pedal points may be reinforced by additional repetitions.[4]

Ex. 9

Silently depress A, then catch with the middle pedal and hold until the end.

Another opportunity for use of the middle pedal is shown in Example 11, from the *Fugue on a Theme of Albinoni,* BWV 950. There can be no question that this work was originally written for pedal keyboard, since the word *Pedal* is given in the original score. If the middle pedal is used, only the low E should be caught and held.

It should always be remembered that none of the piano's pedals is in any way a substitute for a finger *legato* or for well-planned concepts of articulation, phrasing, and dynamic control that must be carried out by

Ex. 10

Ex. 11

the hands alone. In playing Bach's keyboard music on the piano, the
pedals should be regarded primarily as coloring agents and as only occasional aids in keeping a *legato* or in maintaining a pedal point.

THE PEDAL IN TRANSCRIPTIONS

Playing piano transcriptions of Bach's music requires the use of the three
pedals much more than does playing his original scores for the harpsichord or clavichord on the piano. During the nineteenth and early
twentieth centuries, transcriptions were frequently made and performed
by many of the foremost pianists of the day. Then, with a growing
sensitivity to authentic performance practices of earlier music, as well as
a renewed interest in historical instruments, both performers and musi-
cologists increasingly rejected the transcription as justifiable art form. In

their rush to reject the interpretative freedom and, at times, admitted license of the nineteenth-century Romantic performer, their harsh attitude often degenerated into snobbery. But now much of this extreme rejection seems to have passed. Such major artists as Fischer, Gilels, Hess, Horowitz, Kempff, de Larrocha, Michelangeli, Novaes, Petri, Rubinstein, and Sándor have recorded transcriptions of Bach's music. With this distinguished company setting an example, there would seem to be ample justification for discussing pedaling in this important literature.

One of the greatest transcribers of Bach's music was Ferruccio Busoni, whose arrangements for piano of many of the organ works and of the Chaconne in D minor for solo violin still rank among the greatest achievements in the genre. Busoni left a comprehensive analysis of his transcription methods in a supplement (unfortunately omitted in modern reprints) to his edition of *The Well-Tempered Clavier.*[5] The section on pedaling is imaginative, and it is applicable in a wider artistic and practical sense to many compositions not in the transcription category.

Examples 12–19, all of which are in Busoni's essay, show representative uses of the pedals when playing transcriptions. The pedal indications are those found in Busoni's original text; only in a few instances has his notation been altered to make it more understandable.

The Right Pedal
Busoni's trenchant opening remarks in the section concerning the right pedal speak for themselves:

> Do not believe in the legendary tradition, that Bach must be played without pedal. While the pedal is sometimes necessary in Bach's piano-works, it is absolutely essential in these transcribed organ-pieces. True, in the piano-works the inaudible use of the pedal is the only proper one. By this we mean the employment of the pedal for binding two successive single tones or chords, for emphasizing a suspension, for sustaining a single part, etc.; a manner of treatment by which no specific pedal-effect is brought out. . . . Wherever possible, sustain the tones with the hands rather than with the pedal. Sweeping pedal-effects in a pianistic sense are foreign to the style. Where chords (solid or broken) are taken with the pedal, lift the hands simultaneously with the pedal. A vaguely prolonged sound is contrary to the nature of the organ. In passages intended to imitate magnificent "full organ" effects, the pedal is indispensable. The raised dampers produce no ill effect with passing- and changing-notes, and the like. Consider, that the mixtures opened with the full organ contain the fifth and octave, or even the third and seventh, of every tone struck. An approximate imitation of these tone-blendings (tone-tangles) can be obtained, on the piano, only by using the pedal.[6]

Busoni's examples are extremely precise, some even using dotted lines to show exactly where the pedal should be depressed and released. Example 12, from the "St. Anne" Fugue, and Example 13, from the Organ Prelude in D major, demonstrate his precision in the use of the pedal.

Ex. 12

Ex. 13

The Left Pedal

Busoni gives the following suggestions for using the left pedal:

> Touching the soft, or left, pedal (marked *"una corda"* or *"u. c."*) let us say at the outset, that it may be used not only for the last gradations of *"pianissimo,"* but also in *"mezzo forte"* and all the intermediate dynamic shadings. The case may even occur, that some passages are played more softly without the soft pedal than others with it. The effect intended here is not softness of tone, but the peculiar quality of tone obtained.[7]

In Examples 14 and 15, both from the "St. Anne" Prelude, Busoni seems to regard the left pedal as an aid in coloring and uses it to give the effect of changes of organ registration.

Ex. 14

Ex. 15

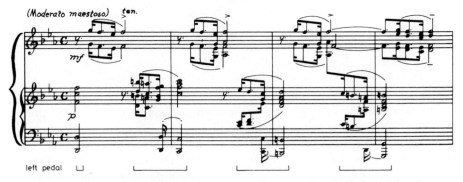

In Example 15, although Busoni gives indications for the left pedal only, the middle pedal should undoubtedly be used to sustain the half-note chords occurring on the first and third beats. If that is done, the right foot should manipulate the middle pedal.

The Middle Pedal

Busoni extensively explores the uses of the middle pedal, writing, "real organ-effects can be obtained only by the combined action of the three pedals."[8] Example 16, from the Organ Prelude and Fugue in D major, uses the middle pedal to sustain pedal points that on the organ would be held by the feet.

In Liszt's transcription of Bach's Fantasie and Fugue in G minor, shown in Example 17, Busoni recommends manipulating the middle pedal with the right foot, since the right pedal is not in use at that moment.

Ex. 16

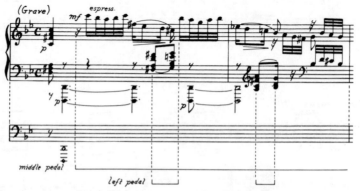

Ex. 17

Busoni feels that the sound of the organ can be better imitated by "the inaudible repetition of sustained tones."[9] In an original example (Example 18), he retains the left-hand D octave by silently re-depressing it to accommodate the shifting harmony above. The right foot must first operate the middle pedal, then shift to the right pedal, since the left foot must hold the left pedal throughout. Although Busoni never mentions the possibility of working both the left and middle pedals simultaneously with the left foot, this solution would help to achieve a *legato* in the first bar.

Ex. 18

Another effect Busoni advocates is that of re-depressing held melody notes, then lifting the damper pedal so that the sound emerges in a manner that highlights the melody. In another of his original examples (Example 19), Busoni's notation of this effect seems to call also for a slow depressing and releasing of the right pedal.

Ex. 19

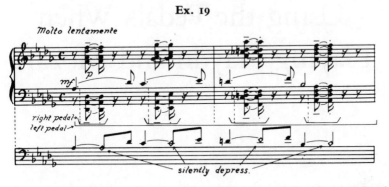

Busoni was a pianist of genius whose ideas on pedaling are startlingly original for his time and in some respects have not been surpassed.

Using the Pedals When
Playing Haydn and Mozart

The Right Pedal
Use of the damper pedal when playing Haydn and Mozart on the piano has always been problematic, and there are some musicians who feel strongly that the pedal should be used sparingly when playing Haydn and not at all with Mozart. Admittedly, some of their earliest keyboard works were also intended to be played on the harpsichord or clavichord, but as the early fortepiano rapidly gained acceptance, both composers soon began to write with this instrument in mind.

The bright, somewhat thin and transparent tone of the fortepiano of Haydn and Mozart's day is difficult if not impossible to reproduce on an undoctored modern piano. That is undoubtedly why many performers have recommended avoiding the right pedal entirely in repertory of this period. But leaving aside personal musical taste, the omission of the damper pedal in performing Haydn or Mozart is not historically accurate. Virtually all the fortepianos of the last three decades of the eighteenth century were equipped with a knee lever to raise and lower the dampers in much the same way as the modern piano's damper pedal does.

As far as is known, Mozart wrote no pedaling indications in any of his keyboard works. Yet he was enthusiastic about the pedaling mechanism of the Stein fortepianos. In an often-quoted letter to his father, dated October 17, 1777, he writes:

> The device which you work with your knee is better than what is found on other instruments. You only need to touch it and it works, and as soon as you move your knee the least bit, you do not hear the slightest remainder of sound.[1]

Although Haydn rarely indicated pedaling in his scores, he did give two indications, shown in Examples 1 and 2, for the damper pedal in the Sonata in C major, Hob. XVI: 50, written around 1794. On the pianos of the time, the long, unbroken pedaling in these passages would have sounded atmospheric and mysterious. These pedalings are marked not because these passages are the only places where Haydn desires pedal but because they create unusual effects. On the vastly more resonant instruments of today, one can roughly reproduce this sound by utilizing an approximate 50 percent release of damper sound or by making partial changes of the pedal when the full sound of open pedal begins to accumulate or blur excessively. The left pedal can also be used to enhance the veiled sonority these passages require.

Ex. 1

Ex. 2

It seems probable that both Mozart and Haydn made at least limited use of the damper-activating mechanism of the day. In using the right pedal on today's instruments, the performer should always remember that in their music, clarity of texture, phrasing, and articulation must never be obscured. As in playing Bach on the piano, the pedal in Mozart or Haydn must be imperceptible.

In any style, one of the most important roles for the right pedal is to give greater resonance and color. That also holds true for Mozart's and Haydn's compositions. Especially in slower, *cantabile* passages that have notes of longer value, the right pedal can help to avoid dryness of tone. The passage from Haydn's Sonata in E-flat major, Hob. XVI: 52, given in Example 3 will sound too dry if no pedal is used.

Ex. 3

Slower passages with Alberti bass or other broken-chord figurations often need some degree of finger pedaling and/or damper pedal to avoid an overly dry sound. Walter Gieseking felt that when a *legato* is indicated, the performer is justified in playing accompanimental figuration in a *legatissimo* manner, in which some degree of finger pedaling is utilized.[2] This approach permits the melody to remain clear and unmuddied but avoids an overly dry texture in the harmonic support below. The degrees to which *legatissimo* finger pedaling and the pedal itself are used of course depend on the individual performer's preference and musical taste. The second movement of Mozart's Sonata in F major, K. 300k, shown in Example 4, contains many passages where such a *legatissimo* touch may be used to excellent advantage. (Alfred Einstein's revisions of Köchel's original numbers are used in all examples cited.)

Ex. 4

Other, more rapid Alberti basses should not receive pedal, and should sound, depending on the register, as though they are being played by an orchestral instrument such as the bassoon or clarinet. In Example 5, use

Ex. 5

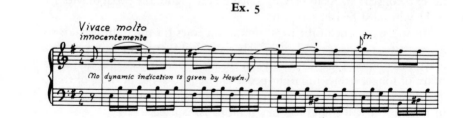

of the pedal in the third movement of Haydn's Sonata in E minor, Hob.
XVI: 34, would make the left-hand texture far too heavy.

Phrasing, slurs, and all other articulation indications should remain
clear, and rests should not be obscured. In Example 6, from the second
movement of Mozart's Sonata in B-flat major, K. 315c, touches of pedal
for color could be given to the first note of each downbeat slur indicated
by the composer, but would not be absolutely necessary.

Ex. 6

Heavy accents can be made more expressive and less percussively dry
by brief touches of pedal, as in the first movement of the Haydn Sonata
in C minor, Hob. XVI: 20, shown in Example 7.

Ex. 7

Some extended broken-chord figurations might demand a more liberal use of pedal, as in the Mozart Fantasie in C major, K. 383a, in
Example 8. The free rhythmic notation is from the original.

Other broken-chord passages of a more melodic character may not
sound as well with long stretches of pedal. In Example 9, from the
Mozart Fantasie in D minor, K. 385g, an unbroken pedal for each of the
first three bars would tend to obscure the melodic contour of the right
hand. Left-hand finger pedaling, combined with an approximate 50 percent release of pedaled sound, will better serve Mozart's style in this
passage. The omission of ties and dynamics is as in the original.

Passages that imitate an orchestral tutti growing to the entrance of the
soloist for a cadenza may require pedal. In Example 10, from the third
movement of Mozart's Sonata in D major, K. 284c, the lifting of the pedal
should make clear the entrance of an imagined "soloist."

Ex. 8

Ex. 9

Ex. 10

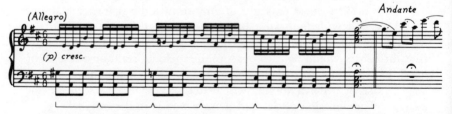

In working out use of the right pedal for either Haydn or Mozart, the pianist should first learn the music without pedal. All articulation should be accomplished by the fingers alone; later, pedal can be added sparingly for color or for a short period to facilitate an awkward *legato*.

The Left Pedal

Except in instances when a definite alteration of tone quality is desired, the left pedal should seldom be used. Although the fortepianos of the day were equipped with a shifting mechanism, no such pedal indications appear in either Haydn's or Mozart's scores. The *pianissimos* given by Mozart in Example 11, from the second movement of his Sonata in C minor, K. 457, are instances in which the left pedal could possibly be used.

Ex. 11

7

Beethoven's Uses of the Pedals

by *William S. Newman*

Background, Facts and Figures, Problems, and Sources

Beethoven was the first front-rank composer to call for the use of the pedals to any appreciable extent. As we have seen, Haydn had made isolated requests for the "open [damper] pedal" late in his pianistic career (in his Sonata in C major, Hob. XVI: 50, first movement) and while he was intrigued by English instruments. And Mozart in his oft-cited letter of October 17–18, 1777, had revealed his admiration for the knee-lever damper controls on the early Stein pianos that he sampled. Indeed, Mozart may well have used damper controls in his own masterly playing, even though he is not known ever to have specified their use in his scores. But with Beethoven it was different. He left little doubt as to the extent, the nature, or the practical application of his pedal uses.

There are two reasons why we might expect Beethoven to have pioneered more use of the pedals. Both suggest a kind of chicken-or-the-egg question of origins. One generation after Haydn and Mozart, did the evolving construction of the piano's pedals finally lead the way to Beethoven's uses, or did Beethoven's more complex, expressive music finally lead the way to their construction? As for the construction, the control of the dampers by a true "pedal" (that is, by a *foot* rather than a *knee* lever), which had been introduced a quarter-century earlier,[1] did not become general until just after 1800. Also, not until about 1800 did action-shifting devices become more widely utilized, so that the hammer could strike only one string *(una corda)* or two rather than all three strings. Yet, as we have seen, devices for both damper control and action shifting had existed for nearly a century, from the time of Cristofori's pianos.[2]

As for Beethoven's becoming ready for the piano's pedals, it was he who had entered—indeed, opened the way to—an era of greater and more intense expressiveness, to which the pedals would be contributing increasingly. Much as he was finding it necessary to qualify his tempos more precisely in his era,[3] so he was finding it necessary to qualify the sounds and textures that he was creating, with respect to both timbre and enrichment. How seriously he took this aspect of his composing can be surmised from the care he seems to have given it in his manuscripts. For instance, in a very abbreviated sketch (dating from 1810) of the popular little piece "Für Elise," WoO 59, Beethoven did not trouble to insert markings for dynamics or slurs, but did trouble to mark the pedaling in detail throughout, which he "evidently regarded as essential to the sonority."[4] Example 1 contains a corner of the sketch. The signs "𝄞𝄢." and "O" may be seen between the staffs.

Ex. 1

Just how much use *did* Beethoven make of the pedals? Considerably more than many performers might suppose, for they seem only occasionally to be aware of the pedal indications in his *Urtexts,* and then chiefly as they may question the more puzzling ones. To be sure, performers cannot be aware of Beethoven's indications at all if they use only an edition that replaces the composer's own editing with the various alternatives preferred by modern editors. Beethoven's own pedal indications occur throughout his music involving piano, not only in his solo music but in his chamber and orchestral music as well. Nearly 800 such indications have turned up in a tabulation of authentic sources done for the present study. Each of these indications calls for an application of either the damper or the action-shifting pedal, followed most of the time, but not always, by its release. Not surprisingly, 98 percent call for the damper "pedal," with only about 2 percent (nearly all in the solo piano sonatas) calling for *una corda*. Furthermore—if the reader will bear with all these statistics in order to get our topic into better perspective—nearly 60 percent of all the indications occur in the solo piano music (three-fourths of these being in the sonatas), about 15 percent in the chamber music, and the remaining 25 percent in the concertos (including the "Triple" Concerto, Op. 56).

Some idea of the years in which Beethoven provided these indications should help the overall perspective, too. He probably used damper controls from the start of his professional piano playing in Bonn in the mid 1780s, or about as soon as they became available to him on the early Stein pianos.[5] But aside from one still earlier indication, he did not begin to indicate the damper controls in his scores until about 1795 (in the manuscripts of his first two piano concertos, Opp. 19 and 15), continuing thereafter right up to his last year of composing, 1826.

The earlier indication, in a sketch dating from 1790–92, is simply an inscription "with the knee" in a series of repeated chords, as shown in Example 2. This happens to be the earliest-known indication for a damper control in a score (that of Haydn, mentioned above, not dating until 1794 or even later). While Beethoven was still using knee levers for those damper controls—that is, up to about 1802 and the completion of his Concerto No. 3 in C minor—he used the terms *senza* and *con sordino* [*sic*], meaning "without" and "with the dampers."[6] Thereafter, he used more modern signs for pedal and release.

Ex. 2

In a letter of November 1802, Beethoven made clear that he already knew about the *una corda* control, for he inquired about a Walter piano that would include a "pull [or knob] with one string."[7] By then he may well have been using this control in his own playing when it was available, but he did not start to indicate it in his scores until later. The first two instances occur in his Piano Concerto No. 4, Op. 58, composed about 1805–1806; some twenty other instances do not occur until the last five piano sonatas, composed from about 1816 to 1822.

None of this information should suggest that once he started inserting them, Beethoven distributed his pedal indications evenly throughout his works for and with piano. On the contrary, he seems to have confined his insertion of them largely to places where he wanted to make a particular point of their effect. In other words, he often bunched them in certain movements (as in the finale of the "Waldstein" Sonata, Op. 53) and left them out entirely in others (as in the first movement of the Sonata in A-flat major, Op. 110), possibly for the very reason that their need might seem obvious to the performer!

In order to get further into the meaning of Beethoven's pedal indications, one has to keep four pertinent questions in mind. First, what pedals did Beethoven have on the pianos that he played and seemed to prefer?[8] For our purposes, the answer really only needs to be that he had at least the two kinds of pedals that he chose to use—the damper and the action-shifting pedals. He also had and knew at least the two most favored among other pedals then in use, the lute or harp pedal and the dampening (as distinguished from the damper) pedal. These extra two pedals, for example, were on his Erard piano (received as a gift from the Paris maker in 1803); and a dampening pedal was on the Viennese Graf piano made for and lent to him during his last three years.[9] But it should be added, as I have argued elsewhere,[10] that Beethoven's first loyalty throughout his life seems to have been to the Viennese pianos rather than to the Erard or to the Broadwood (received as a gift from London in 1818), and that even though the pedals he chose to use had appeared earlier on the British and French pianos, they did appear on the Viennese pianos by the time Beethoven was ready for them. Almost as soon as the Erard arrived, he began to express his general dissatisfaction with it.[11] By the time the Broadwood reached him in 1818, he had already completed much of his piano writing (including, in all probability, the "Hammerklavier" Sonata, Op. 106); and by the time the Graf reached him in 1825 he had but one more pedal indication to insert (in the opening of the transcription, Op. 134, of his *Grosse Fuge* for string quartet, Op. 133).

The second question concerns the nature of Beethoven's pedaling in his own playing. As with the playing of most of the master pianists up to and including Chopin, we have remarkably little specific objective information about Beethoven's playing. Among the numerous, largely glowing, reports that have survived, there are only two that throw any direct light on his pedaling. Both are nuggets that come to us by way of Czerny, a reliable and knowing observer who was right on the scene in Vienna, but both need a bit of interpreting. According to Czerny,

Hummel's partisans charged that Beethoven maltreated the fortepiano, lacked all purity and distinctness, brought only confusing noise through the use of the pedal, and that his compositions were affected, unnatural, melodyless, and, what is more, without proportion.[12]

Presumably Hummel's partisans meant that Beethoven pedaled too much of the time and too long without lifting. The other report is Czerny's own remark that Beethoven used the pedal much more than he indicated in his scores,[13] presumably meaning more often and in more (different) places.

Both statements suggest that Beethoven made much use of the damper pedal, but they juxtapose conservative and progressive attitudes toward this relative innovation. Hummel, a pupil of Mozart, still showed a wary attitude toward it in his treatise.[14] Czerny, himself a pupil of Beethoven, proved more than ready to accept, even promote, the damper pedal.[15] If Beethoven actually did let his "animal spirits" drive him to play loudly and frenetically in excited passages, as some of his observers reported, then he could very well have compounded the whole effect with the "confusion" of the pedal.[16] On the other hand, if he was as intrigued by the pedals' effects as his indications for them suggest, then he could well have cultivated much use of the pedal in his own playing.

A third question is how much Beethoven's deafness may have affected his pedal indications. Did it falsify his reactions to the piano's sounds and therefore influence his judgment as to the pedals' effects? His hearing started to worry him before he was thirty (in 1800). By 1802 it drove him to the despair that brought forth his suicidal *Heiligenstadt Testament,* and by 1822 he was completely deaf. But one must remember that his hearing deteriorated unevenly. There were bad days and good days; there were sounds that failed to penetrate and sounds that came through. More important, as the external ear seemed to regress, the inner, musical ear seemed to become more acute. We can understand that Beethoven would remember the sounds he had heard while he still *could* hear, yet we find it harder to believe that, as instruments developed and ranges increased, he could come to hear internally many sonorities and reverberations that he had *never* heard while his hearing was still satisfactory. Of course, subjective factors enter here. But considering some circumstantial evidence to be mentioned shortly, as well as the more patent success with which Beethoven came to hear new melodic, harmonic, and rhythmic combinations, I for one have come to believe that Beethoven did understand, "hear," and want essentially the pedal effects he indicated.

The fourth question to keep in mind is, How accurately are we interpreting Beethoven's pedal indications themselves? (After which we shall be able to ask, with more confidence, How accurately are we interpreting them in relation to his music?) Is it possible, for example, that Beethoven used *senza sordino* to mean not "with the dampers lifted" but "with the dampening strip (or mute) removed"?[17] No, it may have been possible in earlier uses, but not in Beethoven's contexts. Besides, Czerny's several mentions of *senza* and *con sordino* in Beethoven's music include no references to a dampening possibility. In that connection, Beethoven's use of *sordino* in the singular to mean "dampers" in the plural is just one of the countless linguistic laxities of the time. Of more concern is the uncertainty as to exactly where Beethoven wanted the pedal to be raised or lowered when he inserted the spread-out terms *senza sordino* or *con sordino* in his manuscripts. An example of this last problem may be seen in Example 3, where similar passages from the Sonata in A-flat major, Op. 26, are shown in the autograph, the original 1802 edition, and a modern *Urtext* edition.

Ex. 3

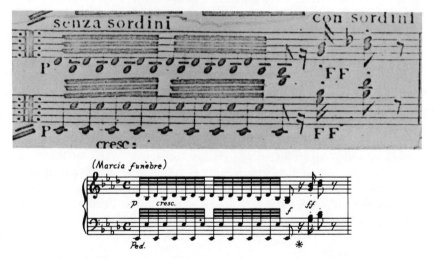

When Beethoven started calling for the actual foot "pedal," he usually preferred the indications " 𝄢 . . . O" rather than the more standard signs recommended by Hummel, Czerny, and others. These standard signs were introduced by Steibelt (see Example 11, below), including an asterisk for the release and another symbol that was used less frequently for the *una corda* pedal. Beethoven sometimes abbreviated *una corda* and *tre corde* or *tutte le corde* as *u. c.* and *t. c.* With slight differences, he worded the progression from one to the other, as in the "Hammerklavier" Sonata, Op. 106, third movement, bars 87–88, as "poco a poco due ed allora tre corde" (or its converse). But, of course, that gradual progression cannot be duplicated today (and could not even then on certain pianos), because the modern *una corda* pedal can shift the action only between two and three, or one and two, strings.

Inquiring readers may sense one further question arising out of the four questions that have now been considered. What are the sources for authentic information about Beethoven's uses of the pedals? As implied earlier, the first priority has to go to his own indications rather than to those found in virtually all "modern" editions that are not reliable *Urtexts*. Beethoven's own pedal indications appear in his autograph manuscripts (even in certain of the sketches as well as in their later versions), early editions (lifetime or immediately posthumous), documents (such as letters, proof sheets, and reports) that relate to those editions, and the modern critical editions. The second consideration is the pedals on the pianos of Beethoven's time that have been kept in working order, for it is only by trying them in their pianistic and musical contexts that one can judge their actual effects and possibilities. To be sure, opportunities to do such "trying" are rare. Third among sources are a very few documentary references that have been gleaned in letters and reports from, to, or about Beethoven. And fourth are the discussions of pedaling, more or less pertinent, in the treatises and methods of Beethoven's time, such as those already cited by Hummel and Czerny. In the present century numerous writings have dealt with questions about Beethoven's uses of the pedals, but only two substantial studies have focused primarily on those uses. One is actually a set of three studies, by Eibner, Jarecki, and Wegerer, that concentrate, respectively, on the historical precedents for Beethoven's indications that create harmonic clashes, on today's ways of handling those clashes, and on the mechanical or technical aspects of the pedals on Beethoven's instruments.[18] The other is the first chapter in an informative, useful, although somewhat hasty little book on Beethoven's piano playing by Herbert Grundmann and Paul Mies.[19]

The Damper Pedal

Among his many indications for the damper pedal, Beethoven seems to have had certain uses particularly in mind. They include sustaining the bass, improving the *legato,* creating a collective or composite sound,

implementing dynamic contrasts, interconnecting sections or movements, blurring the sound through harmonic clashes, and even contributing to the thematic structure. Among those seven uses, which need
to be explored one by one at least briefly, by far the most controversial,
and hence the most discussed, has been the blurring of the sound through
harmonic clashes, whether deliberate or unwitting and inadvertent.

The most obvious use was to sustain the bass, providing harmonic
support while the hands remain free to play elsewhere on the keyboard.
In Example 4, a fragment in a sketch of about 1793 (after Gustav
Nottebohm, *Zweite Beethovenia*), we have early evidence of Beethoven's
concern with the lasting power of the bass.

Ex. 4

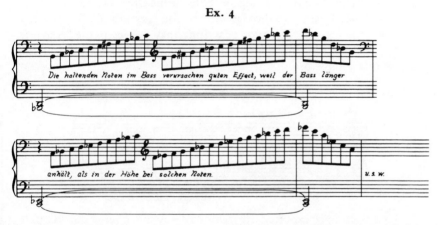

Although Beethoven does not yet indicate the pedal here, he includes
a pertinent annotation (just one of numerous, valuable annotations in his
manuscripts): "The sustained notes in the bass produce a good effect,
since with such notes the bass lasts longer than the high [notes]." A clear
example of Beethoven's use of the pedal to sustain the bass might be
quoted from the second movement of Piano Concerto No. 3 in C minor,
shown in Example 5. Here the pedal sustains the low C throughout the
broken 64th-note tenths and until it resolves to low B.

Ex. 5

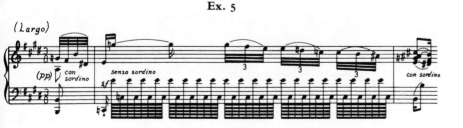

Two of Beethoven's close associates in Vienna, Friedrich Starke and Carl Czerny, emphasized the sustaining of the bass in their discussions of the damper pedal, though for different reasons. Said Starke, "Generally one may use this pedal for *forte* only in [passages] that maintain the same harmony and [only] if a bass or melody note is to be sustained throughout several measures." Said Czerny, "With pedal we are enabled to make the bass-notes vibrate as long as if we had a third hand at our disposal, while two hands are engaged in playing the melody, and the distant accompaniment."[20] Starke seems to have been concerned with the problem of blurring the sound, to be discussed shortly. Czerny was more concerned with ways to facilitate certain passages. Beethoven confirmed his own concern with prolonging the bass, since he ordinarily scored it so that the performer could manage to hold it with the fingers and still play the other strands of the texture. This type of writing may be seen in the "Andante favori," WoO 57 (the original slow movement of the "Waldstein" Sonata), shown in Example 6.

Ex. 6

That Beethoven expected the treble to decay much more quickly than the bass is suggested in the well-known two-note slurs of the Sonata in A-flat major, Op. 110. In bar 5 of the third movement, shown in Example 7, the slur releases may actually have been audible in Beethoven's day, but they must be acknowledged as largely if not entirely visual on today's pianos, with their long-lasting tones. The fingering is by the composer, and the number of beats in this measure is as in the original.

On the other hand, what are we to make of the pedaling in measures 14–17 of Example 8, from the third movement of the Sonata in A major,

Ex. 7

Ex. 8

Op. 101? Beethoven seems to have intended the fifth finger to hold each down-stem bass note until the pedal has to take over, so that the rising tenor line can be reached by the left hand.

The use of the damper pedal to implement *legato* playing could hardly be surprising in Beethoven, considering how importantly the *cantilena* style figures in both his music and his own playing. The versatile aesthetician Johann Friedrich Reichardt referred to the middle movement of the Concerto No. 4 in G major as "a masterly movement of beautifully developed song." Commenting on a performance of it in 1808, he wrote that Beethoven "positively caused it to sing on his instrument, with a deep, melancholy feeling that thrilled me, as well."[21] Undoubtedly, Beethoven's new preoccupation with keyboard *legato* explained the one objection Beethoven had found in Mozart's playing, as Czerny reported at least twice:

> Beethoven told Czerny that he had heard Mozart play; his execution was delicate, but choppy, without *legato* . . . [and further] that his playing was neat and clear, but rather empty, weak and old-fashioned. The *legato* and *cantabile* on the piano were unknown at that time, and Beethoven was the first to discover [these?] new and grand effects on that instrument . . . and excelled all others in his mastery of *legato*.[22]

One technical means of implementing the new *legato*, a means that Beethoven used and actually advocated, was to choose fingerings that would bring the notes within reach.[23] But when the desired *legato* was beyond reach, then an alternative means, understandably, had to be the pedal, as we observed in Example 8. In the first three bars of that example, as in several other passages, there is an apparent contradiction because of the rest in the right hand during each pedal application. The rest is partially psychological in a visual sense (rounding off the right-hand motif each time) and partially real, in that the register an octave higher than the tenor would die away more quickly on Beethoven's instruments, especially with *una corda* prevailing. Note that the down-stem bass notes in bars 17 and 18 have no pedal indications at all. The heavy action and greater distance from the floor made the pedals clumsier to manipulate then, even at the *Adagio* tempo, and would have proved generally impractical with the fast changes that might be expected in what Beethoven himself reportedly called the "finger dancing" of faster passages and tempos.[24]

An interesting question is whether Beethoven and his contemporaries ever used "syncopated pedaling" to achieve *legato*—that is, *raising* rather than lowering the damper pedal exactly as each tone or chord is played so as to clear out previous sounds, followed promptly by lowering it so as to sustain the new tone or chord until the next one is played. Because many sensitive pianists arrive at syncopated pedaling intuitively, if not unavoidably (being easier to do than to describe in words!), one can scarcely believe that such an enterprising, curious experimenter as Beethoven would not have stumbled on the procedure and called attention to it, either in his own scores and documents or by way of contemporary treatises. Yet, Czerny's detailed and precise description of the damper pedal's use would seem to rule out the possibility of syncopated pedaling;[25] and Czerny told Gustav Nottebohm specifically that "Beethoven understood remarkably well how to connect full chords to each other *without the use of the pedal* [italics mine]."[26] As will be discussed later in this book, it is hard to believe that there was no mention of this procedure before 1862, when Louis Köhler published *Der Clavierfingersatz,*[27] and no recognition of it by a master composer until Liszt greeted it late in his own career, in a letter of 1875, as "an ingenious idea . . . especially in slow *tempi.*"[28] If there really was no syncopated pedaling in Beethoven's day, in spite of its seeming today like the most logical aid to keyboard *legato,* then the answer could lie, again, in the cumbersome pedal action, which might well have made it impractical then.

By increasing the duration of a melodic tone, the pedal offered one further way of implementing *legato* (thanks to the sympathetic vibrations created by the partials of the other strings). In that way each melodic tone was more likely to last into and connect with the next. The writers of Beethoven's day appreciated this possibility—for example, Starke, who, however, stretched his point when he said that a tone that would scarcely survive one bar without the damper pedal in an *Adagio* tempo could last "several bars" *with* it.[29]

Generally, Beethoven did not write melodic tones that exceeded the likely duration of keyboard sounds. An exception is the treble octave on B in a lovely line from the second movement of the Sonata in A major, Op. 2, No. 2, as shown in Example 9. The octave lasts three full beats (granted that *Largo appassionato* suggests a little more flow than *Adagio*). If that B octave had been marked with one pedal through its three beats, it would have been more likely to survive into the C-sharp octave on Beethoven's pianos (with their more distinct registers) than on today's pianos. Moreover, the *staccato* bass notes, which themselves help the projection by getting out of the long tone's way, would have come through better as such with pedal. In other words, the same octave today, with our pianos' greater carrying power, is more likely to get lost in the blur of the passing tones, unless our hypothetical single pedal application is replaced by several, more fleeting, pedal applications.

Ex. 9

There is no doubt that another main use of the damper pedal by Beethoven was to implement a collective, composite sound. Example 2, quoted earlier, suggests that Beethoven had this use in mind from the start. And Example 10, from the Bagatelle in E-flat major, Op. 126, No. 3 (completed in 1824), suggests that he still had it in mind in some of his last writing for the keyboard. The experienced keyboardist will sense in these examples the desirability of the full sound that the release of the dampers will produce.

Ex. 10

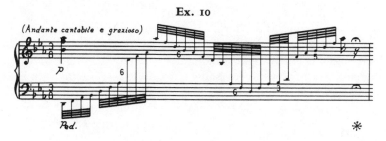

Collective sound through pedaling, especially the elaboration of a single harmony, is what Czerny intended by the term "harmonioso," which he used frequently. In his brief remarks about the way to perform Beethoven's works, he applied this term almost from the start of the sonatas, as in the statement about the Sonata in C major, Op. 2, No. 3, in bars 218–23 of the first movement,[30] giving us another hint that Beethoven was likely to have started using the pedals well before he started indicating their use. Collective sound also seems to have marked the main value of the damper pedal to Daniel Gottlieb Steibelt, in an explanation of pedal signs shown in Example 11. These remarks preface his Sonata in C minor, Op. 35, in an early edition from Longman [and] Clementi, London [1799].

Ex. 11

When Beethoven seems to be building collective sound through pedaling, either graduated or sharply contrasted dynamic change is often in progress. Thus, in the slow movement of the "Archduke" Trio, Op. 97, which suggests many opportunities for "harmonioso" pedaling, four dominant, cadential measures (shown in Example 12) go through both a *crescendo* and a *diminuendo*.

Another instance of "harmonioso" pedaling during sharply contrasted dynamics occurs at the close of the first movement of the "Hammerklavier" Sonata, Op. 106, as seen in Example 13. The absence of a

Ex. 12

Ex. 13

release in this pedal indication and in the final one in Example 14 may or may not have been intentional.

Curiously, Beethoven puts the damper pedal mark right at a *forte* or *fortissimo* mark only infrequently, as in Example 14, from the very end of the same work. I say "curiously" because Starke retained the long-established *Fortezug* ("loud pedal") as his term for the damper pedal, and Czerny acknowledged the prevalence of this term.[31] But both men cautioned against any implication that the pedal indication itself should determine the dynamic level, which was at least as likely to be soft as loud.

Ex. 14

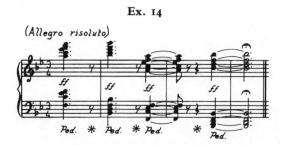

(And both already warned against the use of this pedal to hide a multitude of sins!) Probably the term "loud pedal" originated in the sense of main pedal, or *grande* pedal, as the Frenchman Louis Adam called it.[32] If it had any other meaning of "loud," it was in the sense of bigness produced by collective sound. Thus, it is clearly associated with collective sound in both a *fortissimo* passage (from the third movement of the Sonata in E-flat major, Op. 81a, shown in Example 15) and a *pianissimo* passage (from the second movement of the Sonata for Piano and Violin in G major, Op. 96, shown in Example 16).

Ex. 15

Ex. 16

The absence of a release in the pedal indication of Example 16 is characteristic of an *attacca* connection between movements. The pedaling through rests in Examples 15 and 16 is characteristic of the feelings of echo and reverberation that go with "collective sound," especially on the pianos of Beethoven's time.

Before we get to Beethoven's most controversial use of the damper pedal, two further considerations should be mentioned. One is the occasional bearing of the damper pedal on thematic and even structural aspects of a composition. Especially in his mature years, Beethoven incorporated every musical resource of his composing into the thematic structure and stylistic makeup, not only a trill pattern or a fingering, for example,[33] but even a pedaling. For instance, he applied the damper pedal so as to include both the enunciatory bass note and the succession of tonic and dominant (or vice-versa) in the rondo refrain of the finale of the "Waldstein" Sonata, Op. 53, as shown in Example 17. Used in this way at each restatement, the pedal contributes to both theme and structure by qualifying the refrain's character and identity significantly. In Czerny's words, "without the pedal [this movement] would lose its effect altogether."[34]

Ex. 17

The second consideration is the rather frequent lack of a release sign when the pedal is indicated. Occasionally the omission is an obvious error, as in Example 10, where the release would have to occur at the end of the measure because the pedal is applied again at the start of the next measure (see also Example 25). But more often the omission seems to mean that the sound is left to die away, either at the end of a movement or of the whole work, as at the delicate end of the Sonata in E major, Op. 109; or where one section passes into another, as in Example 18, where the third movement of the Piano Trio in B-flat major, Op. 97, leads to the finale with no pause indicated.

Ex. 18

Sometimes the release is present but occurs on a rest. That such an indication is likely to be deliberate, not accidental, is suggested by measure 113 of the finale of the "Waldstein" Sonata, shown in Example 19. Here "Beethoven used a red crayon to replace a quarter rest [in his autograph] with two eighth rests [apparently] in order to show that the pedal was to be released [exactly] with the second eighth rest."[35]

Ex. 19

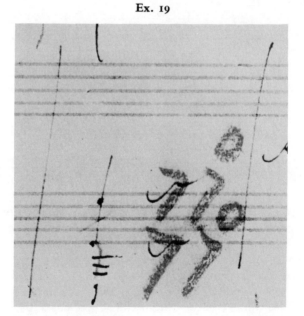

The Problem of Harmonic Blur

How does one account for Beethoven's relatively infrequent yet most controversial uses of the damper pedal, those that provide no change during conflicting harmonies? Should one conclude that Beethoven made such uses in spite of the resultant clashes, or because of them, or with no awareness of them at all? In Example 17, which is cited as much as any other for this problem, the pedal lasts through two alternations of the tonic and dominant harmonies. Such a use can hardly be dismissed as an error when it recurs that way or similarly throughout the movement. Let me first state my own conclusions and then proceed to their defense. In brief, I am convinced by both historical and musical circumstances that Beethoven deliberately cultivated the gently confused sounds in certain passages and that what he got is what he wanted, *at least in terms of the instruments of his time.*

The first point to make is that Beethoven had ample historical precedent for his passages of harmonic blur. To cite just the two closest and most significant precedents, Emanuel Bach had made the important statement in 1762 that the "undampened [undampered] register of the *fortepiano* is the most pleasing, and the most appealing for fantasizing [improvising] if one can exercise the necessary precautions against the reverberations [that is, if one can avoid letting the harmonic clash stand out too much]."[36] And Haydn, after trying the newest English instruments during his second London trip (1794–1795), had devoted his one venture with pedal indications to just such pedaling. His "open pedal," which he requests twice in the first movement of his late Sonata in C major, Hob. XVI: 50, causes the changing harmonies to blur enchantingly during a single, protracted raising of the dampers.[37]

The second point is that Beethoven had ample company among his contemporaries in the use of the pedal to create a gentle blur. Contrary to the assumptions of piano methodologists such as Rudolf Breithaupt, who believed the great master was careless and unaware,[38] Beethoven was responding to a taste that was in the air generally. Several samples of pedal blur by a contemporary can be found in the works of Clementi. Example 20, from the first movement of his Sonata in A major, Op. 50, No. 1, leaves no doubt that he wanted the dampers to remain raised during a number of harmonic changes.

In theory one might find two schools of thought about the harmonic

Ex. 20

(Allegro maestoso con sentimento)

blur. As against the composers we have been citing, conservative writers, such as Milchmeyer, Adam, Starke, and Hummel, expressed decided preferences for a change of damper pedal with every change of harmony.[39] Yet their illustrations, too, showed a taste now and then for pedal blur.[40]

There is even some written documentation that supports a taste for harmonic blur on the pianos (and other chordal instruments) of Beethoven's time. If the reader does not mind how indirect the source is, there is a statement six times removed (!) that goes back to Beethoven himself. According to the Beethoven specialist Paul Mies, the editor Carl Krebs learned from Franz Kullak that Kullak's father, Theodor, had been told by Czerny what Beethoven had in mind when he indicated the celebrated damper release throughout each of the recitative passages in the Sonata in D minor, Op. 31, No. 2, in measures 143–48 and 153–59. Beethoven wanted the effect to recall someone speaking from a vault, where the sounds, reverberations, and tones blur confusingly.[41] Another comment comes from the contemporary Bohemian composer Anton Kozeluch, who likened such effects of the damper pedal to the sound of the then popular (glass) harmonica.[42] Around 1832 the critic Ludwig Rellstab likened them in Beethoven to the sound of the Aeolian harp[43] (or of wind chimes, one might add). Of particular relevance may be Berlioz's reaction to a performance by Liszt in 1837 of the first movement of the "Moonlight" Sonata. Berlioz noted how "the left hand spreads out gently over wide-spaced chords, whose character is solemn and sad, and whose duration permits the piano vibrations gradually to die away into one another."[44] One implication in these comments—that the blur was regarded as most successful in its effect when the music was both slow and soft—is supported clearly by the treatise authors, especially Starke and Czerny.[45]

The first movement of the "Moonlight" Sonata contains the most puzzling of the harmonic-blur passages. Although the first and last pages of the autograph are missing, there is no reason to doubt the authenticity of the *two* inscriptions that appear at the very beginning of all the earliest editions of the sonata: "This whole movement should be played delicately and without damper(s) [that is, with the damper pedal depressed]"; and again, more briefly, "constantly *pianissimo* and without damper(s)." It has to be granted that in most of Beethoven's harmonic clashes created by the damper pedal the bass does not change; only the harmony above it changes. But, of course, if the pedal is to be depressed for a whole movement, there will be many bass changes to consider. In the first movement of the "Moonlight" Sonata, the bass changes at least once in most measures, greatly increasing the blur problem, even on the early pianos and even if the playing is both very slow and very soft (see Example 21).

Ex. 21

To Czerny we owe the most authoritative clarification of the problem, one that is plausible, simple if not obvious, and workable. By about 1840 he had to recommend that performers forsake Beethoven's marking in the first movement of the "Moonlight" Sonata and throughout the opening theme of the slow movement of the Concerto in C minor, Op. 37:

> Beethoven (who played the concerto publicly in 1803) depressed the pedal throughout this whole theme, which worked very well on the weak-sounding pianos of that time, especially if the action-shifting [*una corda*] pedal was used at the same time. But now, with a much stronger tone [on the newer pianos], we must advise that the damper pedal be reapplied with each significant change of harmony, yet so that no break in the tone [continuity] be noticed. For the whole theme must sound like a distant, holy, unearthly harmony.[46]

The only hitch in that clarification is the extent of the blur in the first movement of the "Moonlight" Sonata that still results, even on the earlier pianos, and is still hard to keep within tolerable limits. But other explanations and alternatives that have been suggested have fared less well. One such "explanation" lies in the possibility that the initial inscription in the first movement of Op. 27, No. 2, merely means "keep using the damper pedal throughout," somewhat as we understand the French instruction "Gardez les pédales." But both Beethoven's reworded repetition of the instruction and the consistent mood of the movement make that interpretation less likely.

Another explanation assumes the use of a "divided" damper pedal, which is visible on pictures of Beethoven's Broadwood piano. This pedal enabled one to control the bass dampers separately from the treble dampers. It was installed on many of the pianos of Beethoven's day, both English and Continental,[47] but did not survive. There is a possibility that the bass dampers might have been lowered and raised with each new harmonic bass in the first movement of the "Moonlight" Sonata, leaving the treble dampers unchanged. (Or in other passages the treble dampers might have been lowered, leaving the bass unchanged, as in the Sonata in A major for Piano and Violin, Op. 47, in bars 192–93 of the second movement.) However, Beethoven made only one mention of the divided damper pedal that is known, and then only, in effect, to ask that it *not* be used, in a note at the start of the autograph of his "Waldstein" Sonata: "N.B. Where 'Ped.' is marked, all the dampers are to be raised, [in the] bass as well as the treble; 'O' means they are to be lowered again." Incidentally, the Erard piano, at which Beethoven is often supposed to have composed both the "Waldstein" and the "Appassionata" sonatas, had no divided damper pedal.

Finally, the more distinct octave registers of the early pianos (as against today's uniform scale) have been given as yet another reason why the harmonic blur was more acceptable in Beethoven's day.[48] To those who have lived with the early instruments the point seems well taken. In a bass passage like that in Example 22, from the slow movement of the "Hammerklavier" Sonata, Beethoven would not have assumed that the *staccatos* would have come through the pedaling if he had not regarded the bass register as sufficiently distinct in its own right. The fingering is Beethoven's.

Ex. 22

Yet, in Example 23, from the last page of the Sonata in E major, Op. 109, one must recognize either that Beethoven was too optimistic when he kept repeating five tones within the range of a seventh during one

Ex. 23

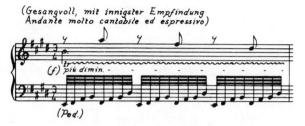

pedal application or (quite possibly) that he really wanted the low quiet rumble that results.

While the foregoing discussion is based on the belief that Beethoven did deliberately cultivate the harmonic blur where his pedaling produces it, it should be obvious, as the treatise writers cautioned, that its handling would vary in actual practice and on the chosen instrument. As the instruments grew in size and carrying power, increasing adjustments of the pedaling had to be made, until today the solutions—more pedal changes, holding some keys down (as in the recitatives of the first movement of Op. 31, No. 2), using the *sostenuto* pedal, and so on—can be quite sophisticated. Some present-day solutions are offered in chapter 8.[49]

The Una Corda *Pedal*

Beethoven knew and wanted an action-shifting pedal at least by 1802[50] and used it in performance at least by 1803, if the implication is clear in Czerny's comment on the Concerto No. 3, quoted above. Furthermore, Czerny himself recommended its use in a still earlier work, Beethoven's Sonata in E-flat major, Op. 7 (completed by 1797), singling out the abrupt "modulation" in the finale (at measure 155) from E-flat to E major and from *fortissimo* to *pianissimo*. [51] But the first indications for the action-shifting pedal that Beethoven put in a score did not appear until the slow movement of the Concerto No. 4, completed by 1806. In that movement he wrote at the start, "throughout the entire *Andante* the pianist should apply the action-shifting *(una corda)* [pedal] without interruption; otherwise the indication 'Ped.' refers to the usual [damper] pedal in accordance with present-day usage." Even so, during the swell (measure 56) that starts the cadenza with the long trill, the pianist is asked to release the action-shifting pedal from *una* through *due e poi tre corde* ("two and then three strings") and then reverse that graduated shift before the end of the cadenza (measure 60).

Neither the graduated shift nor the reduction to one string, which Czerny was still advocating around 1840,[52] is possible on today's pianos.

Otherwise, his concern with the *una corda* pedal was limited to very specialized uses—indeed, as was Beethoven's, to judge by his infrequent use of it. Quoting Czerny once more, dynamic control is best achieved by the fingers, for "it is only in a few passages, very rich in melody, that it is desirable to use this pedal to produce <u>another species of tone.</u>"[53] (Czerny, though not Beethoven, showed at least equal interest in the soft pedal that depended on a shortening of the hammer stroke, without causing any alteration of the timbre.[54])

Beethoven's most extensive, and, to me, most sensitive, uses of both the *una corda* and the graduated shifting between it and *tutte le corde* occur in one of his longest and deepest slow movements, the third movement of the "Hammerklavier" Sonata. One can imagine in Example 24, for instance, that Beethoven used the *una corda* pedal to achieve not only an echo but also a contrast of color, as if created by a different instrumental timbre. In Example 25, which follows shortly after Example 24 in the score, *una corda* is in effect at the start, graduating in measure 87 to *tre corde* in measure 88.

Ex. 24

Ex. 25

The use of the damper and *una corda* pedals together was often recommended in Beethoven's day, as by Starke,[55] among others. (In Example 25 it should be noted that the absence of a release sign for the damper pedal where the bass changes was almost certainly an oversight on Beethoven's part.)

Certain modern authors have wanted to equate the word *pianissimo* or its abbreviation with the *una corda* pedal in Beethoven's day,[56] but I have been unable to find any primary evidence that Beethoven intended these terms to be synonymous. There is circumstantial evidence both pro and con. On the one hand, Czerny advised using the *una corda* pedal wherever *pianissimo* appears in the finale of the "Waldstein" Sonata,[57] quite possibly following Beethoven's own example. On the other hand, why then would *una corda* and *pianissimo* occur together a fair number of times? Furthermore, as Beethoven goes directly from *pp* to *ppp*—that is, to an even softer marking—at the end of the slow movement of the "Hammerklavier" Sonata, he also goes from *una corda* to *tutte le corde!*

Conclusions

When reading Chapter 8, on pedaling Beethoven's music on today's pianos, one should keep in mind certain points raised in this chapter. One is that although throughout his career Beethoven kept wishing for something more in his pianos, he was still writing for the pianos he knew and not for today's instruments. Expecially the matters of less carrying power and greater differentiation between registers would affect the pedaling then and now. Another point is the evidence that Beethoven used the pedal more than he indicated, which must not be taken as license to pedal indiscriminately or without some understanding of what Beethoven most wanted the pedals to do for his music. Still another point is the clumsier pedal action that existed then, which would limit the speed with which the damper pedal, in particular, could be changed. At the same time, one must be careful not to put so much emphasis on the differences in the instruments that one overlooks the taste of the time for the gentle harmonic blur (wind chimes). That taste was a positive and not inconsiderable aesthetic value in itself. Similarly, Beethoven's interest in *legato* and in volume control must not be allowed to obscure his perhaps greater interest in the total sound effect.

As with virtually all aspects of the study of authentic performance practices, there are seldom any final answers, only educated guesses!

Acknowledgments

I am indebted to the following organizations for permission to reproduce some of the musical examples in this chapter:

Beethoven-Haus, Bonn, for Ex. 1, from the opening of "Für Elise," after a facsimile in Max Unger, *Beethovens Handschrift* (1926), Tafel VII; and Ex. 19, from the autograph of the "Waldstein" Sonata.

British Library, London, for Ex. 2, from a diplomatic transcription in *Autograph Miscellany from Circa 1786 to 1799,* vol. II, edited and annotated by Joseph Kerman (London: The British Museum, 1970).

G. Henle Verlag, Munich, for Exx. 3 and 9, from *Beethoven Werke* VII/2/I, Ex. 16, ibid., V/2, Exx. 17 and 21, ibid., VII/3/II; Exx. 7. 13, 14, 15, 22, 23, 24, and 25, after *Beethoven Klaviersonaten,* 2 vols., edited by B. A. Wallner; Exx. 12 and 18, after the edition prepared by Günter Raphael; and Ex. 20, after the edition of Sonja Gerlach and Alan Tyson.

Universal Edition, Vienna, for Exx. 6 and 10, after the edition prepared by Alfred Brendel. Used by permission of European American Music Distributors Corporation, sole U. S. agent for Universal Edition.

Executing Beethoven's Long
Pedals on the Modern Piano

Many of Beethoven's original pedal indications have puzzled performers virtually since the time they were written, especially in passages that are seemingly deliberately smeared (there is no better word for it) by the pedal. William S. Newman's highly illuminating discussion in chapter 7 should be read carefully before considering any of the proposals in the present chapter. If it is admitted that Newman is correct in his conclusion that "Beethoven deliberately cultivated the gently confused sounds in certain passages and that what he got is what he wanted," it is of equal importance to recall that Newman ends this sentence with "at least in terms of the instruments of his time."

The first question a performer must ask is, Should Beethoven's pedal indications always be literally obeyed? If the answer is an unyielding Yes, then the player's problems, although not ended, will be greatly mitigated, since his musical conscience will be clean in that he is following the *Urtext,* regardless of the resulting performance effect. Artur Schnabel was of this persuasion (most of the time), as evidenced by his many Beethoven recordings and by his heavily footnoted edition of the Beethoven piano sonatas.[1]

But if the performer feels that a literal adherence to Beethoven's pedal indications is not always best for conveying the music on a modern resonant concert instrument, then he must then ask, How can I modify Beethoven's pedal indications without losing the intent of the original musical thought? Donald Francis Tovey was of this musical opinion.[2] (It would have been of the utmost fascination to have seen Schnabel and Tovey face-to-face on this question!) The issue of whether or not to modify some of Beethoven's original pedal markings remains hotly contested to this day, and it is not within the scope of the present text to try to settle it. Each player must decide this area of personal musical philosophy for himself. What *is* important is to examine the pros and cons and so have a basis for making an intelligent and well-informed judgment.

If, after carefully digesting Newman's commentary, the player opts for some modifications in Beethoven's pedal indications, then the following sample solutions to a few problem passages may prove useful. They are not offered dogmatically, and they should always be considered in light of the usual factors that influence *any* of the pedaling suggestions given in this text—the instrument, the hall, the dynamics, the tempo, the player's personality, etc. Beethoven's piano music contains nearly 800 pedal indications, many of which are not problematical. In the following sampling, Beethoven's own indications will be examined first, and then alternate pedalings will be proposed. The general procedures used here may be used in other, similar passages, if the player feels that a modification is needed in the first place. For ease of reference, the works examined are given in order of opus number.

Sonata, Op. 27, No. 2
Beethoven's explicit indications to perform the entire first movement of the "Moonlight" Sonata "with raised dampers" cannot be followed on a modern instrument. Even the zealot Schnabel suggests normal changes of pedal at shifts of harmony, and for once he has no footnote comment on the necessity of obeying Beethoven's score to the letter.[3] But there is a way to capture something of the same veiled, floating sound that Beethoven may have wished to achieve through an extended use of pedal. The solution, suggested by the well-known musicologist and editor Howard Ferguson,[4] takes advantage of sympathetic partials. Ferguson suggests that before starting to play, one silently depress all the notes on the keyboard below the lowest note in the piece, then catch them with the middle pedal. That means that all the notes from the lowest E down will be depressed and held. This solution will sound well on most instruments only if the left pedal is also brought into operation throughout. (Here the player has an excellent opportunity to learn to operate both the middle and left pedals with the left foot alone, as explained in chapter 4.) The right foot must of course be reserved to make appropriate changes of pedal with the harmony. A slight overlap and delayed pedal change on each new harmony, especially in the softest sections, will aid in capturing the *misterioso* effect Beethoven seems to want for this work. Some partial changes of pedal, especially between harmonies that are more related by common tones, will be needed. Occasional finger pedaling can also be used to blur slightly harmonies having common tones, as in bar 4, where a strict change of pedal on each quarter beat, as suggested in most edi-

Ex. I

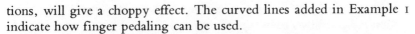

tions, will give a choppy effect. The curved lines added in Example 1 indicate how finger pedaling can be used.

No pat solutions to the difficult pedaling demanded in this movement can be given. The performer must find a middle ground between a clinically antiseptic pedaling that changes clearly at each harmony and the hopeless muddle that would result if Beethoven's original long, extended use of pedal were to be followed.

Sonata, Op. 31, No. 2

The original pedalings in these passages have long been a thorn in the side of many a pianist. They are in a sense much more controversial than those in the preceding example, since today no one tries to follow the single, long pedal in the "Moonlight" Sonata on a modern instrument. But opinion is strongly divided as to whether the extended pedals in the recitative passages of the first movement of the Sonata, Op. 31, No. 2, should be literally obeyed. Newman has cited precedents for such "Aeolian harp" effects, as well as Beethoven's well-known remark that these passages should sound like someone speaking from a vault (tomb). There seems little doubt that an atmospheric, poetically evocative blur was intended by the composer. But how much?

Several solutions are possible, including, surprisingly enough, playing the recitative passages exactly as written. Bars 143–48 are shown in Example 2 with Beethoven's original pedaling. The player must tempo-

Ex. 2

rarily forget about any real shaping of the melodic line in a vocal sense, as would normally be done. In bars 145–47, for instance, there should be no *crescendo* or stress on the E's. Also, the B flat in bar 144 should be under played slightly, since it forms a minor second with the A's heard immediately before and afterward. Even the *appoggiaturas* (written as quarter notes) on the downbeats of bars 146 and 148 should not be stressed, as would normally be done if this line were to be played in a more openly vocal manner. In short, do not stress notes of the melody that do not belong to the prevailing dominant (of D minor) harmony, carried from bar 143 to bar 148. And although the implied harmony changes to a tonic in bar 148, Beethoven still keeps the pedal. On his instrument the rolled dominant chord of bar 143 would have long since faded.

Example 3 shows bars 153–59, again with Beethoven's original pedaling. The second recitative passage, in bars 155–58, creates an even more difficult problem, if the player chooses to keep the original unbroken long pedal. As before, correct shaping of the melody is of the greatest importance, especially as the register of the writing drops in bars 155–56. Although Beethoven writes *con espressione,* any surge in dynamics will result in an overpowering blur. If anything, the player should make a small *decrescendo* from the second half of bar 156 through the first half of bar 157. In both recitative passages, the player will also probably wish to use the left pedal.

Ex. 3

Careful dynamic shaping and underplaying of certain melody notes is but one solution to Beethoven's long pedal indications, and it will play a role in some other possibilities for these two passages. Another solution uses finger pedaling. In Example 4, several notes of the rolled chord are held by the fingers, while partial pedal changes are made during the melody. Even though finger pedaling now makes complete clarity of the melody possible, some atmospheric haze should be retained. Finger pedaling simply gives one more control over the amount of such haze than would be possible with a long pedal or with partial changes of pedal alone.

Ex. 4

A third solution to these recitative passages is by means of the middle pedal, as shown in Example 5. It is similar in effect to a use of finger pedaling, except that more of the notes of each rolled chord can be held for the full length of the passage. If this solution is used in bars 153–58, great care must be taken to play the C on the downbeat of bar 156 very softly, since this note will already be caught with the middle pedal and might be overly reinforced when repeated. If the left pedal is used, the player must work both the left and middle pedals with the left foot, while reserving the right foot for the damper pedal.

Yet another solution to these passages, given by Tovey,[5] is shown in Example 6. He suggests silently depressing and holding a handful of notes below each rolled chord, then making changes of pedal in the melody when necessary. Tovey feels that "even if the bass has been played with the softest touch it will be too concrete a sound to be desirable if prolonged beyond its written length. . . . This effect will not carry in

Ex. 5

Ex. 6

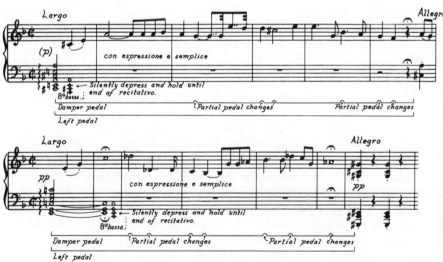

a large concert room. But neither would the tone of Beethoven's pianoforte."[6]

All these "solutions" to Beethoven's original pedaling have both advantages and drawbacks, but each one should be tried to determine which works best in a given performance situation.

Sonata, Op. 53

The Róndo theme of the last movement of the Sonata, Op. 53, with Beethoven's long pedal indications, has consistently perplexed both listeners and performers. Beethoven definitely intended some blurring, perhaps as a price for maintaining the low pedal points that occur at the start of each new pedal indication. Unfortunately that means that the player must satisfactorily handle the resulting blurring of tonic and dominant harmonies in bars 1–12, then the mixing of major and minor mode in bars 15–22. It is perhaps significant that much of the time when the Rondo theme is heard later, either in its original full form or only in part (in bars 31–38, 98–105, 114–36, 144–51, 313–20, 403–11, 427–34, 485–505, and 515–22), this same pedaling idea—namely the holding of a bass pedal point—recurs. At other statements of the Rondo theme (in bars 39–62, 152–75, 221–32, and 321–44), the pedal is lifted at an expected change of harmony. In a number of these passages, the reason for some of the changes of pedal seems to be related to a change of dynamic level from loud to soft (as in bars 221–32), to a filling-out of the texture (as in bars 41–49), or to clarifying a change in the articulation (as in bars 57–58, where the left hand is marked with *staccatos*).

With regard to passages marked with long pedal indications, one might ask why Beethoven wrote such a long pedal. Schnabel says of bars 1–4, "To change the pedal in the third and fourth bars would destroy the very apparent intention of always letting the fundamental note sound until the next fundamental note follows." In other words, each pedal point must be maintained at all cost. If the player feels that is the primary reason for Beethoven's long pedaling, then an obvious solution is to use the middle pedal (possibly combined with the left pedal), as shown in Example 7.

The next question that must be asked is, Should some blurring still be kept with a use of the damper pedal? Probably the player will wish to do so by making partial changes of pedal at each new harmony, with the resulting amount of haze and blur depending on personal taste.

A second solution to these passages, shown in Example 8, is simply to make partial changes of pedal at each shift of the harmony, while still maintaining at least a portion of each pedal point. This solution, favored by many performers, has the advantage of leaving the left foot entirely free to use the left pedal if desired, instead of necessitating the use of the left and middle pedals simultaneously.

A third solution is to follow Beethoven's long pedal markings literally, as shown in Example 9. Voicing and balance then become even more important. Each pedal point will have to be stressed enough so that it

Ex. 7

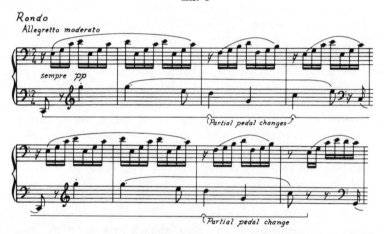

Ex. 8

carries through clearly and also supports—even "soaks-up"—any blur-ring from shifting harmonies above. Notes not belonging to the basic implied harmony of the pedal point should be slightly underplayed.

Any of these three methods can be made to work. The player would be wise to have all three at his disposal, to be able to surmount any contingencies in a concert situation.

Sonata, Op. 57

Bars 233–37 of the first movement of the Sonata, Op. 57, are difficult to play convincingly with Beethoven's original long pedal indications, shown in Example 10. Even though the same harmony is outlined

Ex. 9

Ex. 10

throughout, the shift to *piano* in bar 235 and the low register in which the
D flat–C motif is given create problems. Examples 11 and 12 offer
alternatives to the original pedaling. In both, partial pedal changes will
keep the effect of a long, unbroken pedaling, while enabling the D flat–C
motif to remain reasonably clear.

Ex. 11

Sonata, Op. 101

In the second movement of the Sonata, Op. 101, bars 30–34 seem related
to the famous "open pedal" bars in Haydn's Sonata in C major, Hob. XVI:
50. The performer should probably retain a good amount of the haze and
blur that are consequences of Beethoven's original pedal indication, as
shown in Example 13. But unlike the situation in the Haydn passages, the
role of the pedal here is to maintain the D-flat pedal point. If the pianist
feels that the resulting blur is overpowering, the middle pedal can be
used, with partial pedal changes being made at each shift of harmony.

Ex. 12

Ex. 13

How clear these changes are will again depend on personal taste and performance conditions.

It should be evident from the foregoing examples that even when Beethoven's pedaling is modified to suit the modern instrument, the original idea of an atmospheric haze should be maintained. Some scholars object to any tampering with Beethoven's original pedalings because the results are often radically different when the pedaling is modified by insensitive players. Especially when the middle pedal is used, care is needed to prevent the total effect from sounding dry and clearly etched. The above solutions are ways of better controlling and projecting Beethoven's original sound concept on modern instruments. But doing nothing at all and putting up with the resulting excessive blurring is perhaps preferable to badly handled modifications of the composer's pedalings.

9

Pedaling the Piano Works of Chopin

by Maurice Hinson

The correct way of using the pedal remains a study for life.
—Frédéric Chopin

Frédéric Chopin was a true pioneer in the use of pedaling. He constantly explored the rich new territory that the invention of the damper pedal had made possible, and no pianist before him used the pedal with so much skill. Chopin made frequent use of the pedal, and through an intuition born of genius he knew when to depress it as well as when to raise it. Antoine François Marmontel commented that sometimes when Chopin performed, his foot seemed to vibrate as he rapidly pedaled certain passages,[1] and that "No pianist before him has employed the pedals alternately or simultaneously with so much tact and ability."[2] Alfred Hipkins of the Broadwood firm heard him play in London in 1848 and said that Chopin used ample pedal, especially in left-hand arpeggio passages, "which swelled or diminished like waves in an ocean of sound."[3]

Realizing how important the pedal was to his music, Chopin was very careful in his manuscripts to indicate his intentions regarding its use. Unfortunately, many of his publishers were careless in following his directions. There is still no published version of his works that includes all his original pedal indications, although both Henle and Vienna Urtext have made great strides in that direction, as has the Norton Critical Scores edition of the Préludes. A new and more reliable edition of a few volumes published by Edition Peters, Leipzig, and edited by Paul Badura-Skoda and Thomas Higgins is gradually becoming available. All pianists should use the more accurate and reliable editions.

The Pedals on Chopin's Preferred Pianos
Soon after arriving in Paris in 1831, Chopin was introduced to the Pleyel piano. For the rest of his life he thought it was the *non plus ultra* of keyboard instruments. Chopin never changed his opinion of this piano and liked both the upright and grand instruments. When he was living in Majorca he sent for a small Pleyel upright to replace a rented, poorly made Spanish piano. The sound of the Pleyel grand is silvery, bright, and clear, and in its day its clarity was greatly admired. This instrument was very responsive and produced all the tone color Chopin required without sounding harsh or ugly in loud passages. Hipkins writes that "his *fortissimo* was the full pure tone without noise, a harsh inelastic note being to him painful."[4] Chopin's pedal markings make perfect sense when performed on a Pleyel grand similar to the ones he used. Even the absence of pedal for many bars seems correct. When the pianist remains faithful to Chopin's avoidance of pedal, its use—when indicated—is like a breath of fresh air. Slight blurring also sounds correct at specific places. Often these purposely blurred passages sound almost "impressionistic," and give the music a kaleidoscopic and multicolored effect. Franz Liszt described the sound of Chopin's Pleyel as "the marriage of crystal and water."[5] Chopin told Liszt in an often-cited remark:

> When I am indisposed, I play on one of Erard's pianos and there I easily find a ready-made tone. But when I feel in the right mood and strong enough to find my own tone for myself, I must have one of Pleyel's pianos.[6]

Chopin's Pedal Markings in the Autographs
In the interpretation of Chopin's piano music, the damper pedal is the most important tool, the pianist's most powerful, subtle, and versatile means of expression. According to Vladimir Horowitz:

> The pedal is everything. It is our lungs and we breath through the pedal. You can blend two harmonies which are completely dissonant for one millionth of a second and create possibilities for endless varieties of color.[7]

It behooves every pianist to try Chopin's pedal indications, for many of them are extremely revealing, daring, and unusual; they often make wonderful musical sense, even on today's more resonant instruments. Careful use of Chopin's pedal indications frequently helps clarify structure and gives character to a work. Chopin used the 𝄞. and ✳ signs in his autographs to show the depressing and raising of the pedal. In some instances these indications are not as precise as our twentieth-century symbol ⌞____⌟. Yet in other instances there is no doubt about Chopin's meaning, his indications being so precise. Although Chopin never indi-

cated the use of the *una corda* pedal, it would be pedantic to conclude that
it should never be used in playing his works.

Jean Kleczynski, who was personally acquainted with such Chopin
pupils and close friends as Princess Marcellina Czartoryska and Julian
Fontana, refers to Chopin's use of the *una corda* pedal:

> We arrive at the combination of the two pedals, at which Chopin excelled
> to perfection. How well we know these musical flourishes which are so
> attractive to the ear, with the soft pedal (the Nocturne in F sharp, Op. 15
> No. 2, second part, the Nocturne in D flat, Op. 27, No. 2, etc., etc.).
> Chopin would often pass from the hard (damper) pedal to the soft almost
> instantaneously, particularly in discordant variations of pitch. These had a
> very special fascination, chiefly on the Pleyel pianos. Examples are: the first
> measure of the *larghetto* in the Concerto in F minor on the note E flat; the
> Polonaise in C minor, Op. 40, No. 2, at the moment of returning to the
> motif of the trio; the Mazurka in A minor, Op. 17 (No. 4), eighth measure;
> the Polonaise in C-sharp minor, Op. 26, No. 1, second part, ninth measure,
> and so on.[8]

Kleczynski gives an example from the Polonaise in C minor, Op. 40,
No. 2, shown in Example 1.

Ex. 1

In his example from the Mazurka in A minor, Op. 17, No. 4, shown in
Example 2, the performer would expect that Chopin would stress rather
than soften bar 4. The left pedal in this instance was perhaps used by

Ex. 2

Chopin to allow for a greater intensity of tone within a soft dynamic area, as well as to give a pronounced change of tone color at this climactic point in the phrase.

It is clear that Chopin's use of the left pedal was highly innovative and followed the dictates of an acutely sensitive ear, rather than any set of hard and fast "rules."

Editors' Changes in the Préludes

In Prélude No. 5 in D major, shown in Example 3, Chopin marks pedals through harmonic changes where dominant harmony resolves to tonic.

Ex. 3

In Examples 4 and 5, both from Prélude No. 6 in B minor, Chopin indicates pedal only in bars 13, 14, and 23. It was an idiosyncrasy of his writing to omit the release sign expected near or at the end of many compositions, including this Prélude. This piece is usually heard with a pedal in every bar.

Ex. 4

In the familiar Prélude No. 7 in A major, shown in Example 6, the majority of Chopin's pedals are held across bar lines where the pedal sustains the low bass tones. However, in many modern editions these pedals are disregarded in favor of a timid change on each second beat, which obliterates the fundamental tone in the bass. When the piece is played *piano dolce,* the slight blurring of ornamental tones in the melody

Ex. 5

Ex. 6

is attractive and suggests a dance heard from afar. Bars 3, 5, 7, 11, 13, and
15 have the nonharmonic tones in the melody blurred into their resolu-
tions.

Washes of pedal are given in Prélude No. 13 in F-sharp major, shown
in Example 7. At first, the purpose of these pedals seems to be the
maintaining of a *legato* across the large skips in the left hand, but close
examination shows them to come at important points in the phrase.

In Prélude No. 15 in D-flat major, Example 8 shows a pedal carried
through a new slur, and Examples 9 and 10 show pedals carried through
melody notes.

In Example 11, from the autograph of Prélude No. 16 in B-flat minor,
bars 2 and 3 show some striking pedal changes made by Chopin. Origi-

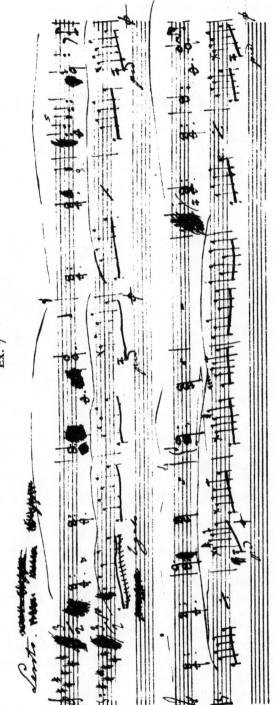

Ex. 7

Ex. 8

Ex. 9

Ex. 10

nally he indicated a normal pedaling that changed every two beats; then, deliberately crossing them out, he left the entire three bars with one pedal! The right hand consequently becomes a total blur. This is one of the best examples of Chopin's use of long pedal. And even though the pianos of his day admittedly had less resonance, a pronounced blurring effect would still have come through in these three bars. Another example of extreme pedal blur in this Prélude is shown in Example 12. In bars 18–21, with the subdominant merged with the tonic at bar 21, Chopin produces what is perhaps the most extreme example of pedal cacophony in all his music. A pedal release comes only at the end of bar 21.

In Example 13, from Prélude No. 19 in E-flat major, Chopin's pedal notation shows great subtlety. Bars 5 and 7 are exactly alike, except for

Ex. 11

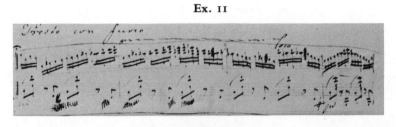

Ex. 12

Ex. 13

one note in the left hand, a nonharmonic auxiliary B-natural in bar 7. Here Chopin discreetly and very briefly avoids pedal so the B-natural can be heard.

In Example 14, from Prélude No. 21 in B-flat major, a charming effect is produced by an unusual pedal beginning on the last beat of bar 12. It crosses the bar line and ends at the chains of chords in both hands in bar 13. This pedal is preserved in many old and new editions, among them the nineteenth-century *First Critical Revised Edition* of Breitkopf und Härtel (edited by Liszt, Brahms, Bargiel, Franchomme, and Rudorff, published in the United States by Edwin Kalmus), Peters (Scholtz), Wiener Urtext (Hansen), and Henle (Zimmermann). Among these volumes of the Préludes, the Henle edition is the best. But the *First Critical Revised Edition* and the Peters edition have many departures from the text that were no doubt intentional (the four other editors of the *First Critical Revised Edition* were not as faithful as Brahms to Chopin's texts). Another interesting edition is the one by Willard A. Palmer, published by Alfred.

Ex. 14

What is the explanation for the lack of pedal indications in several of the Préludes, such as those in E minor and C minor? Pedaling is so obvious in these two Préludes—a change on each new chord—that Chopin simply left most of it out. In such a work as the Etude in A-flat major, from the *Trois Nouvelles Etudes,* however, Chopin simply did not complete the manuscript, since this Etude is impossible to perform gracefully without pedal.

Editors' Changes in Other Works

In the autograph of the Etude in F minor, Op. 25, No. 2, one can see the care with which Chopin introduced his pedals. The version given to the copyist had only six pedal indications: in bars 18–19, 49–50, 57, 66, and 68. After this copy was made, Chopin extended the release in bar 26, extended the pedal in bar 57 through the all-important *portato* markings, and deleted his final release sign in bar 69. He also added eighteen additional pedal marks, and in the process, changed the position of his release in bar 24 three times, finally deciding to extend the pedal through the whole bar.

Example 15 contains one of the most problematic passages in all of Chopin, bars 54–73 of the Ballade in A-flat major, Op. 47. In the "rocking-horse" second theme, which is first stated at bar 54, Chopin marks a pedal at the beginning of each bar to catch the bass. It also catches the dissonant chord that is added on the third beat, allowing it to ring through the bass note on beat 4. Then the pedal is raised, so that the chord on beat 6 is dry. These indications suggest that Chopin is pedaling the bass or phrasing the bass with the pedal. Note that he writes the pedal release just after beat 4, but, initially at least, before the rest on beat 5. Here there should be a minute break in the sound.

After the first four-bar statement, Chopin begins to vary the pedaling. In bars 58 and 59, he moves the pedal release over to the rest on beat 5. Then in bar 60, he indicates no pedal at all. Is this carelessness or a considered decision to alter the texture of the sound at this point? Most editors assume the former and give bar 60 the same pedaling as in bar 59.

At the *crescendo* in bars 63–65, some very interesting compositional changes begin to take place. There are accents and longer notes in the treble, and the principal bass notes are no longer eighth notes but quarters, all of which imply a gathering of greater intensity and stress. Then at the climax of the *crescendo* (bar 65), Chopin keeps the pedal down through the entire bar, dissonance and all!

In bars 66–67 the pedaling crosses the bar lines, and in bars 67 and 69 there is an accented, unpedaled chord on beat 3. The whole line has a slight lurching quality that is quite eloquent. If Chopin had kept on with the regular pedaling, controlled by the bar line, a very regular passage would have resulted. But he seems fanatically concerned with de-regularization, which the notation expresses in an amazingly precise manner. Many times Chopin (and other great composers as well) leave the performer a lot of freedom concerning the pedal. But in most of the second theme of this Ballade, he gives fastidious indications for the pedal in order to avoid a feeling of squareness.

Many pedaling problems occur in the Etude, Op. 25, No. 10, for pedal indications appear only in bar 35 in the Chopin-edited copy and in the first German edition. The pedal is desperately needed to connect the ascending intervals in the right hand—a fifth, a third, and another third—and to prolong the low C sharp. Chopin apparently changed his mind when he corrected the proofs of the first French edition. It contains several more pedal indications, which help to achieve a *legato* when the left hand must move after stretching the interval of a tenth; namely, in bars 31, 32, 34, 39, 40, 42, 59, 60, 62, 79, and 82; and another was no doubt intended in bar 80. Even though Chopin's keyboard was slightly narrower—the span of a tenth was about a quarter-inch less than on a modern Steinway—most players would also need pedal in bars 36, 49, 53, 69, 71, 73, and 89 for other left-hand connections. The edition of Paul Badura-Skoda for Wiener Urtext has the best solution. Since Chopin's autograph is lost, Badura-Skoda used the Chopin-edited copy as a principal source, but also included the pedals from the first French edition, identifying this source in the opening bars of the B-major section. This middle section, with its inner parts, also remains difficult, as do the opening and closing *Allegro con fuoco* sections in B minor, with their inner parts nowhere aided by Chopin's pedal. This Etude is not only a study in octaves but also in *legato*.

In discussing the autograph of the Ballade in F major, Op. 38, Camille Saint-Saëns comments on Chopin's sometimes sparing use of the pedal:

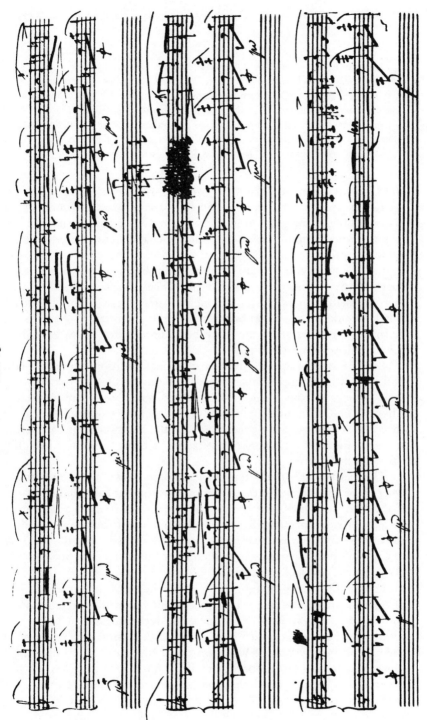

This manuscript shows us with what reserve Chopin used the pedal; in several passages where he had indicated it, it was afterwards suppressed. The reason it is frequently indicated in his works is that he did not wish it to be used when not indicated. To dispense with this help is no easy matter. For many it would even be impossible, so general has the abuse of the pedal become. To play without the pedal calls for a degree of suppleness in the hands, of which everyone, however talented, is not capable.[9]

But Chopin is reserved *and* unreserved in his use of pedal, for some places are full of pedal markings, while others are very sparse. In most of the piano writing of the generation of the 1830s, full pedaling is normal: the piano is expected to vibrate most of the time, and an unpedaled sonority is the exception.

In the majority of Chopin's compositions in one or another primary source, his pedal notation is sufficient. When Chopin omits the pedal, there is usually a good reason. In long passages where Chopin has deliberately avoided the pedal in order to preserve other values, some use of pedal may be necessary if the piano being used is not bright enough to sound well without it.

Even in some of the most respected of today's editions, there are pedal problems. One example is the Scherzo in B minor, Op. 20, bars 387–88, as it appears in the Henle edition, edited by Ewald Zimmermann. Chopin's original manuscript is lost. In the first German edition, a pedal covers both bars, but the Henle has none at all. The two-bar pedal is a fine solution, for the mixed sonority it creates is one of the most beautiful effects in the entire piece.

The performer should try using Chopin's own pedal indications where they are extant, for they offer great variety of color and phrasing. If they do not work because the modern grand is more resonant or because of room acoustics, delicate adjustments of touch and a proper balance between the different registers should be made. But the majority of Chopin's pedals work quite well on most modern pianos provided the player listens and adjusts continually.

Chopin obviously thought deeply about the pedal, and a careful study of his pedaling in the autographs (both for Chopin interpretation itself and for the cultivation of subtle pedaling techniques) is strongly recommended. Some scores are now available in facsimile form, most of them published by Polskie Wydawnictwo Muzyczne. When studying a work in manuscript form for the first time, it is amazing to see the layers of "tradition" peel away, so that one experiences the music fresh for the first time.

Observations on Chopin's Use of the Pedal

1. Chopin uses pedal to connect many final chords in his works, but more for the purpose of adding resonance than to help the *legato;* e.g., the final chords of Préludes Nos. 18 and 21, but not of Nos. 2 and 8, which have very quiet conclusions. In bar 198 of the Ballade in F major, Op. 38, shown in Example 16, Chopin deleted the pedal directions, thereby showing that he distinguished between pedaled and unpedaled chords.

Ex. 16

2. Chopin uses pedal in scale passages. See the E-major scale at the end of the Scherzo in E major, Op. 54, shown in Example 17. The pedal is depressed only at the beginning and end of the scale.

Ex. 17

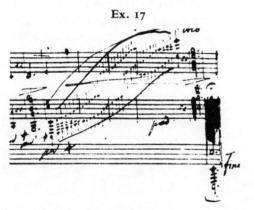

Pedal may be used throughout an upward-moving scale that is firmly supported by underlying harmonic material, as in Prélude No. 24 in D minor, shown in Example 18. On occasion Chopin may even use pedal in a long downward-moving scale, as in the Barcarolle, Op. 60, shown in Example 19. The original pedaling, which clearly extends to the very end of the run, is frequently shortened even in the more careful editions.

Chopin uses pedal in these scale passages to avoid dryness and to give needed brilliance and glitter.

Ex. 18

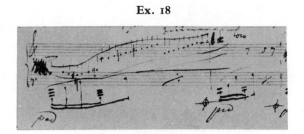

Ex. 19

3. Chopin frequently pedals through nonharmonic tones in a melody (see Example 6 above).

4. The pedal may be used by Chopin to reinforce the sound, as in Prélude No. 8 in F-sharp minor, shown in Example 20. Here the passing notes and foreign tones are profuse, yet they blend when Chopin's pedaling is used.

Ex. 20

5. Changes of harmony are often blurred with the pedal by Chopin, as in Example 21, where the dominant-seventh harmony in D-flat at bars 97–98 of the Ballade in F major, Op. 38, moves to a subdominant chord without pedal change.

6. Chopin's pedal marks do not always agree with slurs and/or phrase marks, as is evident in Example 22, from the Barcarolle, Op. 60. Here his pedals are intended more for keeping the harmony than in delineating the slurs in the left hand.

Ex. 21

Ex. 22

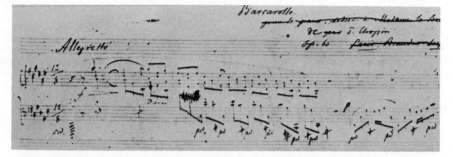

7. Themes of contrasting character are often given contrasting pedaling by Chopin. Example 23 shows bars 243–76 of the Scherzo in B-flat minor, Op. 31. Chopin indicates pedaling in bars 249–64, yet in the more lyrical sections found in bars 197–248 and 265–80, he gives none.

8. In much of Chopin's music the pedal is indicated to be held through rests. The Scherzo in B-flat minor, Op. 31, as seen in Example 24, has many instances of such pedaling.

9. Chopin frequently omits a pedal release sign at the end of a composition. In fifteen of the twenty-four Préludes, Op. 28, he omits the release in Nos. 1, 6, 7, 9, 11, 13, 16, 17, 18, 19, 20, 21, 22, 23, and 24. He seems to leave it to the performer's discretion.

10. In performing Chopin, standard textbook suggestions regarding pedaling cannot always be trusted. It is known that Chopin sometimes varied the pedaling in similar or identical passages. In the Ballade in F major, Op. 38, he gives one pedaling for bars 46–49, shown in Example 25, and another for the identical passage in bars 140–43, shown in Example 26. Thus, an inflexible rule always to pedal identical passages in the same manner cannot be followed when playing Chopin's music.

Ex. 23

Ex. 24

Most textbooks relate a change of pedal to a change of harmony. Chopin's pedaling is frequently independent of the harmony, as when harmonies are deliberately blurred together. Chopin also uses pedal with scales, something many pedaling guides say is not permitted.

Ex. 25

Ex. 26

Chopin's original pedal indications create more blurring on modern pianos than they would have on his instrument, and that must be taken into account by today's performer. But this fact alone does not justify ignoring his directions. The pianist who evens out Chopin's pedal indications may be missing an important element of the compositional intent.

General Suggestions for Pedaling Chopin's Music

There is no correct pedal "in general"; in art we know that nothing pertains "in general." Broad rules about pedaling bear the same relation to artistic pedaling as a chapter on syntax does to poetic language. There are many variables in pedaling, and no particular set of pedal markings should be followed slavishly. The pedal demands meticulous study. It should be used with the same intelligence and definiteness as the fingers. The performer must adjust the pedaling to the acoustics of the room, to the piano itself, and to his own touch. And so with these ideas in mind and a reminder to the pianist always to pedal with a purpose, the following are offered as suggestions for pedaling Chopin's piano works:

1. Frequently the pedal should be changed after the beat, in what is known as "synocopated" or *legato* pedaling. ("Play first, pedal afterwards.") Example 27, from the Nocturne in G minor, Op. 37, No. 1, needs this type of pedaling.

2. Play *staccato* notes with pedal with the same touch and attack as when playing them without pedal. *Staccato* notes with pedal have a slightly different tone than the identical notes played *legato* with pedal. In Example 28, from the Polonaise in A-flat major, Op. 53, Chopin's own pedaling is given.

Ex. 27

Ex. 28

3. Catch the bass of the harmony with the pedal when it cannot be sustained by a finger. Pedaling must respect the basses. Example 29, from the Ballade in A-flat major, shows Chopin's original pedaling.

Ex. 29

4. Pedal more lightly in the bass register than in the treble, perhaps using half-pedaling. Half-pedaling in the upper register can be effective for color and slight blurring. In Example 30, from the Concerto in F minor, a series of half-pedal changes or some degree of partial damper release of sound is more effective than a full holding of the pedal.

5. Use the pedal to give impulse to an accent. Many of Chopin's mazurkas contain opportunities for this kind of pedaling, as shown in Example 31, an excerpt from the Mazurka in C major, Op. 24, No. 2.

6. Pedal vibrato or flutter pedaling is advised for fast scale passages and/or for clearing out harmonies in a thick texture before the final chord is sounded. Melodies that use turns, mordents, trills, and rapid passing, neighboring, or appoggiatura tones may also require this type of pedaling to compensate for the accumulation of many close sonorities. The passage

Ex. 30

Half-pedal changes

Ex. 31

in Example 32, from the Fantaisie in F minor, Op. 49, will benefit from a rapid flutter pedal rather than longer stretches of pedal, which would tend to group the sound into overly thick masses.

Ex. 32

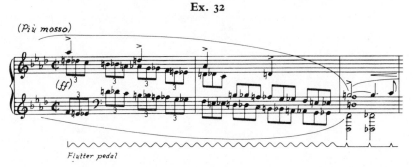

Flutter pedal

7. Since the majority of Chopin's music requires pedal, any un-pedaled passages should be regarded as having a special color. The Etude, Op. 25, No. 4, shown in Example 33, has a number of such passages.

Ex. 33

8. Hold the pedal through rests when indicated by Chopin. There is usually a good reason for the indication. In Example 34, from the Fantaisie in F minor, the pedaling is his.

Ex. 34

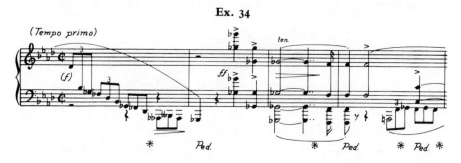

10

Using the Pedals
When Playing Schumann

Using the Right Pedal

Most of Schumann's markings for the right pedal fall into two categories: general indications for the use of pedal throughout an entire section or piece at the player's discretion and markings that are intended to be followed explicitly in a given passage. There are many instances in which Schumann simply marks *Mit Pedal* ("with pedal"), *sempre col Pedal, sempre tenuto per il Pedale, Pedale grande,* or *Pedal,* often at the beginning of a piece, and he does not always indicate the release. In "Pierrot," from *Carnaval,* Op. 9, the word *Pedal* is written in bar 1 and a release sign (✲) occurs 43 bars later! Over half the pieces in *Kinderszenen,* Op. 15, contain only a single pedal indication, in the opening bar. With the words *senza Pedale,* Schumann on occasion requests that no pedal be used.

An extremely interesting footnote appears at the bottom of the first page of the Sonata in F-sharp minor, Op. 11, in both the first edition of 1836[1] and the second edition of 1840:

> The composer uses the pedal in nearly every measure, always as the changes of harmony demand. Exceptions, where he wishes that it not be used, are marked ⊕ ; with the next *"Pedale"* marking, its constant use begins again.[2]

This important comment by Schumann, which is unfortunately omitted in the collected Schumann edition of 1879–93,[3] edited by Clara Schumann (with Brahms as co-editor), and her so-called instructive edition of Robert's piano works, ca. 1886,[4] throws valuable light on the composer's general attitude toward the damper pedal. A clear example of his "always as the changes of harmony demand" use of the pedal is given in Example

1, from *Kreisleriana* No. 8, Op. 16. In this and the following examples, all pedal indications are by Schumann.

Ex. 1

There are revealing accounts of Schumann's own playing from Oswald Lorenz, a personal acquaintance of his in Leipzig during the 1830s, and from Alfred Doerffel, a piano student of his after 1839. Lorenz mentions Schumann's liberal use of pedal, yet maintains that no excessive blurring of harmonies was evident;[5] but Doerffel contradicts him, describing what he terms Schumann's "organ style" of playing.[6] Doerffel claims that Schumann usually played with the dampers somewhat raised, and that "It seemed as if the pedals were always half down, so that the note groups mingled."[7]

Sometimes it is difficult to determine whether Schumann is asking for only a general use of pedal at the player's discretion, or if he specifically wishes a long stretch of unbroken pedal. One such instance occurs in the Finale of his *Etudes en Forme de Variations,* Op. 13, shown in Example 2. Such doubtful passages should be tested with the original pedaling, always bearing in mind that the pianos in use when Schumann's earlier piano works were written still did not have the resonance of today's concert instruments.

Schumann on occasion indicates that notes are to be held longer with the pedal by means of curved or straight lines after the notes. These forms of notation are found in the original editions of the Sonata in F-sharp

Ex. 2

minor, shown in Example 3, and the Phantasie in C major, Op. 17, shown in Example 4.

Ex. 3

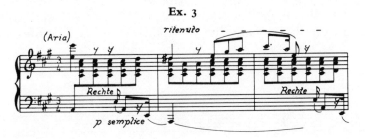

Ex. 4

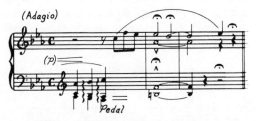

He may also call for a long stretch of unbroken pedal to capture a special effect of atmosphere and color. In Example 5, also from the Phantasie in C major, a feeling of distance and withdrawal is achieved through Schumann's explicit pedaling. This long pedal is especially effective in a large resonant concert hall; the dominant and tonic harmonies will tend to blend and merge better there than in a small room. If the

Ex. 5

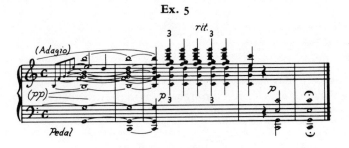

dynamics in this passage are carefully handled, there should be no need for a change of pedal in the penultimate bar.

On occasion, Schumann can be extremely exacting with his directions for pedal, as in Example 6, from "Chopin" (from *Carnaval*). Here he seems to parody not only Chopin's compositional style but his pedal notation as well.

Ex. 6

Schumann sometimes uses the pedal to bridge over one section to another, even when rests are indicated. Example 7, from the first movement of the Sonata in F-sharp minor, is shown here as in the original. Both the collected edition[8] and so-called instructive edition[9] by Clara Schumann have an extra pedal release sign under the rest and fermata immediately before the *Allegro vivace*, in clear violation of the composer's intent.

Ex. 7

Schumann may use the pedal for contrast and variety, even in sections having the same articulation throughout, as in the excerpt from "Pantalon et Colombine" (from *Carnaval*), shown in Example 8.

Ex. 8

His pedaling can be boldly experimental for its time. In Example 9, from the Finale of *Papillons,* Schumann indicates that the pedal should be held unbroken for some 27 bars. This effect was inspired by an episode in a novel by Johann Paul Friedrich Richter and portrays the confused chattering of partygoers leaving a ballroom as the clock strikes six.[10] Schumann's original pedaling should at least be attempted, although many players may wish to resort to a bit of unobstrusive half- or quarter-pedaling, possibly combined with use of the middle pedal to hold the low D in bar 47. A musical "disappearing act" occurs a few bars later in the same work, where Schumann's unusual writing, shown in Example 10, gives the effect of a slow pedal release.

In Example 11, another famous instance of Schumann's originality in pedaling occurs in "Paganini" (from *Carnaval*). Here the composer uses the pedal to create an echo effect as well as a swell on one chord. After the four loud *sforzando* chords, the notes of the *pianississimo* chord have traditionally been sounded by first depressing the keys silently, then releasing the pedal. This interpretation is highly questionable, since the partials of the final soft chord do not match those of the *fortissimo* F-minor harmony. Schumann's effect will be much better presented if the *pianississimo* chord is actually sounded and the pedal is released immediately after the keys have been played, then quickly re-depressed. If this proce-

Ex. 9

Ex. 10

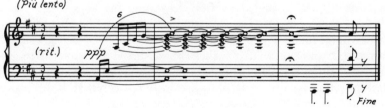

Ex. 11

dure is followed exactly, there will be a slight *crescendo* before the E-flat seventh chord entirely fades away.

Using the Left Pedal

Schumann occasionally indicates that the left pedal is to be used by writing the word *Verschiebung* ("shifting"), as seen in his "Frühlings-gesang" (from *Album für die Jugend*), in Example 12.

Ex. 12

Some of Schumann's original pedaling indications were changed in subsequent posthumous editions, including as has been seen, the long respected one by Clara Schumann. Although the composer's indications for pedaling are vastly incomplete, when they are found, they usually highlight some special effect. In his striving for new sonorities, Schumann often achieves marvelously original pedaling effects. Like Liszt, Schumann many times uses the right pedal to highlight a musical, as well as a poetic or pictorial, idea. The two men, along with Chopin, were the nineteenth century's most brilliant pedaling innovators.

Using the Pedals
When Playing Liszt

Using the Right Pedal

From both the implied pedal effects and the explicit pedal notation found in many of his piano works, it is evident that Liszt must have possessed an understanding of pedaling that was far ahead of his time. At least in his later years, he used syncopated or *legato* pedaling, a technique then considered advanced but now universally used and taught. In a letter to Louis Köhler dated July 27, 1875, Liszt wrote, "The entrance of the pedal after the striking of the chords . . . is very much to be recommended . . . especially in slow tempi."[1] Moriz Rosenthal, a student of Liszt's during the years 1878–79 and 1884–86, wrote in 1924 that Liszt knew of syncopated pedaling and that he undoubtedly would be immensely pleased at its general adoption in the four decades after his death.[2] The lack of general use of a syncopated pedal technique by pianists in Liszt's day is further evidenced by Rosenthal's remark in the same article that syncopated pedaling is "the most distinctive difference between the piano playing of forty years ago and of today."[3] A later article quotes Rosenthal as saying:

> I consider the discovery of the syncopated pedal the most important event in the history of piano playing. It constitutes the high water mark between the older and the present school. No more painstaking *legato* playing of chords by dint of fingering; no more dry playing without pedals in order to avoid blurs. The syncopated pedal was the emancipation of the wrist and arm from the keyboard.[4]

Liszt's writing generally calls for a rich, full use of pedal, especially when it is needed as a support for long pedal points. In his piano tran-

scriptions of works for voice and as well as for other instruments, a liberal
or almost constant use of pedal is an absolute necessity. Liszt advised his
students to pedal all long melody notes, particularly those in a high
register, even when they are not supported by underlying harmonic
material.[5]

Liszt's original pedal indications have often been changed in later
editions. Consequently much of his music suffers from underpedaling,
not only through performers' slavish following of corrupt editions but
also because of a basic misunderstanding of true Lisztian sonority. It can
be safely stated that Liszt played *without* pedal is the exception. As with
such composers as Beethoven and Schumann, Liszt's pedal indications
frequently indicate an exceptional effect rather than a customary use that
would ordinarily be done at the player's discretion. Any number of these
special effects can be found, many of them in response to definite poetic,
pictorial, or even psychological ideas.

In addition to the conventional 🎹 and ✳, Liszt uses a variety of
indications to request use of the right pedal. His placing of the word
armonioso in the score always means a rich blending of harmonies through
a liberal use of pedal. Example 1 shows one such passage, from "Harmonies du soir" (from *Etudes d'exécution transcendante*). Changes of pedal
should perhaps not be completely clear, but always leave a small amount
of haze to blend into the next rolled chord. Liszt's use here of the word
armonioso and the consequent implied slightly delayed changes of pedal
anticipate by over half a century the pedal overlap used by Debussy.[6]

Ex. 1

Liszt occasionally gives the indication *les deux Pédales* to show that he
wishes both the right and left pedals to be depressed simultaneously.

The rare indication *Ped. ogni battuta* simply means to take a new
change of pedal on each downbeat. An instance of this marking in *Die
Trauer-Gondel* No. 2 is shown in Example 2.

Liszt often indicates long pedals to create massive sonorities, even
during a series of unblending harmonies. Example 3, from "Pensée des
morts" (from *Harmonies poétiques et religieuses*), and Example 4, from

Ex. 2

Ex. 3

Ex. 4

"Wilde Jagd" (from *Etudes d'exécution transcendante*), contain passages of this typical Lisztian sonority.

Many of Liszt's pedal indications follow an expected pattern of carrying over basic underlying harmonies or implied pedal points, as in Example 5, from "Bénédiction de Dieu dans la solitude" (from *Harmonies poétiques et religieuses*).

An effect of three hands playing, so brilliantly used by both Liszt and his famous rival Sigismond Thalberg, always calls for a liberal use of pedal, even when, as in Example 6, from *Réminiscences de Norma,* it is not explicitly indicated in the score.

Ex. 5

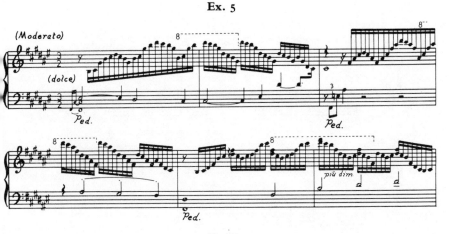

Ex. 6

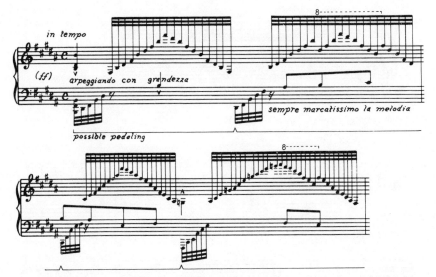

Liszt may ask for longer stretches of pedal as a means of imitating other musical instruments or to evoke impressionistic, extramusical sound effects. The number of such effects is extensive, and the following examples are by no means exhaustive. In all of them Liszt's original pedal indications are given.

Some of the most imaginative long pedal effects that imitate other instruments are in the *Hungarian Rhapsodies*. The resonant, reverberating jangling of the cimbalom, a large dulcimer used by the Hungarian gypsies, is frequently portrayed. One such passage, from *Hungarian Rhapsody No. 3*, is given in Example 7. Liszt may also write *quasi zimbalo* to

Ex. 7

Ex. 8

indicate that a passage must sound like a cimbalom. Even if he does not indicate the use of pedal, as in Example 8, from *Hungarian Rhapsody* No. 11, its use would be assumed.

Another instrument of the gypsy orchestra is the double bass. The sound of this instrument is captured in Example 9, from *Hungarian Rhapsody* No. 3, with the aid of Liszt's original thick pedal indication.

Ex. 9

The muffled sound of funeral bells is heard in Example 10, from "Michael Mosonyi" (from *Historische ungarische Bildnisse*), where the composer himself writes *wie Glocken* ("like bells"). From a master class, Lina Ramann quotes Liszt concerning the interpretation for this passage: "The double stops of the tolling . . . *quasi legatissimo* . . . the notes ringing into each other."[7]

Ex. 10

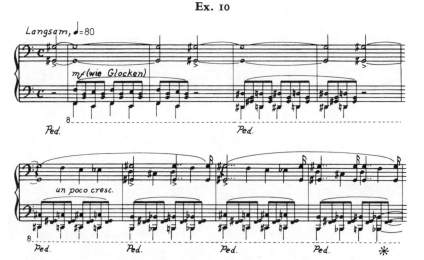

Liszt's use of the pedal to paint extramusical images can be striking. The imitation of wind-driven stormy waves is graphically enhanced by long stretches of pedal in "St. François de Paule 'marchant sur les flots' " (from *Légendes*), shown in Example 11. Wind gently swaying the ancient trees in the gardens is the extramusical effect Liszt wishes to capture with long pedaling in Example 12, from "Aux Cyprès de la Villa d'Este" No. 2 (from *Troisième Année de Pèlerinage*).

The image of whirling snow is masterfully evoked if the performer follows Liszt's original long pedal indication in Example 13, from "Chasse-neige" (from *Etudes d'exécution transcendante*). *Trübe Wolken* ("Grey Clouds"), an experimental work of Liszt's dating from 1881, exhibits an impressionistic smearing of pedal, as shown in Example 14.

Ex. 11

Ex. 12

Ex. 13

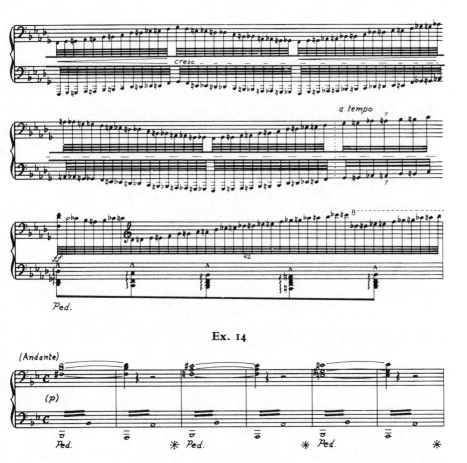

Ex. 14

A famous example of long pedaling, typically Lisztian in its linking of a musical and a poetic idea, occurs in Example 15 in the so-called *Dante Sonata* (from *Deuxième Année de Pèlerinage*). Here the deliberate blurring of sonorities is intended to suggest the lamentations of Hell's damned.

Liszt occasionally uses an unusual pedal indication for what can only be construed as a psychological effect. In Example 16, from *Mephisto Waltz* No. 1, his original pedal, which blurs the accented minor seconds in the left hand is seldom followed; most pianists change the pedal on the second 32nd note of each bar. But Liszt's intended effect, coming at the climax of the frenzied orgiastic dance instigated by Mephistopheles in Lenau's poem, gives a strident, savage, animal-like snarling sound that is entirely in keeping with the programmatic content of the music.

Liszt occasionally demands that no pedal be used. In Example 17, from "Feux follets" (from *Etudes d'exécution transcendante*), although there is no written indication for pedal before the *senza pedale* marking, he

Ex. 15

Ex. 16

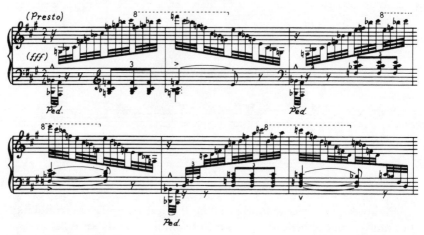

must have assumed it would have been used. The pedal indication two bars later is by Liszt.

Using the Left Pedal

Liszt usually indicates use of the left pedal by writing *una corda* and occasionally asks for a simultaneous use of the left and right pedals by writing *les deux Pédales* ("the two pedals"). When he wishes the left pedal to be released, he customarily writes *tre corde,* but he sometimes neglects to do so.

It should not be assumed that Liszt uses the left pedal only in extremely soft passages, for there are a number of instances when he requests it as a modifier of tone quality in passages of a higher dynamic

Ex. 17

Ex. 18

level. In Example 18, from "Bénédiction de Dieu dans la solitude," it is used to achieve greater intensity of sound in the melody. The pedaling is as found in the original.

At other times the left pedal may be used to achieve extramusical effects. In Example 19, from *Die Trauer-Gondel* No. 1, the left pedal is again used during a passage of relatively high dynamic level. This use, in combination with the long stretches of pedal given by Liszt, helps to create the macabre image of a lament, muffled funeral bells, and the lapping of water during a funeral procession by gondola on the canals of Venice.

Liszt cautioned his pupils against using the left pedal in passages louder than a *mezzo-forte*. He felt that the piano would be much more likely to go out of tune if it were played for long periods at a higher dynamic level while using this pedal, since on most notes the hammers would strike with full force on two instead of three strings.[8]

It should not be assumed that Liszt always uses the left pedal in extremely soft passages. In the *Mephisto Waltz* No. 1, he indicates an

Ex. 19

unbroken use of the left pedal in bars 339–451 (but gives no release for the *una corda*). During this long stretch, the general dynamic level is *piano*. Then starting in bar 452, the beginning of Example 20, when the dynamic level drops to *pianississimo,* there could be a return to a brighter *tre corde* tone quality. The intended effect is extramusical, since this passage imitates the hard, sardonic laughter of Mephistopheles.

Ex. 20

Using the Middle Pedal

Liszt was definitely acquainted with the middle pedal, although we are not sure when he was first shown a mechanism of this type. The piano firm of Boisselot et Fils exhibited an instrument equipped with a *sostenuto* device at the 1844 Paris Exposition. Then Louis Boisselot, the son, went on Liszt's concert tours of Spain and Portugal in 1845–47.[9] He apparently presented Liszt with one of his the firm's instruments. In a letter to Carl Weitzman, dated August 14, 1861, Liszt mentions it as still in his possession.[10] It is not clear whether it is the same instrument that was exhibited at the Paris Exposition. It is not the Boisselot instrument with which Liszt toured, for that one remained in Portugal and is now in the State Instrument Museum in Lisbon.[11] A later Chickering piano that Liszt owned apparently had a *sostenuto* pedal mechanism for the lower half of the keyboard.[12] It is now in the Liszt Museum in Budapest and is most likely the instrument that Chickering delivered to Liszt in Rome at Christmas 1867. He later donated it to the Royal Hungarian Academy of Music.[13]

In 1883 Liszt was sent a grand by the Steinway firm in New York. The piano, serial number 49382, had been finished on December 12, 1882 in Hamburg, just a few years after Steinway had begun incorporating the *sostenuto* pedal on its instruments.[14] It is now in the *Museo teatrale alla Scala* in Milan. In a letter of November 1883 to the Steinway firm, shown in Example 21, following some generally flattering remarks about the piano, Liszt wrote:

Regarding the use of your most welcome *sostenuto* pedal with sustaining tones, I am sending to you the two enclosed examples, "Danse des Sylphes" by Berlioz, and the third of my "Consolations." Today I have only written the opening measures of both pieces, with the condition that if you wish it,

Ex. 21

Ex. 22

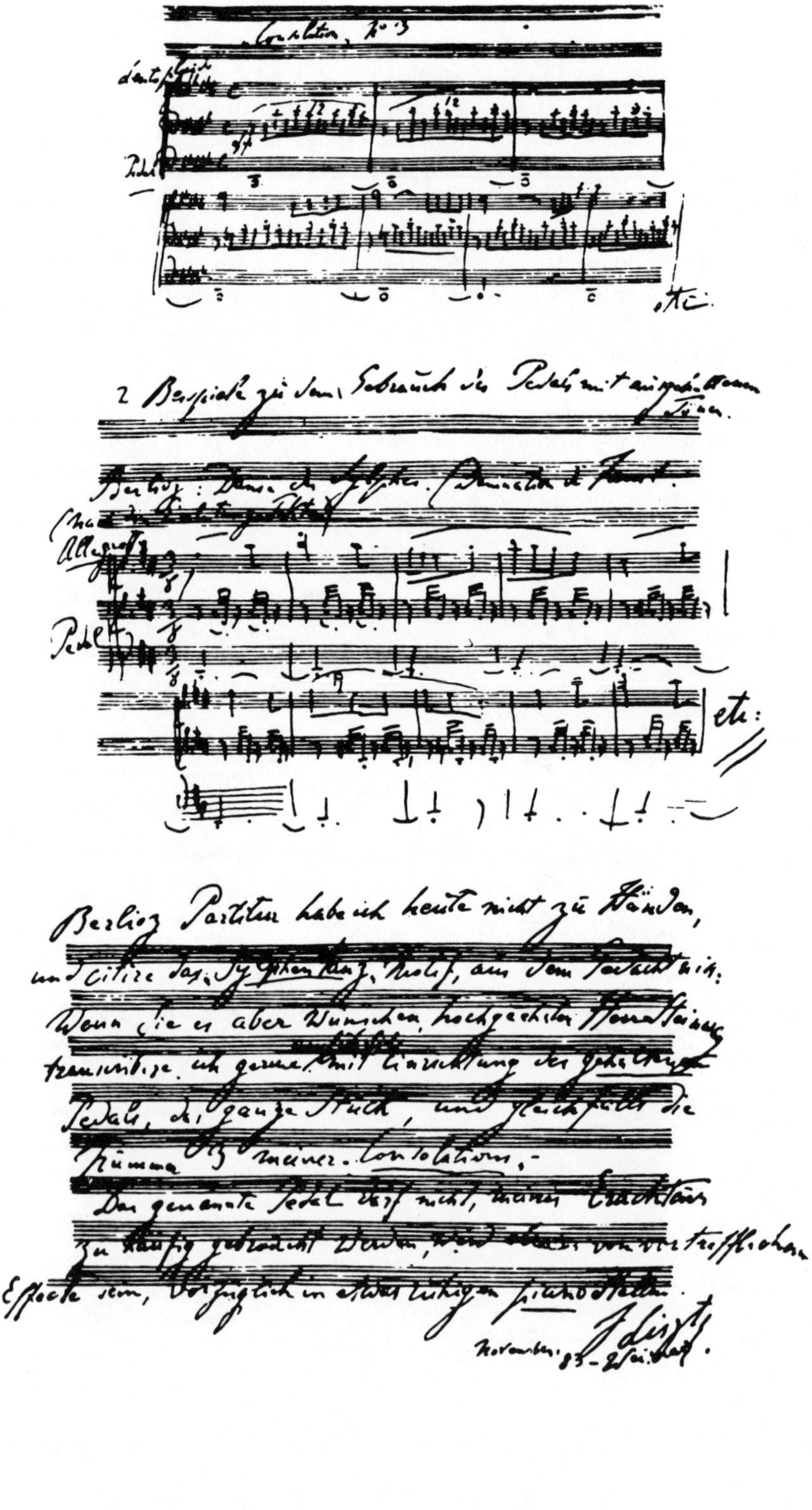
Consolation, No. 3

dans le Pédale

2 Beispiele zu dem Gebrauch des Pedals mit ausgehaltenen Tönen.

Berlioz: Danse des Sylphes. (Damnation de Faust.)

Allegro

Pedal

etc.

Berlioz Partitur habe ich heute nicht zu Händen, und citire das Sylphen Tanz Motif aus dem Gedächtniss. Wenn Sie es aber wünschen, hochgeehrter Herr Steinway, transcribire ich gerne, mit Anwendung des gehaltenen Pedals, das ganze Stück, und gleichfalls die Nummer 3 meiner Consolations.

Das genannte Pedal darf nicht, meines Erachtens, zu häufig gebraucht werden, wird aber von vortrefflichem Effecte sein, vorzüglich in etwas ruhigen Pianostellen.

F. Liszt

November 83 – Weimar.

I shall happily finish the entire transcription, complete with exact adaption for your *sostenuto* pedal.

In a postscript he added:

The pedal referred to should not, in my opinion, be used with too much frequency, but will be of excellent effect, especially in somewhat tranquil soft passages.[15]

Handwritten excerpts from the opening bars of both pieces were enclosed in the letter (see Example 22). Liszt divides the writing over three staves. On the lowest staff, in both pieces, he writes in tied notes the pedal point he wishes held by the *sostenuto* pedal. This letter and the manuscript examples have been reproduced at various times in several periodicals and books, but their present location is unknown.

Liszt, who was one of the great musical innovators of all time, was the first major nineteenth-century composer to acknowledge and welcome the appearance of the newly invented *sostenuto* pedal. Although there are no other documented examples of his using it, his enthusiastic response to Steinway would seem to open the door for its use in some of his works.

12

The Catalan School of Pedaling

In the Teaching of Enrique Granados and Frank Marshall

by Mark Hansen

The "Catalan" school of piano playing is characterized by special attention to clarity of voicing, tone color, and, most especially, subtle use of the pedals. It is a tradition that was begun by the Catalan pianist Juan Bautista Pujol (1835–1898), who was the teacher of such famous virtuosi as Enrique Granados, Ricardo Viñes, and Joaquin Malats. This tradition has been carried into the twentieth century by his pianistic "heirs," Frank Marshall and Alicia de Larrocha.[1]

The piano literature of nineteenth-century Spain demands a virtuoso pedaling technique. Perhaps the most notable advancement in this direction was accomplished by Granados and his pupil Frank Marshall. Granados's special abilities in the use of the pedal are documented by the American pianist-conductor Ernest Schelling (1876–1939), as he refers to his own attempts to play "Coloquio en la Reja" from *Goyescas*:

> I heard him [Granados] play it many times and tried to reproduce the effects he achieved. After many failures, I discovered that his ravishing results at the keyboard were all a matter of the pedal. The melody itself, which was in the middle part, was enhanced by the exquisite harmonics and overtones of the other parts. These additional parts had no musical significance, other than affecting certain strings which in turn liberated the tonal colors the composer demanded.[2]

Throughout his life Granados combined teaching and performing, leading him to establish the Académia Granados in Barcelona in 1901. The school quickly gained a national reputation for its progressive educational policies. Granados was extremely devoted to teaching and kept handwritten records of his pupils' progress. These became the basis for his treatise *Método Teórico Práctico para el Use de los Pedales del Piano* ("Theoretical and Practical Method for the Use of the Piano Pedals").[3]

Granados's most famous pupil was Frank Marshall. Born in Spain in 1883 of English parentage, Marshall soon was serving as Granados's teaching assistant, personal secretary, and copyist. He was later named associate director of Granados's school. Marshall, like Granados, dedicated much of his time to teaching, and his two written works, *Estudio Práctico sobre los Pedales del Piano* ("Practical Study of the Piano Pedals")[4] and *La Sonoridad del Piano* ("Piano Sonority"),[5] further advance both his and Granados's pedagogical concepts regarding pedaling. Both of Marshall's books are presently used at the Academy. Upon Granados's death in 1916, Marshall was appointed director. The name of the school was later changed to Acadèmia Frank Marshall. Upon Marshall's death in 1959, the directorship was assumed by his prize pupil, Alicia de Larrocha.

An examination of the written pedagogical works of Granados and Marshall helps to illuminate the "Catalan" approach to pedaling and piano sonority. In a conversation with the author, de Larrocha put in perspective the role these written methods play. Her remarks are quoted at appropriate times in this chapter.

Granados's *Método Teórico Práctico* outlines three basic functions of the pedal: its use with individual notes to maintain a *legato* line or to enhance tone quality, as a means of connecting groups of notes into consonant and/or dissonant sonorities, and as a coloring device for melodic lines while contrasting textures of both dynamics and touch occur in other voices. Granados subdivides note values into what he calls *valores reales e imaginários* ("real and imaginary values"), which form the basis for depression and release of the pedal. He also establishes his own system of pedal notation. Granados's rhythmic subdivision is the basis of what is commonly termed "synocopated" pedal. In Example 1, the pedal is to be depressed on the second quarter of time, the hands lifted at the "L," and the pedal held for the duration of the horizontal line.

Ex. 1

Granados's imagined subdivisions of notes and rates of pedal change are related to the length of the notes themselves. The longer the note, the slower the rate of pedal change, as shown in Example 2.

Ex. 2

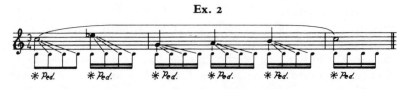

Granados's concept of perceptible and imperceptible dissonance holds that the degree of dissonance is strongly dependent on tempo: the faster the tempo the greater the number of nonharmonic tones that can be combined in an unbroken pedal. See Example 3.

Ex. 3

In addition to exploring such common pedaling problems as bridging leaps, isolating grace notes from the prevailing harmony, and pedaling contrasting touches, Granados explains how to create a *legato* pedal effect by using finger substitution. See Example 4.

Ex. 4

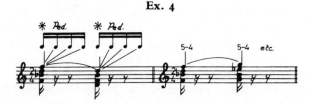

Granados devotes special attention to applying different amounts of pedal according to the register of the writing, as illustrated in Example 5.

In an excerpt from Grieg's *Berceuse,* shown in Example 6, Granados shows how the pedal can be used both for accenting and in syncopation.

The Granados method is presently out of print and, according to de Larrocha, has not been used for many years at the Marshall Academy. Neither Granados's nor Marshall's methods can be said to give a complete key to the "Catalan" school of pedaling, for, as de Larrocha stressed, they "are only the most basic texts—the primer level of pedal study."[6]

Ex. 5

Ex. 6

Although *Estudio Práctico* treats pedaling in more depth than does the Granados method, Marshall acknowledges that his method is but the starting place for pedal mastery and that real artistry is achieved mostly by intuition. And although he believes that "laws serve no purpose,"[7] he nonetheless feels that talent can, with the proper foundation and discipline, build artistic refinement and direction.

As with Granados, Marshall builds his pedaling approach upon a concept of imaginary note value subdivisions, as shown in Example 7. His exercises for the application of this basic concept are extremely thorough and precise, as illustrated in Examples 8–11.

Marshall stresses the sustaining of a melodic line concurrently with the release of harmonic material below, a pianistic layout that occurs often

Ex. 7

Ex. 8

Ex. 9

Ex. 10

Ex. 11

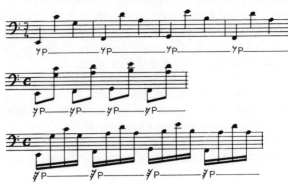

Ex. 12

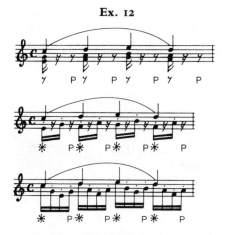

in Spanish piano music. According to de Larrocha, "The *Goyescas* are full of this problem."[8] Example 12 shows several representative exercises given by Marshall.

Marshall's second volume, *La Sonoridad del Piano,* contains works from the standard Romantic literature. It presents practical applications of the principles found in the *Estudio Práctico,* as well as further pedaling concepts. Marshall indicates voicing and sonority problems by means of varying note sizes, with the larger notes receiving more tone. In Example 13, the note sizes in bars 2–4 indicate that the order of emphasis is to be soprano, tenor, bass, and alto.

Marshall gives several examples of use of pedal as a coloring agent. In Example 14, from Schumann's "Vogel als Prophet" (from *Waldszenen*), in

Ex. 13

bars 1, 2, and 4, right after each *staccato* eighth note on each second beat, a quick spot of pedal is used for sonority. In Example 15, from Schumann's Scherzino, Op. 124, No. 3, pedal is applied in bar 2 to contribute to the phrasing on the third beat and to enhance the sonority on the fourth and fifth beats.

Ex. 14

Ex. 15

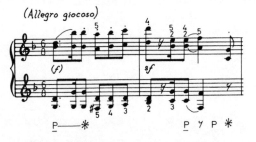

In Example 16, from "Der Dichter spricht" (from Schumann's *Kinderszenen*, Op. 15), accented pedal is used to obtain a richer sonority, even at the *pianissimo* level of this passage. Marshall's use of dashes under certain pedal signs indicates that an "accented" pedal is to be depressed with the attack of the note. Further uses of "accented" pedaling combined with syncopated pedaling are shown in Example 17, from the *Largo* movement of Beethoven's Sonata, Op. 7.

The two Marshall texts are presently used at the Marshall Academy. De Larrocha indicated that while Marshall's notation in some respects takes a different visual form from the Granados method, it nonetheless

Ex. 16

Ex. 17

serves to reinforce the same principles. Marshall's books, she pointed out, are simply a means of establishing a basic habit with the young, inexperienced student; and the concept of a rhythmic division of note values should be strictly advocated only at an early stage of learning.

De Larrocha strongly emphasized that pedaling technique is a constantly evolving element, something that changes with every new piano, new hall, and new acoustic. The "Catalan" school, she feels, belongs more to intuition than to isolated, rigid, and compact rules. She was quick to add that the pedaling ideas found in both Granados's and Marshall's books represent only one possibility and approach.

De Larrocha explained that her own pedaling has evolved and changed with time. For example, instead of executing the accented pedal right with a note, as Granados and Marshall advocate, she has now come to the point of applying the pedal, where possible, before the note is struck in order to obtain maximum sonority. When questioned about the validity of pedaling according to subdivided note values, she stated that in her own playing, the speed of application has become faster and faster, to allow the pedal to enhance the sound for the longest possible period. She also stated that she usually practices without pedal, applying it later, when she had determined exactly what the fingers can accomplish.

When asked about the uniqueness of the "Catalan" school of piano playing, as compared with other "schools" of pedagogy and performance, she replied that it was not that the pedaling was so unusual, but that Granados and his followers were the first school of players to put so much emphasis on the pedal, its sound potential, and its pedagogical aspects.[9]

Some markings in the scores of Enrique Granados have a basis in his pedal method. Example 18, from his *Escenas Románticas,* contains a practical application of the subdivided note-value approach to pedaling. The

Ex. 18

Ex. 19

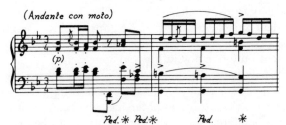

excerpt from *Danzas Españolas*, Vol. 4, No. 11, shown in Example 19, contains uses of accented pedal to increase sonority.

In Example 20, from the *Escenas Románticas*, there is a most curious pedal indication in bars 1, 3, and 5. Is the inverted "V" an indication of a half-pedal change to maintain the prevalent harmonic sonority throughout the bar? Full pedal changes are indicated at points where the bass line and/or tenor line have rests. Such a subtle pedaling would contribute to a clearer musical realization of the score.

Ex. 20

The above examples are indicative of the concern that Granados had for pedaling. An awareness by today's performer of the existence of such pedaling indications, as well as of the pedaling concepts outlined in both Granados's and Marshall's methods, can provide a foundation for better understanding the "Catalan" school of playing.

Gieseking's Pedaling in Debussy and Ravel

by Dean Elder

Walter Gieseking (1895–1956) was and still is universally acclaimed as the greatest interpreter of the piano works of Debussy and Ravel. He once remarked to me, "I have to hear beautiful sounds come from my piano." This seemingly mild truism, which I understood only with time, is the key to interpreting the impressionists. "Their music," said Gieseking, "must be played with technical perfection [and it was almost impossible to play well enough for him] in a classic, rather strict frame, always voicing with color and singing the melodies spontaneously, uninhibitedly from within."

If one approaches these works primarily from the point of view of the form, phrasing, harmonic structure, and technique, or in too romantic or too percussive a style, something will always be out of balance. It is in the piano that the magic and beauty of impressionism are built. These sounds can rise only by being heard by their re-creator. The pianist must think of the total impression of the piece and strive to hear those sounds.

Walter Gieseking was a "natural" pianist. He had a fantastic ability to play by ear; an abnormally acute, photographic memory; and a lightning-fast motor mechanism. He possessed a wonderful talent for playing fluttery, even classic, techniques and for controlling the vibrations of every note. His tone was one of the most easily recognizable of all the great pianists. It was transparent, nonpercussive, of great dynamic range—qualities that resulted from his phenomenal ear for prolonging vibrations, his Pan-like inwardly felt melodic outpouring, and, perhaps above all, his masterful pedaling. Throughout his career, he performed Debussy or Ravel or both on nearly every program that did not consist of one composer.

Pedaling According to the Bass Harmony

Gieseking believed the correct use of the pedal to be of enormous importance. "Just as one learns correct finger technique from the head and not the fingers, so one learns correct pedaling from the dictates of the ear and not the foot." He reiterated that often the pedal sign in Debussy and Ravel is the bass note, and that the pedal should be held as long as the bass harmony. Thus long pedals must be held for bars or even pages when the harmony remains the same. In bar 71 of the Prélude from Debussy's *Pour le piano,* shown in Example 1, at the start of the D–E trill, Gieseking wanted the pedal held to the reprise, which comes nearly a page and a half later, in bar 97. On his recording,[1] however, he starts changing the pedal at bar 91, six bars before the reprise, where the texture thins and the line descends. "In small rooms and on recordings, you can't use as much pedal as you can in Carnegie Hall," he said.

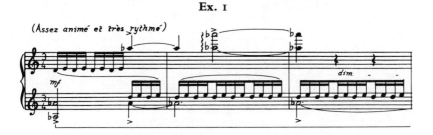

Ex. 1

←—bars 74-94—→

Later, on bars 134–42 of the same piece, shown in Example 2, he suggested there be "one pedal for bars 134, 135; one pedal for bars 136, 137; and one pedal for bars 138–42 (or in bars 140 and 141 change the pedal each two beats for the two-note phrasing)."

During the whole-tone scale, five-finger page before the *piano subito* jungle drums in *L'isle joyeuse,* shown in Example 3, he wanted the pedal held for the entire page! Yet, he would use flutter pedal if the instrument and the hall did not permit a long, unbroken pedal.

Ex. 2

Although Gieseking pedaled each composer individually, in the classics and the romantics his pedaling did not change much on the spur of the moment. In the impressionists, on the other hand, his pedalings would sometimes vary spontaneously. Once during the Saarbrücken classes, after advising holding the pedal for all of bars 166–85 in *L'isle joyeuse,* he played the page in question. Afterward he turned around and said, "You see!" As we had seen him unconsciously use flutter pedaling, we said, "Yes, *maître,* we see."

Even single bars of *L'isle joyeuse* often suffer from unsonorous pedaling. (In this and all later examples, Gieseking's suggestions are given in quotation marks.) "In bar 6, hold the pedal. In bars 7–8 use pedal during the entire guitar figures (which should be fingered 5–3–2–1)." Example 4 shows these three bars.

Perhaps the most remarkable long pedal effects are to be found in Debussy's "Voiles," (Prélude 2, Book 1). Gieseking achieved a Monet-like canvas of "drifting sailboats" with his extremely even, tender, watery

Ex. 3

←— bars 170-181 —→

Ex. 4

touch and pedaling. From bar 15, he requested that the pedal be held until bar 42 *(En animant)* or to the last triplet eighth note of bar 41 (see Example 5). "Up to this pentatonic harmony, it is all one whole-tone harmony."

"Hold the pedal through the pentatonic harmony from bar 42 *(En animant)* until the last three bars, with possible changes or half-changes at bars 45 *(Très retenu)* and 48 *(au Mouv')* [as shown in Example 6]. In principle, after bar 15 change the pedal about three times in this piece, according to its three-part form and harmony."

Ex. 5

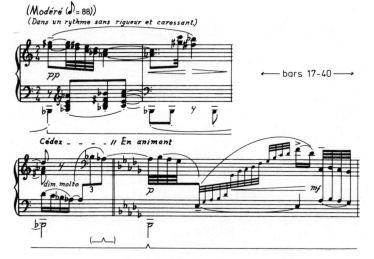

←—— bars 17-40 ——→

Ex. 6

Voicing as an Aid in Holding Long Pedals

Some pianists do not hold these long pedals, thinking they will result in too blurred a sound. They pedal Debussy and Ravel the way they pedal Chopin or Schumann and delineate unevenly and with crude gradations of touch. In using long pedals, the melodic notes must be brought out, nonharmonic notes voiced more softly than harmonic ones, and everything else weaker in sonority.

Examples abound in which the bass should be sustained throughout the same harmony. In bars 52–56 of the Prélude from Debussy's *Suite bergamasque*, shown on Example 7, "Don't change pedal for four bars; the left-hand eighth notes need to be very soft."

Gieseking, of course, took pains to achieve subtle shading with the fingers when using these long-pedal effects. "Blur so there is a nice

Ex. 7

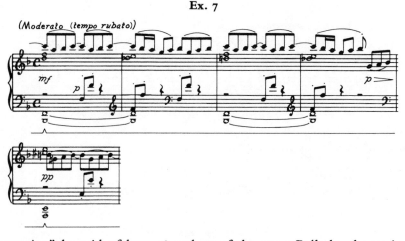

sonority," he said of bars 28 and 29 of the same Prélude, shown in Example 8. "You can pedal through each two beats if you play the top D sharp more *pianissimo* than anything else in the first two beats, more on the G sharp than on the C sharp–D sharp–E–F sharp in the third and fourth beats."

Ex. 8

In bars 56–60, shown in Example 9, "Don't change pedal for four bars. Nuance delicately and softly, with a slight accent on the right-hand whole notes C sharp–E in the first bar and almost inaudible right-hand whole notes C–D sharp in the second bar. Bring out the left-hand *staccato* notes slightly in the second and fourth bars."

In bars 30–35 of the Menuet from the same suite, shown in Example 10, Gieseking again advised changing the pedal with the bass changes. "Hold one pedal for bars 33–34." In bars 35–38, "Pedal for three bars, it's the same harmony. If it doesn't sound good, you aren't giving enough nuance with your fingers."

In Example 11, bars 132–38 of the Passepied from the suite, before the final return of the opening theme, "Don't change the pedal for six bars. The low E is the implied bass and is important for the sonority."

Ex. 9

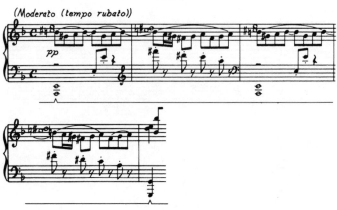

Ex. 10

In the excerpt from "Pagodes" (*Estampes* No. 1), shown in Example 12, "one pedal for bars 1–7, one pedal for bars 7–11, and one pedal for bars 11–15." One often hears pianists changing the pedal frequently in this opening, striving for clarity. They misunderstand Debussy's oriental,

Ex. 11

Ex. 12

pentatonic, vibrating *délicatement et presque sans nuances* ("delicately and nearly without nuances"). Throughout this piece the basses need to be sustained and the upper parts delicately melanged to bring out the melodic and harmonic atmosphere. In bar 75, "Catch the left-hand low D sharp in the pedal and hold the pedal to bar 80 *(Tempo I)*." (See Example 13.)

Ex. 13

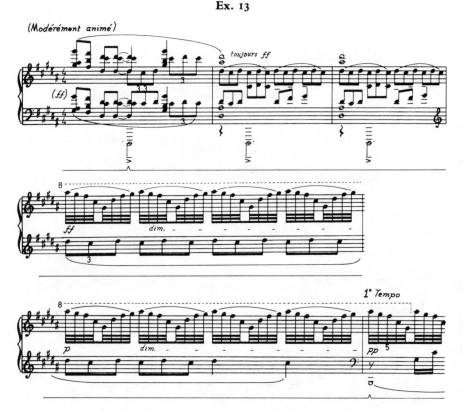

Gieseking wanted "one pedal for the first six bars" of "La soirée dans Grenade" (*Estampes* No. 2), shown in Example 14. All too frequently, however, the pedal is changed every bar in this opening, thereby destroying the piece's languid, Spanish atmosphere.

At bar 126 of "Jardins sous la pluie" (*Estampes* No. 3), shown in Example 15, Gieseking suggested pedaling the lowest note of the arpeggio and holding it at least into the next bar. Then in bar 133 of the same piece, "Bring out the left-hand three accented quarter triplet notes and hold the pedal from the low E of the first beat for three bars" (Example 16).

It is important to maintain the sonority by holding the basses as underpinning to the harmony above. Many pianists striving for pinpoint clarity get a brittle, uninteresting tone. Even in the toccata-like pieces of Debussy and Ravel, Gieseking strove for an impressionistic sonority. In fact, he kept their total *oeuvre* within a unified tonal canvas and wanted their music to have as beautiful a sonority as possible. Many times

Ex. 14

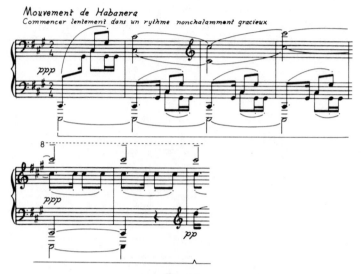

Ex. 15

Ex. 16

Gieseking held the pedal through two consecutive chords of the same harmony, not only to sustain the bass but also to produce a richer sound. In bar 2 of the Sarabande (from *Pour le piano*), shown in Example 17, "Connect the second eighth note to the half note in the same pedal." In bar 8, shown in Example 18, "Hold one pedal in spite of the written quarter note."

Ex. 17

Ex. 18

In the opening nine bars of "Clair de lune" (from *Suite bergamasque*), "Pedal only to connect or to add vibrations to individual notes. But starting from bar 10, the basses must be held through the bar as Debussy has indicated." Here the principle of playing nonharmonic notes more softly than harmonic ones is exemplified in a simple way: "Play the last E flat a little louder than the other notes." (Example 19 shows bars 8–11.)

Ex. 19

In "Reflets dans l'eau" (*Images* 1, No. 1), it was not enough to hold the pedal for the first two bars, shown in Example 20. The voicing had to be

Ex. 20

Ex. 21

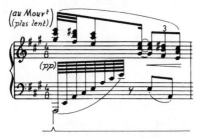

subtle: "Bring out the upper notes of the right-hand chords somewhat. Play the chords very softly and evenly in tone." In bar 67 of the same piece (Example 21), "In order to hold the pedal through the bar, you have to play the right hand very delicately."

In bars 43–47 of "Hommage à Rameau" (*Images* 1, No. 2), the basses must be held throughout the same harmony, with the upper sonorities and vibrations subtly mixed. "Pedal for four bars, pedal bar 47, and pedal bars 48–50." (Example 22 shows bars 43–51.)

In "Jimbo's Lullaby" (from *Children's Corner*), "Hold one pedal from bar 19 to bar 29 [Example 23], or at least as long as it works to hold the ostinato-like bass. The melody doesn't need to be brought out very much." "Hold one pedal from bar 66 until the last quarter note of bar 69," as shown in Example 24. As before, correct voicing of the melody is necessary to manage this long pedal.

In "Danseuses de Delphes" (Prélude 1, Book 1), adhering to the composer's dynamics should make it easy to follow Gieseking's direction to "Pedal by the bar in bars 18–20 [Example 25] to sustain the basses," yet in many recordings pianists do not follow Debussy's pedal indications. Gieseking also instructed the player to "Bring out the tops of the right-hand octave melody."

In "Les collines d'Anacapri" (Prélude 5, Book 1), "One pedal for bars 66–68" (Example 26), again to sustain the bass and aid in the *crescendo*.

Ex. 22

Ex. 23

Ex. 24

Ex. 25

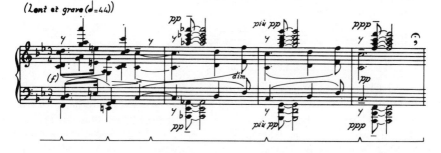

Bars 43–47 of "Brouillards" (Prélude 1, Book 2), shown in Example 27, offer an example of holding the bass for impressionistic effect and exploring pedaling effects in *pianissimo*. "Hold the pedal, if possible, according to your instrument, from the C of the first beat of bar 43 to bar 47. Some pianos and halls won't allow this and you have to change the pedal with the low C in each bar."

Ex. 26

Ex. 27

In bars 41–44 of "Feuilles mortes" (Prélude 2, Book 2), shown in Example 28, "Try holding the pedal longer than one bar, perhaps for the full three bars." As before, voicing is of the utmost importance in achieving this imaginative pedaling. Although Gieseking does not use these long pedalings in this passage on his recordings,[2] he nonetheless suggested experimenting, in his striving for the beauty his ears heard at the moment.

In "Ondine" (Prélude 8, Book 2), Gieseking told one student to hold the pedal for the entire last page, starting at bar 65, shown in Example 29. (Gieseking does so on his Columbia recording.[3]) He instructed another student to pedal each two bars, holding the arpeggiated chord in bar 72 with the fingers. "The pedal must be cleared on bar 73" (and Gieseking

Ex. 28

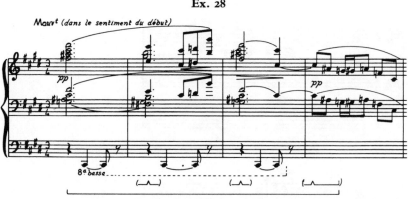

does that on his later Angel recording[4]). To make possible this delayed change of pedal after the sounding of the final arpeggiated chord, Gieseking used the distribution of notes shown in Example 29 and wanted this final chord played loudly enough, perhaps even *forte,* so that the tonic chord would sound above the held pedal sound.

Ex. 29

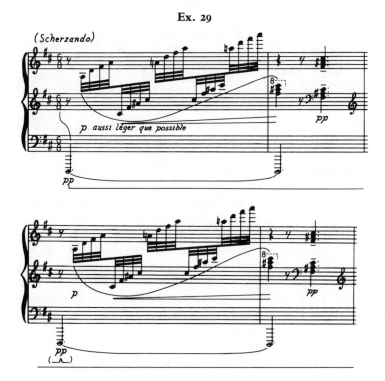

Ex. 29 Cont.

Although Gieseking instinctively produced a clearer, more classic sonority in the works of Ravel than in those of Debussy, his pedaling of these two composers was very similar. In *Jeux d'eau,* he held the pedal through bars 64–66, as shown in Example 30.

Gieseking would often hold the pedal through implied pedal points. In Ravel's "Alborada del gracioso" (*Miroirs* No. 4), "Pedal bars 191 and 192 and bars 193 and 194 (or pedal through to the arpeggiated chord of bar 195) [Example 31]. The ostinato harmony of each two-bar sequence is the same and is played with a *crescendo.*" In the last six bars of the piece (Example 32), "Hold the pedal from the low F sharp of bar 224 through the notes of the next three bars."

At the end of "Noctuelles" (*Miroirs* No. 1), "Hold the bass D-flat octave in one pedal from bar 126 through the first beat of bar 131 [Example 33]. The bass needs to be held as underpinning."

Ex. 30

Ex. 31

At the cadenza *(Lent)* of "Oiseaux tristes" (*Miroirs* No. 2), "Play the left-hand low A flat–E flat rather full and hold them in the pedal through to the *ppp* " (Example 34). Ravel also indicates that pedal should be used, although he does not indicate for how long.

Ex. 32

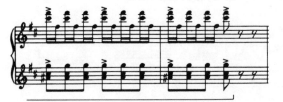

Ex. 33

In "Une barque sur l'océan" (*Miroirs* No. 3), "Hold the pedal from bar 132 through the last four lines of the piece" (Example 35).

In the excerpt from the third movement of Ravel's *Sonatine* shown in Example 36, Gieseking held the pedal from bar 106 to bar 111 (as well as

Ex. 34

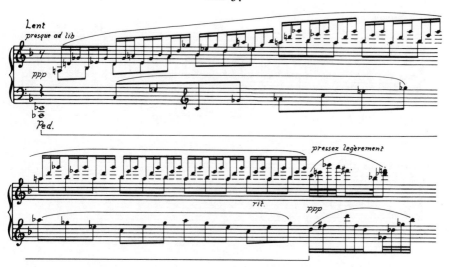

Ex. 35

← bars 133–136 →

in analogous passages). Although the bass E of bar 106 is only a half note, the sonority can be beautiful if one takes the pedal for several bars. Such pedaling, however, requires Gieseking's extraordinarily delicate, equal touch to make the left-hand sixteenth notes *pianissimo* while the quarter notes F sharp, E, and B (the main theme from the first movement) sing. If pupils could not achieve the desired sonority, he let them change the pedal with the upper right-hand melody notes.

Ex. 36

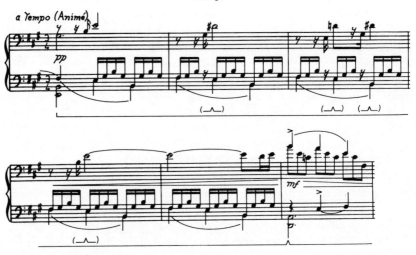

Holding Basses with Pedal through Rests

In the opening bars of the Prélude from Debussy's *Suite bergamasque,* shown in Example 37, Gieseking said to "Hold the bass through the rests to obtain a full sonority. The low F's and C's are important. The sixteenth notes will sound clear if you play them absolutely evenly." This pedaling sounds better than taking the pedal off in the second bar because of the rests. Gieseking's pedaling always encompassed the composition's total effect, sonority, and mood.

Ex. 37

Sometimes *staccato* upper-score notes should be held by the pedal while the bass is sustained. In bars 47–48 *(Mouv¹)* of "General Lavine" (Prélude 6, Book 2), "Catch the pedal after the second right-hand chord and hold it through the following bar" (Example 38). Some pianists blur the first beat or use the *sostenuto* pedal and do not hold pedal through the second bar. The rests mean more to them than the overall tonal effect.

Ex. 38

Gieseking recommended one pedal for bars 6–9 of Ravel's "Noc-tuelles" (*Miroirs* No. 1), shown in Example 39. (On his Angel recording, however, he sustains the pedal for only two bars; but in the same passage, which is repeated in bars 90–93, he holds pedal for almost four bars.[5])

Ex. 39

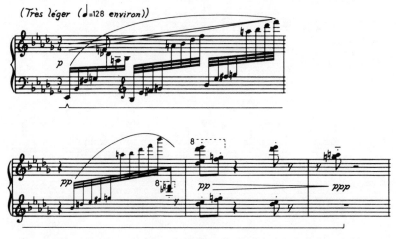

To avoid any Czerny-like dryness, he held the left-hand F's in an unbroken pedal in bars 80–84 (Example 40).

In "Une barque sur l'océan" (*Miroirs* No. 3), "Hold the pedal starting at bar 88 for two bars" (Example 41). A few bars later, he said to "Hold the pedal starting in bar 94 for four bars" (Example 42). The bass underpinnings need to be sustained through the ensuing upper-register filigree, to give a wavelike, impressionistic color. There are other examples of this type of pedaling throughout the *Miroirs,* in "Ondine" (from *Gaspard de la nuit*), and in the last movement of *Sonatine.*

Ex. 40

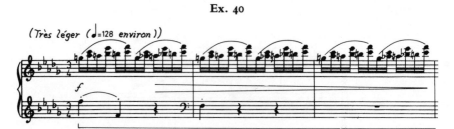

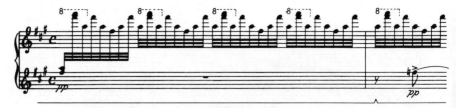

Ex. 41

Ex. 42

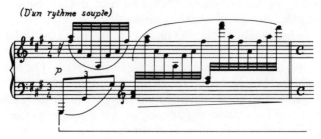

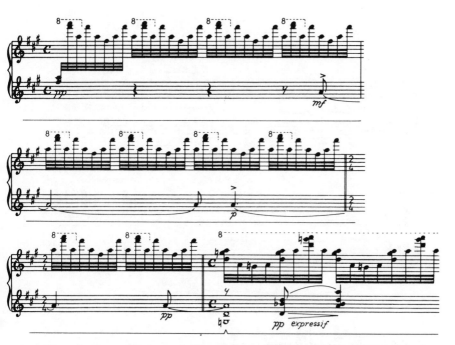

The opening of Debussy's "Les collines d'Anacapri" (Prélude 5, Book 1), shown in Example 43, is another instance of Gieseking's holding floating harmonies through ensuing rests. "In bars 1–2 keep one pedal. Hold the pedal from bar 5 to bar 10. Let bar 6 vibrate through the rests of bar 7. In bar 7 start the arpeggiated chords *piano* and begin to *crescendo* immediately to the *forte* of bar 10." In contrast, Gieseking wanted the *Vif* of bars 3 and 4 "clear and without pedal."

In "Les sons et les parfums tournent dans l'air du soir" (Prélude 4, Book 1), "Hold the pedal from the second quarter of bar 7. Pedal again from the second quarter of bar 9." (Example 44 shows bars 7–10.)

During the descending *pianissimo* quarter notes at the conclusion of "Des pas sur la neige" (Prélude 6, Book 1), shown in Example 45, "Play these *portato* notes with a relaxed arm, all with the fifth (or the fourth) finger and hold the pedal." Some pianists, seeing the *portato* signs, pedal each note. Gieseking's pedaling and dynamics pictorialize "footsteps dissolving in the distance."

Using Very Little Pedal

Although long pedals and pedaling according to the harmonies are frequent, much of the music of Debussy and Ravel needs sparse pedaling. Gieseking's pedaling was imaginative and stylistically correct, yet where

Ex. 43

Ex. 44

Gieseking used considerable pedal, some pianists play dryly; and where he used very little or no pedal, some pianists use considerable pedal.

Gieseking wanted no pedal until the second page of "Le vent dans la plaine" (Prélude 3, Book 1), the opening of which is shown in Example 46. (In contrast, Arturo Benedetti Michelangeli[6] uses considerable pedal;

Ex. 45

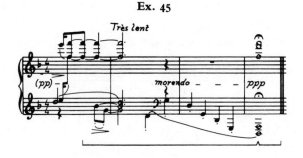

Ex. 46

Claudio Arrau[7] uses a lot. Both pianists conjure up "water" more than "wind.")

Of bars 32–35 of the Prélude from *Suite bergamasque* (Example 47), Gieseking said, "Clear, very little pedal, nice *legato*." To facilitate, take the lower whole-note A in bar 33 with the left hand.

Ex. 47

In "Les sons et les parfums tournent dans l'air du soir" (Prélude 4, Book 1), "The beginning should be played with a perfect *legato*. The

Ex. 48

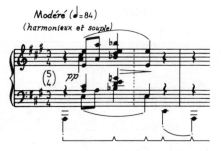

pedal must change with the harmonies, the third and fourth beats, and again on the fifth beat to observe the rest" (Example 48).

In Example 49, bars 1–2 of "Serenade of the Doll" (from *Children's Corner*), "Change the pedal or use *staccato* pedal on each quarter. Play with extreme evenness." Debussy indicates that the entire piece should be played with the *una corda* pedal depressed.

Ex. 49

Tempo, touch, and pedaling are interrelated. In "The Snow Is Dancing" (from *Children's Corner*), "Not too slow. Snow falls a little faster than your tempo. The dots aren't *staccato* markings, but dots under a large phrase mark. Use very little pedal." At another time he said, "Slow, poetic, a snow drizzle, still and soft, no snow storm! The beginning almost without pedal" (Example 50).

In the opening of "Des pas sur la neige" (Prélude 6, Book 1), shown in Example 51, "Don't pedal the D–E and E–F intervals of a second. Pedal only after the E and after the F. Throughout this piece, the pedal should be used only for connecting consecutive notes. None of the notes should grow hazy, dissolve, merge, or melt into one another."

In "Les tierces alternées" (Prelude 11, Book 2), shown in Example 52, "Almost *legato,* almost without pedal; in the left hand you can hold the accented thirds somewhat longer than the other thirds, or take a very little pedal on them. Observe that the left hand accents only the first third." Gieseking kept the tempo, sonority, and dynamics within an impressionistic frame even in the motoric pieces.

Ex. 50

Ex. 51

Ex. 52

In the opening of Ravel's *Sonatine,* shown in Example 53, Gieseking cautioned, "In the beginning, almost no pedal. It must be clear despite the interlocking hands. The 32nd-note accompaniment notes must be clear too but softer than the melody. Keep the melody and accompanying part on two levels of sound."

Ex. 53

Ex. 54

In the Menuet of the same work, shown in Example 54, he cautioned about using too much pedal. "Keep a clear sonority; the harmonies should not sound thick."

Gieseking was unusually demanding that the pedal be used sparingly in order for the basses to be clear. In "Les collines d'Anacapri" (Prélude 5, Book 1), from bar 32, "The bass theme should be brought out like a folk song, very clearly, with almost no pedal and as if from the distance; otherwise it sounds ordinary" (Example 55).

Ex. 55

In "Hommage à S. Pickwick Esq., P.P.M.P.C." (Prélude 9, Book 2) again the basses need to be clear. "The first bars without pedal; otherwise the left hand is not clean. You can only use a little connecting pedal for the right hand" (Example 56).

Ex. 56

Using No Pedal
In the opening of Menuet from *Suite bergamasque,* shown in Example 57,
"When you have four voices, don't use pedal. The left hand is *pizzicato.*"
At the end of the piece, shown in Example 58, "Don't pedal the *glissando.*
Pause slightly before playing the top note."

Ex. 57

Ex. 58

In Example 59, bar 26 of "Ce qu'à vu le vent d'Ouest" (Prélude 7,
Book 1), "Take the pedal off on the second quarter; pedal again on the
third quarter, so that the seagull cry is clear—*Angoissé:* someone is
drowning."

Ex. 59

Pedaling without Blurring Melody or Harmony
When diatonic movement should be clear, Gieseking took pains to use the
pedal only to connect inner voices that could not be connected with the
fingers. Regarding the Prélude from *Suite bergamasque,* he said, "Bergamo
is an ancient city in Italy, older than Rome. It has a sunny, free, open

Ex. 60

landscape. Keep the textures clear. In bar 3 [Example 60] catch the pedal only after the soprano G in order to connect the lower voices."

In bars 9 and 10 of the Sarabande from *Pour le piano,* shown in Example 61, "Don't blur the two sixteenth notes in the pedal."

Ex. 61

Gieseking also wanted the openings of "Jardins sous la pluie" (*Estampes* No. 3) and "Minstrels" (Prélude 12, Book 1), to be played "without pedal." At the beginning of "Les fées sont d'exquises danseuses" (Prélude 4, Book 2), "No pedal if possible. Possibly hold the left-hand notes with the fingers a little longer instead of using pedal," as shown in Example 62.

Ex. 62

In the opening of "La sérénade interrompue" (Prélude 9, Book 1), Gieseking did not play the *staccato* sixteenth notes with pedal, but he did make use of the *una corda* pedal. At bar 25, where the interlocking fifths commence, "*una corda* only, no damper pedal" (Example 63).

Sometimes Gieseking would play *staccato* or *portato* notes without pedal, saving it for the following melody, to achieve a new color. In "The Snow Is Dancing" (from *Children's Corner*), "Play bar 63 without pedal;

Ex. 63

bars 64, 65, and 66 with pedal; and bar 67 without pedal. Play close to the keys without movement" (Example 64).

Ex. 64

Pedaling for Pictorial Effect

Gieseking often had a picture in mind when gauging dynamics and pedaling. In bars 22–23 of "The Snow Is Dancing," shown in Example 65, he thought that Debussy's articulations were technically unrealizable. "Use pedal; it must remain in fog."

He knew the Mediterranean well and often remarked on the clarity and bright colors of its air and landscape. At bar 49 of "Les collines d'Anacapri" (Prélude 5, Book 1), shown in Example 66, "The theme should be free and clear; Anacapri knows no fog . . . hardly any pedal but not dry."

Ex. 65

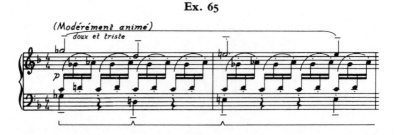

Ex. 66

In bars 16–17 of "Brouillards" (Prélude 1, Book 2), shown in Example 67, Gieseking wanted one pedal held through and a real *più pianissimo*. "The whole Prélude is fog."

Ex. 67

In bars 49–56 of "The Snow Is Dancing," shown in Example 68, "*Senza pedal*. Above all, blatant *sforzandos* and drum rolls, gradually changing to softer and longer-held notes. In bar 56, gradually add pedal."

In Example 69, bar 14 of "Reflets dans l'eau" (*Images* 1, No. 1), "Pedal only the second, fourth, sixth, and eighth sixteenth notes." In Example 70, in bars 30, 31, and 32, "No pedal on the sixteenth-note triplet. Catch the pedal on the last eighth of this bar and hold through the 64th notes of the following bar."

Ex. 68

← bars 51-55 →

gradually add pedal

Ex. 69

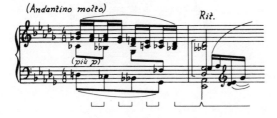

Ex. 70

Ex. 70 Cont.

In Example 71, bar 29 of "La danse de Puck" (Prélude 11, Book 1), "Pedal first on the G flat." In Example 72, bar 17 of "Canope" (Prélude 10, Book 2), "Hold the upper-score notes with the right hand. Pedal only on the left-hand quarter notes."

Ex. 71

Ex. 72

In bars 63 and 64 in the middle "Tristan" section of "Golliwogg's Cake Walk" (from *Children's Corner*), shown in Example 73, pianists often do not know what to do about the half note *vis-à-vis* the following *staccato* notes. Gieseking said, "The answering effect is like a mocking tap dance and shouldn't be too fast. In bar 63, hold the pedal until the second beat. Don't pedal bar 64."

At the end of the cadenza in the Prélude from *Pour le piano,* Gieseking advised holding pedal just to the last E: "Then a new pedal on this E, which is a new harmony" (Example 74). (Gaby Casadesus recommends this pedaling too.)

Ex. 73

Ex. 74

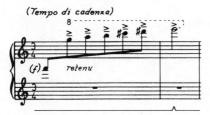

Crescendo and/or Accent Pedaling
In Example 75, bars 65 and 66 of the Prélude from *Pour le piano,* "Crescendo pedal should be used on the third beats."

Ex. 75

In Example 76, bar 13 of "Le vent dans la plaine" (Prélude 3, Book 1), "Pedal the *sforzando.*" At bar 17, Example 77, "Use some pedal on the small *crescendos.*"

Ex. 76

Ex. 77

Vibrating or Flutter Pedaling

In bar 31 of "Doctor Gradus ad Parnassum" (from *Children's Corner*), "Hold the pedal—vibrating, not deep—to the second beat of bar 32" (Example 78).

Ex. 78

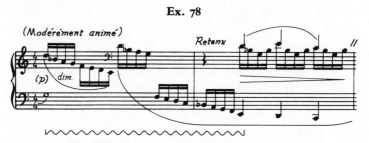

For the *quasi-tambourine* bars of "Minstrels," Gieseking recommended, "In a large hall pedal for three bars; use vibrating pedal in bar 4, changing often; and use no pedal in bar 5" (Example 79). At the end of the piece, where the drum is *pianissimo,* he wanted no pedal.

Ex. 79

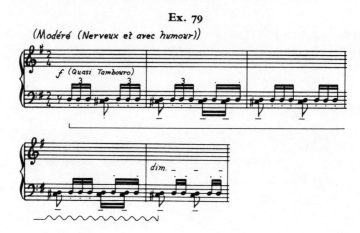

For the final *Rapide et fuyant* run of "La danse de Puck" (Prélude 11, Book 1), shown in Example 80, Gieseking gave a number of recommendations: 1. "Take the pedal off in the second half of the bar. The important thing is that the run is even but not too fast." 2. "Use vibrato-pedal, like a tender, airy, intuitive rustle, the run neither unclear-fast nor fast-clear!" 3. "Half-pedal. Use the entire hand as a unit." 4. "No pedal in the final *rapide*. The entire run and final note need to be light and under one slur. Hold the final bass note because of the fermata but without pedal."

Ex. 80

At bar 109 of "Mouvement" (*Images* 1, No. 3), "Play with a real *fff*, then flutter the pedal during the *diminuendo molto* of bars 111–14" (Example 81).

Ex. 81

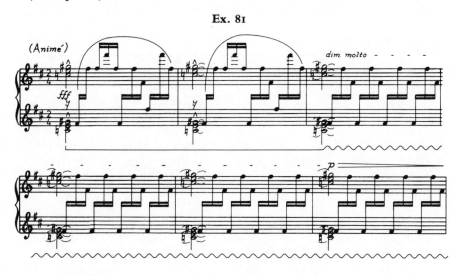

Using Half-Pedal

In the last four bars of the Menuet of Ravel's *Sonatine,* shown on Example 82, "Play the *crescendo* in tempo, *sans rubato,* very calmly. Change the pedal with the bass notes, using half-pedals on the descending chords of

Ex. 82

the last two bars; pedal the last chord and hold it through the bass fifth. Don't use the *sostenuto* pedal."

Using Finger Pedaling

At the reprise in "Clair de lune," shown in Example 83, from bar 51, "Play the top notes of the sixteenth-note arpeggios with the right hand to enable using as little pedal as possible. Use the pedal only briefly for connecting a change of chord. Sustaining the sixteenth notes with the fingers allows the upper notes of the right hand having the melody to sing clearly and beautifully."

Ex. 83

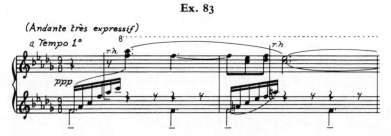

At bar 21 in "La puerta del Vino" (Prélude 3, Book 2), Example 84, Gieseking wanted the rolled notes struck almost together, like chords, without finger movement, and the notes held with the fingers. "Pedal

Ex. 84

(*Mouvᵗ de Habanera*)

only on the half notes, the right-hand E and left-hand G, and then hold
the pedal. These *fortes* are ironical."

In general, straight pedal should be used on rolled tenths or arpeggiated chords, as in bars 18 and 19 of the Sarabande from *Pour le piano,*
shown in Example 85. For accenting, Gieseking wanted straight pedal on
the chords of bar 18 of "Minstrels," shown in Example 86.

Ex. 85

Ex. 86

Anticipatory Pedaling
Gieseking suggested depressing the damper pedal, but not the *una corda,*
before playing the first note of Debussy's "La fille aux cheveux de lin"
(Prélude 8, Book 1), shown in Example 87; and both the damper and *una
corda* pedals before beginning Ravel's "Oiseaux tristes" (*Miroirs* No. 2),
shown in Example 88.

Ex. 87

Ex. 88

Retaking Chords Because of Rests

Where Debussy wrote long-note chords in one voice and shorter notes with rests in another, Gieseking would silently retake the long-note chords. The main examples of this technique are in bars 42–45 of "La cathédrale engloutie" (Prélude 10, Book 1), where the whole notes of each bar are repeated *diminuendo* (see Example 117, below), and in bars 49–52 of "Les sons et les parfums tournent dans l'air du soir" (Prélude 4, Book 1) (see Example 89).

Pedaling Endings of Pieces

"Les sons et les parfums tournent dans l'air du soir" is also an example of the pains Gieseking took with the pedaling and the nuancing of voices at the end of a piece. For the last line, shown in Example 89, he advised, "Play the grace notes on the beat. Pedal after the first eighth note and hold. Bring out the grace notes and the first eighth notes and play the other notes very softly. On the third beat, retake the chord and change the pedal. The sixteenth and 32nd notes need to be rhythmically exact and without pedal. The whole line should be clear, and the last two bars as quiet as possible."

Ex. 89

For the last line of "La puerta del Vino" (Prélude 3, Book 2), shown in Example 90, he said: "Hold the pedal for the last six bars; hold the

left-hand octave with the pedal as long as the right-hand notes sound."
Another time he said, "Vibrato-pedal." And still another time, searching
and listening for the effect he thought most beautiful, he said, "Change
the pedal after the final octave so as to leave only the right hand singing
for the next two counts."

Ex. 90

For the last three bars of "Feuilles mortes" (Prélude 2, Book 2), shown
in Example 91, he gave several recommendations: "Hold the pedal of bar
50, change the pedal on the second beat of bar 51, and release it on the
second beat of bar 52. Hold the C sharps as indicated. . . . Make a
ritardando in the upper voice of bar 51 so that the F sharp and E sharp don't
sound together in the pedal. Vibrate the pedal on the last chord until only
the C sharp is sounding."

Ex. 91

Pedaling Ending Staccato *Chords*
In several pieces Debussy and Ravel have written ending *staccato* chords
followed by rests. Gieseking did not find their way of writing the most
effective. For example, for the last two chords of the Prélude from De-

bussy's *Suite bergamasque,* he recommended, "Hold the pedal through the next-to-last bar; then play the last chord less *fortissimo* and short" (Example 92).

Ex. 92

But for the three *ppp* chords of the Passepied from the same suite, he said, "Don't hold the pedal through the rests; release the pedal after each chord" (Example 93).

Ex. 93

In bar 70 of Ravel's "Alborada del gracioso" (*Miroirs* No. 4), shown in Example 94, "Hold the bass fifth, which is *ff subito,* to the chord on the fourth beat. Then play this chord *staccato.*"

Ex. 94

Using the Una Corda *Pedal*
At bar 27 and in the *pianissimo quasi-glissando* bars of the cadenza on the last page of the Prélude from *Pour le piano,* Gieseking suggested using the

una corda pedal. He wanted the entire "Serenade of the Doll" (from *Children's Corner*) to be performed with the *una corda* pedal, even the *forte* passages. In "La danse de Puck" (Prélude 11, Book 1), he also wanted the *una corda* pedal used throughout except for a few places.

For the last line of "Clair de lune," he suggested using the *una corda* pedal, and releasing it for the final arpeggiated chord. "If you play the last chord with the *una corda* pedal, it sounds dull."

In bar 28 of "Le vent dans la plaine" (Prélude 3, Book 1), shown in Example 95, "Play these three *forte* chords with a *crescendo* but without rushing in tempo. It is difficult because it is fast. Lift the pedal on the second eighth note of the bar, so that the *piano* chord can be heard. Immediately depress the *una corda* on the *piano* chord."

Ex. 95

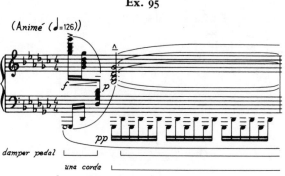

Using the Sostenuto *Pedal*

Some pianists, misunderstanding Debussy's and Ravel's bass indications, use the *sostenuto* pedal to hold the basses so the upper parts can be clear. But neither Debussy nor Ravel composed for pianos with a *sostenuto* pedal, and they had a different effect in mind from what one gets with the *sostenuto* pedal.

For the most part, Gieseking felt that using the *sostenuto* pedal was not the way to produce the desired tonal effect in the music of these two composers, and he seldom employed it. He did, however, recommend it for Debussy's "Pour les quartes" (Etude No. 3). In bar 20, the first bar of Example 96, "Hold the low C in the *sostenuto* pedal." In bar 65, at *Tempo I,* shown in Example 97, "Hold the bass-clef chords with the *sostenuto* pedal."

Gieseking usually employed the *sostenuto* pedal in the Prélude from *Pour le piano*. In bar 6 (Example 98), "Directly after playing the bass A, with no other note down, depress the *sostenuto* pedal."

Ex. 96

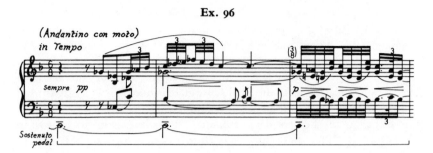

Ex. 97

Ex. 98

Avoiding the Sostenuto *Pedal*

When playing the same piece on a piano that had no *sostenuto* pedal, Gieseking relegated all the sixteenth notes to the right hand: "In bars 6–14, play all the sixteenth notes with the right hand. In bar 14, from the second beat on, play the chords with the left hand. In bars 16 and 18, play the first beat with the right hand, then the chords with the left hand." (Example 99 shows bars 13–18.)

Gieseking did not like the *sostenuto* pedal employed in the middle chorale section of "La cathédrale engloutie," nor did he wish it used at the ending of "La soirée dans Grenade" (*Estampes* No. 1). In bars 122–28, "Pedal each two bars. Don't change the pedal on these arpeggios. If you nuance the nonharmonic tones more softly than the harmonic ones (the

Ex. 99

(Assez animé et très rythmé)

Ex. 100

Mouv¹ du début

D's *ppp*), the arpeggios can be held in the pedal and the total sound will be a clear harmony" (Example 100).

Gieseking's suggestion for playing the last four bars of "Canope" (Prélude 10, Book 2), shown in Example 101, without employing the *sostenuto* pedal was ingenious. In bars 30 and 32, "Play the chord and hold the left-hand notes down, then strike the right-hand A with the fifth finger. Silently re-depress the G and D of the whole-note chord, and play the upper-score notes with the fifth finger, using only enough pedal to point up the phrasing and the *legato*. At the end of the piece play the fifth-finger E *portato,* as marked. While still holding the G and D with the fingers, return and depress middle C silently."

In bar 40 of "La terrasse des audiences du clair de lune" (Prélude 7, Book 2), "Play the C-sharp octaves *staccato.* Don't hold them in the pedal. Take the D–G–B chord all with the left hand" (Example 102).

Ex. 101

Ex. 102

Rather than using the *sostenuto* pedal or blurring to hold tied bass notes, Gieseking would redistribute notes between the hands. In bar 43 of "Doctor Gradus ad Parnassum" (from *Children's Corner*), "Delay a bit before the downbeat; play the A flat with the right hand, likewise the E flat in bar 44. That way you can hold the bass note without having to sustain the pedal." (Example 103 shows bars 41–44.)

Ex. 103

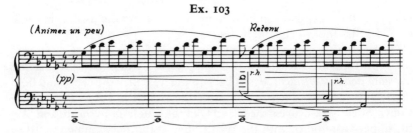

At the end of "Jimbo's Lullaby," "In bars 78 and 79, after playing the E flat and D flat, replay the F and G silently, and change the pedal immediately after each holding, to stop the *staccato* E flat and D flat." (Example 104 shows bars 77–81.)

In bars 88 and 89 of "Golliwogg's Cake Walk," shown in Example 105, Gieseking suggested: "Take the F with the left hand so that the complete half-note chord can be held without pedal, for the right-hand *staccati*

Ex. 104

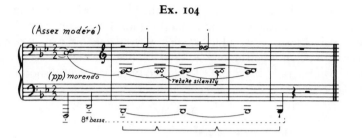

Ex. 105

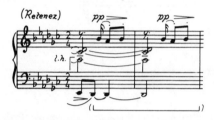

should be short." For pianists who could not stretch the tenth, he suggested catching the pedal after the bass D flat and holding it.

Four bars from the end of "Hommage à Rameau" (*Images* 1, No. 2), "Silently replay the left-hand G sharp octave and pedal each half note" (Example 106).

Ex. 106

In bars 15 and 16 of "Feuilles mortes" (Prélude 2, Book 2), shown in Example 107, Gieseking gave several solutions for holding the notes as marked and observing the rests without using the *sostenuto* pedal: 1. "If you can reach a major tenth, take the bottom notes F and G of the top-score chords with the left hand. Play the bottom-score treble-clef eighth notes with the right hand. This way you can hold two or three of the dotted half notes with the left hand and change the pedal. Lift the pedal on the fourth eighth note of each bar." 2. "Take the bottom-score eighth notes with the right hand." 3. "In bar 15 take the eighth notes of the bottom score, B and E, with the left hand. Retake the bass-score fifth silently. Play the following right-hand eighth notes without pedal, but sonorously. In bar 16, it's all the same how you divide, the silent retaking of the fifth being superfluous." 4. "You can play the bottom-score eighth notes with the right hand and silently retake the dotted half notes of the top score."

Ex. 107

Pedaling Different Harmonies without the Sostenuto *Pedal*
Gieseking wrote,

> It goes without saying that in holding the pedal through different har-
> monies, you must obtain a delicate melange of sonorities and not an obscure,
> thick pulp of notes. . . . The playing of a succession of melodic notes with
> the pedal down necessitates the most careful nuances when it concerns
> diminishing sonorities. Each note must sound longer than the preceding
> notes, an effect which can be obtained by a very careful, undetectable
> *crescendo.* When it concerns a melodic line of increasing sonority, the nu-
> ancing of the fingers is much simpler.[8]

Thus when Gieseking held the pedal in Debussy or Ravel through many bars of the same harmony, he was communicating with a singing, *en dehors* melody. That is not the same as holding the pedal and giving all elements equal emphasis.

Gieseking even suggested playing the inner note of a chord more softly to help sustain two harmonies in one pedal. In bar 4 of "Danseuses de Delphes" (Prélude 1, Book 1), the first bar of Example 108, "Play the B flats more softly with the second fingers, in the first-inversion B-flat chords. In this way you can hold the low D bass octave in one pedal through the following D-minor chords."

In bars 11–12 of the same piece, shown in Example 109, where Debussy indicates that the bass octave is to be held through two bars, one can use Gieseking's idea of each successive chord obliterating the vibra-tions of the preceding chord. "Make the top notes of the right-hand

Ex. 108

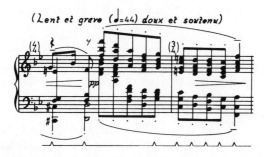

octave melody the loudest. The ascending lower-voice chords have to be *ppp*." His solution was to hold the pedal until the third or fourth eighth note of bar 12.

Ex. 109

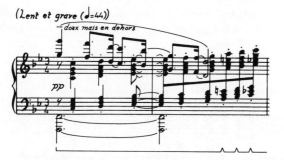

In bar 48 of "Feuilles mortes" (Prélude 2, Book 2), "The top voice should be very bright. Pedal bar 48; play bar 49 very softly, bringing out only the upper voice, which is the quickest to disappear in the pedal." (Example 110 shows bars 47–49.)

Ex. 110

MASTER LESSON ON DEBUSSY'S
"THE SUNKEN CATHEDRAL"
(Prélude 10, Book 1)

The following lesson—combined from several lessons—on "La cathé-drale engloutie" illustrates how Gieseking integrated pedaling into his overall interpretation. His playing of this piece was highly imaginative and descriptive, and much detail went into his tonal painting. Every nuance was extremely well thought through and worked out.

Bar 1. ♩ = 69 and slower. The outside dotted whole-note chords should ring, especially the top right-hand and bottom left-hand notes, the top right-hand notes being the loudest. Play the inner chords extremely softly and evenly in tone. In playing these chords, keep the hand and arm firm and play from the shoulder, with no finger motion. Keep the hand on the keys, holding the wrist low, the fingers firm, the arm dropped slightly, and using the least possible weight. Use the same fingering on each chord, shifting position with the entire hand. Hold the pedal through the first two bars and then through the second two bars (Example 111).

Ex. 111

Bar 2. The bass notes are the vibrations of a low bell.

Bars 4–7. Here for the first time, in bar 5, the third descending bass chord can be emphasized somewhat more. Hold the pedal from the first chord, clearing it gradually in bar 6, and etching the top right-hand notes. Change the pedal on the C sharp of bar 7; thereafter change the pedal with the bell tones on E (Example 112).

Bar 7. Remain slow at the *Doux et fluide;* play no faster. (N.B. Giese-king thought he was the only one to play this piece in time, that even Debussy, on his Welte Mignon recording, played it incorrectly.[9] A re-viewer in Paris once criticized Gieseking for not changing the tempo here, but Gieseking said, "This man did not know that he was wrong and not I." The remark about bar 7 also concerns bars 7–14 and 22–28.)

Ex. 112

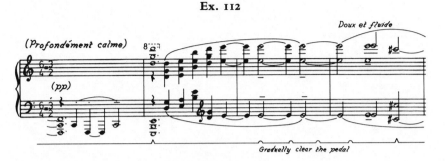

Bars 8–10. Note two printing errors found in some scores: The top note of the left-hand C-sharp octave should be tied over from the last beat of bar 7 to the first beat of bar 8. The G-sharp octave in bar 9 should be tied to the first beat of bar 10. Here, "The first spires of the sunken cathedral are emerging from the water."

Bars 14–15 (Example 113). Hold the pedal for two bars. "Pedal everywhere according to the basses."

Ex. 113

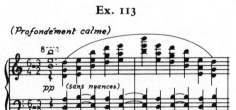

Bar 16. Not too slow a tempo. ♩ = 69. Now there are triplets to the beat instead of quarter notes. Use an *en face* fingering in the left hand on the third and fourth beats, as shown in Example 114. Bring out the top notes of the right-hand melody chords and hold one unbroken pedal through these next three bars of B pentatonic harmony.

Bar 17. Play the chords in the right and left hands exactly together and *marqué*, bringing out the top notes and making a big difference between the *piano* of the chord and the *pianissimo* of the rest of the bar.

Bars 19–21 Hold one unbroken pedal for these three bars of E-flat pentatonic harmony. Lead the *crescendo* with the left-hand middle voice up to *fortissimo* in bar 22. Etch the top notes of the right-hand chords.

Bars 22–25 (Example 115). Keep the exact tempo of the beginning (♩ = 69), and do not go faster. Hold the pedal from the first beat of bar

Ex. 114

Ex. 115

22 to the second half note of bar 25. Thereafter, perhaps change with every bass note. The right-hand quarter-note octaves are like the tolling of the cathedral bell.

Bar 27. Allargando on the last two bass octaves.

Bar 28. Play the two low C's as an octave, using the third fingers of both hands, for power and sonority. Throughout this great chorale section, play the chords with arm weight from the shoulders. "Do not use *sostenuto* pedal." Hold each pedal as long as possible, obliterating the preceding harmony with the new one. If the tone becomes too blurred, depending on the instrument and the hall, raise the pedal halfway or change it to clear the sound. In principle, change only with the playing of the new bass octave; certainly where the harmonies are the same or almost the same, keep the same pedal. Keep this section *fortissimo* but without hardness of tone. (Example 116 shows bars 26–30.)

Ex. 116

Bars 42–45. Here Gieseking felt that Debussy wanted the special effect
of the main chord diminishing, as if the *sostenuto* pedal were being used.
To achieve this effect, silently depress or retake the first chord after
playing the second chord. Change the pedal on the quarter rest so that on
the sixth beat just the first chord will be left sounding. (Example 117
shows bars 42–45.)

Ex. 117

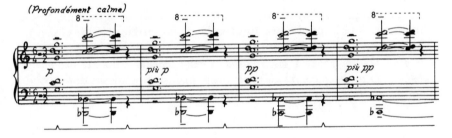

Bars 46, 47. In bar 46, play the transition bass note A flat/G sharp very
softly, so that the following theme, though resonant, is still *pianissimo*,
"like a beautiful cello melody, right from the first note." Begin bar 47
somewhat faster, ♩ = 63, and hold that tempo throughout, pedaling
with each right-hand note. (Example 118 shows bars 46–50.)

Ex. 118

Bar 49. Play the third half note (G sharp) clearly and the following bass G sharp softly. (Perhaps it should be tied.)

Bars 51–52. Keep one pedal for two bars. (Example 119 shows bars 51–55.)

Bars 53–54. Again pedal for two bars.

Ex. 119

Bars 55–62. Hold the pedal from the low G sharp until the third beat of bar 62. The pedal should be unbroken for 7⅔ bars! Here the harmony remains the same. (Example 120 shows bars 55–63.)

Bars 58, 60. The jumps from the grace notes have to be rapid. In bar 60, Gieseking played the A octave on the last beat ahead of the right hand in order to give himself more time for the downward leap to the G sharp. "It also sounds better," he said.

Bars 60–62. Make a big *crescendo* to the *fortissimo*. In bar 62, *molto diminuendo* to the second half note (many pianists pound out this second half note!), bringing out the upper voice.

Ex. 120

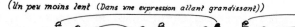

Bar 63. Pedal clearly with each chord, bringing out the top notes.
Bars 66, 67. The low G sharps are like bells. (Example 121 shows bars 64–67.)

Ex. 121

Bars 68–70. Reverse the hands from the way they are distributed, playing the low F sharps and G sharps with the right hand and the C's with the left hand. The lower bell, the F sharps and G sharps, should be louder than the C's. In bar 70, maintain the tempo, playing even, murmuring eighth notes. Finger the left hand as shown in Example 122 (bars 68–72).

Ex. 122

Bar 71. For this last measure of transition, lift the pedal and connect the eighth-note figure smoothly into bar 72.

Bar 72. Begin the *au Mouv'* section resonantly; the listener must hear that the theme is the same as before. Gieseking suggested using one of Cortot's ideas: "Bring out the thumb notes of the chord rather than the upper voice (or bring them both out)." In any case, keep the left hand completely even in tone and *pianissimo.* Finger the left hand 2–1–2–3–5 and play *legatissimo,* with an overlapping or holding-over of the notes, especially the G's, which act as the axle of the eighth-note figuration. The low C's are important as the foundation of the tonal structure. Change the pedal with the melody to preserve the *pianissimo.*

Bar 80. After a small *crescendo,* the enchanted cathedral sinks. (Example 123 shows bars 80–81.)

Ex. 123

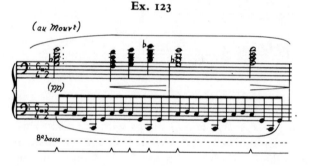

Bar 84 to the end (Example 124). ♩ = 66. Catch a clear low C in bar 84 and hold the pedal for the last six bars! "If one or two tones have the wrong number of vibrations, the whole effect is lost. Everything must be equal. If you keep every note absolutely as it should be, you will have pure C major sounding at the end. You end with the sonority of the beginning. Count these bars. The cathedral sinks back, devoid of expression."

Bars 86, 87. Play the whole-note C-major chord somewhat stronger than the first half-note chord, thereby subtly damping out any non–C-major vibrations that may carry over. In the bottom left-hand C–G–C chord, bring out the fifth finger and play the G weaker for the sake of balance.

Gieseking knew *his* way of performing the works of Debussy and Ravel was right for him, but if a somewhat different approach moved or convinced him, he liked it. He was satisfied with and modest about his acclaim. As for his pedaling, his ear dictated what he did to produce some of the most beautiful sounds ever to come from the piano.

Ex. 124

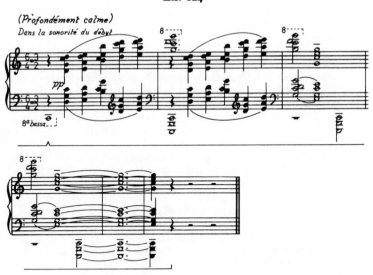

Examples 111–124, from "La cathédrale engloutie"
© 1910 Durand S.A.
Used by permission of the Publisher
Theodore Presser Company
Sole Representative U.S.A.

NOTES

2. The Right Pedal

1. Wolfgang Amadeus Mozart, *Concerto in D minor for Pianoforte and Orchestra,* edited by Friedrich Blume (London: Ernst Eulenburg Ltd., n.d.), pp.41–42, bars 344–47.

2. Johann Joachim Quantz, *On Playing the Flute,* translated and with an introduction and notes by Edward Reilly (New York: Schirmer Books, 1966), p.276.

3. Leopold Mozart, *A Treatise on the Fundamental Principles of Violin Playing,* translated by Editha Knocker, with a preface by Alfred Einstein (London: Oxford University Press, 1948), p.219.

4. Edwin Fischer, recorded performance of Beethoven's Sonata in C minor, Op.13 ("Grande Sonata pathétique") (His Master's Voice, D.B. 3666 and 3667, n.d.).

5. Edwin Fischer, *Beethoven's Pianoforte Sonatas: A Guide for Students and Amateurs,* translated by Stanley Godman, with the collaboration of Paul Hamburger (London: Faber and Faber, 1959), p.47.

6. Edwin Fischer, recorded performance of Beethoven's Sonata in C minor, Op.13 ("Grande Sonata pathétique") (Odeon o 80 673, n.d.).

4. The Left Pedal

1. Percy Grainger, *Guide to Virtuosity* (New York: G. Schirmer, Inc., 1927), p.viii.

5. Using the Pedals When Playing Bach

1. Johann Sebastian Bach, *Two-Part Inventions,* edited by Joseph Banowetz (Park Ridge: General Words and Music Co., 1979), pp.3–4.

2. *The Bach Reader: A Life of Johann Sebastian Bach in Letters and Documents,* edited by Hans T. David and Arthur Mendel (New York: W. W. Norton and Co., Inc., 1945), p.311

3. Ibid., p.197.

4. Carl Philipp Emanuel Bach, *Essay on the True Art of Playing Keyboard Instruments,* translated and edited by William J. Mitchell (New York: W. W. Norton and Co., Inc., 1949), p.159.

5. Ferruccio Busoni, "On the Transcription of Bach's Organ-Works for the Pianoforte," first appendix to Volume I of J. S. Bach's *The Well-Tempered Clavichord* [sic] (New York: G. Schirmer, 1894), pp.154–90.

6. Ibid., p.176.

7. Ibid., p.177.

8. Ibid., p.178.

9. Ibid., p.182.

6. Using the Pedals When Playing Haydn and Mozart

1. *The Letters of Mozart and His Family,* edited and translated by Emily Anderson, 2nd ed., prepared by A. Hyatt King and Monica Carolan (New York: St. Martin's Press, 1966), vol. I, p. 329.

2. Reimar Riefling, *Piano Pedalling,* translated by Kathleen Dale (London: Oxford University Press, 1962), pp. 37–38.

7. Beethoven's Uses of the Pedals

1. See Franz Josef Hirt, *Stringed Keyboard Instruments,* translated by M. Boehme-Brown from the original German of 1955 (Zurich: Urs-Graf-Verlag, 1981), p. 89.

2. Rosamond E. M. Harding, *The Piano-Forte, Its History Traced to the Great Exhibition of 1851,* 2d ed. (1933: reprint, Surrey: Gresham Press, 1978), pp. 28–29, 31.

3. See William S. Newman, "Tempo in Beethoven's Instrumental Music," *The Piano Quarterly* 117 (Spring 1982): 22.

4. See Paul Mies, *Textkritische Untersuchungen bei Beethoven* (Munich: G. Henle Verlag, 1957), p. 189.

5. See William S. Newman, "Beethoven's Pianos Versus His Piano Ideals," *Journal of the American Musicological Society* XXIII (1970):484–504, especially pp. 486–87 (with further references).

6. Cf. Carl Czerny, *Über den richtigen Vortrag der sämtlichen Beethoven'schen Klavierwerke* (from Czerny's "Erinnerungen" and Op. 500/IV), edited and with commentary by Paul Badura-Skoda (Vienna: Universal, 1963), p. 51. But Czerny was wrong if he was implying that the change did not begin until Op. 53; it began with the three sonatas in Op. 31, completed in 1802 (the year *before* Beethoven received his Erard piano), although Beethoven reverted to *senza sordino,* etc., in his Piano Concerto, Op. 37.

7. Newman, "Beethoven's Pianos," p. 494. Translations not otherwise acknowledged in the present chapter are my own.

8. Newman, "Beethoven's Pianos," pp. 493–96.

9. See William S. Newman, *Performance Practices in Beethoven's Piano Sonatas* (New York: W. W. Norton, 1971), pp. 34–43, with illustrations. More details are given in Kurt Wegerer, "Beethovens Hammerflügel und ihre Pedale," *Österreichische Musikzeitschrift* XX (1965):201–11.

10. Newman, "Beethoven's Pianos," pp. 484–85 *et passim.*

11. See Wilhelm Lütge, "Andreas und Nannette Streicher," *Der Bär (Jahrbuch von Breitkopf und Härtel)* IV (1927): 65.

12. Carl Czerny, *Erinnerungen aus meinem Leben,* edited and annotated by Walter Kolneder (Strasbourg: P. H. Heitz, 1968), p. 19.

13. Badura-Skoda, *Über den richtigen Vortrag,* p. 22.

14. Johann Nepomuk Hummel, *Ausführliche theoretisch-practische Anweisung zum Piano-Forte-Spiel . . .,* 2d ed. (Vienna: Tobias Haslinger, 1828), p. 452.

15. Carl Czerny, *Theoretical and Practical Piano Forte School . . .,* Op. 500, 3 vols. (not including the supplementary vol. IV, which takes up Beethoven), translated from the original German by J. A. Hamilton (London: R. Cocks, [1839?–1842?]), vol. III, pp. 57–58.

16. See the reports in Theodor von Frimmel, *Beethoven-Studien,* 2 vols. (Munich: Georg Müller, 1906), vol. II, pp.240–49, 254–57.

17. As argued at first in Derek Melville, "Beethoven's Pianos," in *The Beethoven Reader,* edited by Denis Arnold and Nigel Fortune (New York: W. W. Norton, 1971); but cf. *The Musical Times,* Dec. 1971, p.1171, and April 1972, pp.361–62.

18. Franz Eibner, "Registerpedalisierung bei Haydn und Beethoven," Gerschon Jarecki, "Die Ausführung der Pedalvorschriften Beethovens auf dem moderne Klavier," and Kurt Wegerer, "Beethovens Hammerflügel und ihre Pedale," *Österreichische Musikzeitschrift* XX (1965):189–96, 197–200, and 201–11 respectively.

19. Herbert Grundmann and Paul Mies, *Studien zum Klavierspiel Beethovens und seiner Zeitgenossen* (Bonn: H. Bouvier, 1966).

20. Friedrich Starke, *Pianoforte-Schule,* 3 vols. (Vienna: 1819–1821), vol. I, p.16; Czerny, *Piano Forte School,* vol. III, pp.58–61.

21. See Franz Kullak, *Beethoven's Piano-Playing,* translated from the original German of 1881 by Theodore Baker (New York: G. Schirmer, 1901; reprint, New York: Da Capo Press, 1973), p.13.

22. Ibid., pp.4–5; Gustav Nottebohm, *Zweite Beethoveniana* (1887; New York: Johnson Reprint, 1970), p.357.

23. See William S. Newman, "Beethoven's Fingerings as Interpretive Clues," *Journal of Musicology* I (1982):171–97.

24. See Anton Schindler, *The Life of Beethoven,* 2 vols., translated and edited by Ignaz Moscheles (London: Henry Colburn, 1841), vol. II, p.129.

25. Czerny, *Piano Forte School,* vol. III, pp.58–61.

26. Nottebohm, *Zweite Beethoveniana,* p.356.

27. Louis Köhler, *Der Clavierfingersatz* (Leipzig: Breitkopf und Härtel, 1862), pp.104–106. I owe this information to Yona Knorr.

28. *Letters of Franz Liszt,* edited by La Mara (Marie Lipsius), translated by Constance Bache (London: H. Grevel, 1894), vol. II, p.278. I owe this information to Geraldine Keeling.

29. Starke, *Pianoforte-Schule,* vol. I, p.16.

30. Cf. Badura-Skoda, *Über den richtigen Vortrag,* p.30.

31. Starke, *Pianoforte-Schule,* vol. I, p.16; Czerny, *Piano Forte School,* vol. III, pp.57 and 63.

32. Louis Adam, *Méthode de piano,* facsimile reprint of the Paris edition of 1805 (Geneva: Minkoff, 1974), pp.218–26.

33. See William S. Newman, "The Opening Trill in Beethoven's Sonata for Piano and Violin, Opus 96," in *Gedenkschrift Günter Henle* (Munich: G. Henle Verlag, 1980), pp.384–93; Newman, "Beethoven's Fingerings," pp.188–91.

34. Czerny, *Piano Forte School,* vol. III, p.64.

35. Kenneth Drake, *The Sonatas of Beethoven as He Played and Taught Them* (1972; reprint, Bloomington: Indiana University Press, 1981), p.151.

36. Carl Philipp Emanuel Bach, *Versuch über die wahre Art das Clavier zu Spielen,* 2 vols., edited from the original edition of 1753 and 1762 by Lothar Hoffmann Erbrecht (Leipzig: Breitkopf und Härtel, 1957), p.327.

37. "Open pedal" is wrongly identified with a muting device in H. C. Robbins Landon, *Haydn: Chronicle and Works,* 5 vols. (Bloomington: Indiana University Press, 1976–1980), vol. III. pp.444–45; cf. the review of vol. III by William S. Newman, *The Piano Quarterly* 100 (Winter 1977–1978):46.

38. See Barbel Friege, "Beiträge zur Interpretationsgeschichte der Klavier-sonaten Ludwig van Beethovens," Ph.D. diss., University of Halle-Wittenberg, 1970, p.60.

39. Johann Peter Milchmeyer, *Die wahre Art das Pianoforte zu spielen* (Dresden, 1797), pp.58–59; Louis Adam, *Méthode de piano*, p.218; Starke, *Pianoforte-Schule*, vol. I, p.16; Hummel, *Piano-Forte-Spiel*, p.452.

40. E.g., Hummel, *Piano-Forte-Spiel*, p.453.

41. Mies, *Textkritische Untersuchungen*, p.189.

42. See Richard Kramer, *Notes, Journal of the Music Library Association* 29 (1972–1973):28.

43. See Wilhelm von Lenz, *Beethoven et ses trois styles*, reprint of the original edition of 1852 (Paris: Gustave Legouix, 1909), p.199. Czerny also uses this term (*Piano Forte School*, vol. III, p.61).

44. Cf. Newman, "Beethoven's Pianos," p.496.

45. Starke, *Pianoforte-Schule*, vol. I, p.16; Czerny, *Piano Forte School*, vol. III, p.61.

46. Badura-Skoda, *Über den richtigen Vortrag*, pp.43 and 101–102.

47. See, e.g., Hirt, *Stringed Keyboard Instruments*, pp.35, 39, 48, and especially 42. I have found only one brief mention of the divided damper pedal in Harding, *The Piano-Forte*, on p.44.

48. See Grundmann and Mies, *Klavierspiel Beethovens*, pp.40–41.

49. Cf., also, Gerschon Jarecki, "Die Ausführung der Pedalvorschriften Beethovens auf dem modernen Klavier," *Österreichische Musikzeitschrift* 20 (1965):197–200.

50. See note 8 above.

51. Badura-Skoda, *Über den richtigen Vortrag*, p.33.

52. Czerny, *Piano Forte School*, vol. III, pp.64–65.

53. Ibid., p.65.

54. See Harding, *The Piano-Forte*, p.124.

55. Starke, *Pianoforte-Schule*, vol. I, p.16.

56. E. g., Harding, *The Piano-Forte*, p.127.

57. Badura-Skoda, *Über den richtigen Vortrag*, p.51.

8. *Executing Beethoven's Long Pedals on the Modern Piano*

1. Artur Schnabel, ed., *Ludwig van Beethoven 32 Sonatas for the Pianoforte*, 2 vols. (New York: Simon and Schuster, Inc., 1935).

2. Harold Craxton, ed., *Ludwig van Beethoven Sonatas for Pianoforte*, with commentaries and notes by Donald Francis Tovey, 3 vols. (London: The Associated Board of the Royal Schools of Music, 1931).

3. Schnabel, vol. 1, p.300.

4. Howard Ferguson, ed., *Style and Interpretation*, vol. 3: *Classical Piano Music* (London: Oxford University Press, 1964), p.8.

5. Craxton and Tovey, vol. 2, p.125.

6. Ibid.

9. *Pedaling the Piano Works of Chopin*

1. Antoine François Marmontel, *Les pianistes célèbres* (Paris: A. Chaix et Cie., 1888), p.67.

2. Ibid., p.68

3. Edith J. Hipkins, *How Chopin Played*, from contemporary impressions collected from the diaries and notebooks of the late A. J. Hipkins, F. S. A. (London: J. M. Dent and Sons, 1937), p.7.

4. Ibid., p.5.

5. Franz Liszt, *Frédéric Chopin*, translated with an Introduction by Edward N. Waters (New York: Vienna House, 1973), p.90.

6. Derek Melville, *Chopin* (London: Clive Bingley, 1977), p.28.

7. Glenn Plaskin, *Horowitz, a Biography* (New York: William Morrow and Co., 1983), p.100.

8. Jean Kleczynski, *Frederick Chopin—An Interpretation of His Works*, translated by W. Kirkbride (Palma de Mallorca: Mossèn Alcover, 1970), pp.71–72.

9. Camille Saint-Saëns, "A Chopin Ms.," in *Outspoken Essays on Music*, translated by Fred Rothwell (London: Kegan Paul, Trench, Truber and Co., Ltd., 1922), p.105.

10. Using the Pedals When Playing Schumann

1. Robert Schumann, *Pianofortesonate, Klara zugeeignet von Florestan und Eusebius*, Op. 11 (Leipzig: Friedrich Kistner, 1836), p.1.

2. Robert Schumann, *Grande Sonate pour le Pianoforte composée et dédiée à Mademoiselle Clara Wieck Pianiste de S. M. l'Empereur d'Autriche*, Op. 11, 2d ed. (Leipzig: Friedrich Kistner, 1840), p.1.

3. *Robert Schumanns Werke*, 14 series in 31 vols. edited by Clara Schumann and Johannes Brahms (Leipzig: Breitkopf und Härtel, 1879–93).

4. Robert Schumann, *Sämtliche Klavierwerke für Pianoforte zu zwei Handen, mit Fingersatz und Vortragszeichen versehene instruktive Ausgabe, Nach den Handschriften und persönlicher Ueberlieferung herausgegeben von Clara Schumann*, 3 vols. (Leipzig: Breitkopf und Härtel, ca. 1886).

5. Annie Patterson, *Schumann* (London: J. M. Dent, 1903), p.156.

6. Ibid., p.157.

7. Ibid., p.158.

8. *Robert Schumanns Werke*.

9. Robert Schumann, *Sämtliche Klavierwerke*.

10. Johann Paul Friedrich Richter, *Flegeljahre* (reprint, Weimar: Hermann Böhlau, 1934).

11. Using the Pedals When Playing Liszt

1. *Franz Liszts Briefe*, vol. II, edited by La Mara (Leipzig: Breitkopf und Härtel, 1893), p.223.

2. Moriz Rosenthal, "If Liszt Should Come Back Again," *The Etude* XLII/4 (1924):224.

3. Ibid.

4. Clarence Lucas, "Debussy and the Pedal Blur," *The Etude* LIII/3 (1935):145.

5. Arthur Friedheim, "Artistic Pedalling and How to Achieve It," *The Etude* L/8 (1932):537.

6. Maurice Dumesnil, "Debussy's Influence on Piano Writing and Playing," in *Proceedings of the Music Teachers National Association*, Series 39, Pittsburgh, 1945, pp.39–42.

7. Lina Ramann, *Liszt-Pädagogium, Klavier-Kompositionen Franz Liszts,* III Serie (Ungarisch) (Leipzig: Breitkopf und Härtel, 1901), p.11.

8. Friedheim, p.537.

9. Arthur Loesser, *Men, Women and Pianos: A Social History* (New York: Simon and Schuster, 1954), p.406.

10. Carl Friedrich Weitzman, *A History of Piano-forte Playing and Piano-forte Literature* (New York: G. Schirmer, 1897), p.285.

11. Fernando Laires, "Franz Liszt in Portugal," *The Piano Quarterly* 23 (Spring 1975):35.

12. David Wilde, "Transcriptions for Piano," in *Franz Liszt: The Man and His Music,* edited by Alan Walker (New York: Taplinger Publishing Co., 1970), p.185.

13. Weitzman, p.285.

14. Victor Wolfram, *The Sostenuto Pedal* (Stillwater: Oklahoma State University, 1965), p.28.

15. Ibid., pp.28–29.

12. The Catalan School of Pedaling

1. Albert McGrigor, "The Catalan Piano School," record jacket notes from *The Catalan Piano Tradition,* International Piano Archives recording no. 109 (New York: Desmar, 1979).

2. Ibid.

3. Enrique Granados, *Método Teórico Práctico para el Uso de los Pedales del Piano* (Madrid: Union Musical Española, 1954).

4. Frank Marshall, *Estudio Práctico sobre los Pedales del Piano* (Madrid: Union Musical Española, 1919).

5. Frank Marshall, *La Sonoridad del Piano* (Barcelona: Editorial Boileau, n.d.).

6. Conversation with Alicia de Larrocha, Dallas, Texas, 14 April 1983.

7. Marshall, *Estudio Práctico,* p.1.

8. De Larrocha, conversation.

9. Ibid.

13. Gieseking's Pedaling in Debussy and Ravel

1. Walter Gieseking, recorded performance of Debussy's *Pour le piano,* Angel Records, no. 35065.

2. Walter Gieseking, recorded performances of Debussy's "Feuilles mortes," in *Préludes,* Bk. II, Columbia Masterworks, M–382 (ML 4538); and Angel Records, no. 35249.

3. Ibid., Columbia Masterworks.

4. Ibid., Angel Records.

5. Walter Gieseking, recorded performance of Ravel's "Noctuelles," from *Miroirs,* in three-record set of Ravel's complete piano works, Angel Records, no. 3541–5S.

6. Arturo Benedetti Michelangeli, recorded performance of Debussy's "Le vent dans la plaine," in *Préludes,* Bk. I, Deutsche Grammophon, no. 2531200.

7. Claudio Arrau, recorded performance of Debussy's "Le vent dans la plaine," in *Préludes,* Bk. I, Philips, no. 9500676.

8. Walter Gieseking, "Wie spielt man Ravels Klaviermusik?" *Melos —
Zeitschrift für Neue Musik* 14 (December 1947):412–14. Translation by Dean Elder.

9. Claude Debussy, recorded performance of "La cathédrale engloutie," from
Préludes Bk. I, in *The Welte Legacy of Piano Treasures: Debussy and Ravel Perform
Their Own Compositions in 1913,* Recorded Treasures, Inc., no. S663.

BIBLIOGRAPHY OF SOURCES
IN ENGLISH

Ahrens, Cora B. and G. D. Atkinson. "Pedals and Pedaling." In *For All Piano Teachers*. London: The Frederick Harris Music Co. Limited, 1955. Pp.27–34.

Anderson, Emily, ed. and trans. *The Letters of Mozart and His Family*, 2d ed. Prepared by A. Hyatt King and Monica Carolan, 2 vols. New York: St. Martin's Press, 1966. P.329.

Bacon, Ernst. "Of the Pedals." In *Notes on the Piano*. Syracuse: Syracuse University Press, 1963. Pp.51–55.

Badura-Skoda, Eva and Paul. *Interpreting Mozart on the Keyboard*, translated by Leo Black. London: Barrie and Rockliff, 1962. Pp.10–11, 13–17, 153–57.

Banowetz, Joseph. "Schumann's Pedaling." In *Robert Schumann: An Introduction to the Composer and His Music*. An edition of Schumann's *Album for the Young* and *Scenes from Childhood*, edited and with a preface by Joseph Banowetz. Park Ridge: General Words and Music Co., 1975. P.19.

———. "Pedaling Technique." In *Teaching Piano*, vol. I, edited by Denes Agay. New York: Yorktown Music Press, Inc., 1981. Pp.91–122.

Barnes, John. "Some Practical Advice on the Use of the Pedal." *The Etude* 31 (June 1913):406.

Bastien, James W. *How to Teach Piano Successfully*, 2d ed. San Diego: General Words and Music Co., 1977. Pp.247–48.

Benward, B. "Use the Pedal—Don't Abuse It." *The Etude* 67 (November 1949):14.

Bernstein, Seymour. "Pedaling." In *With Your Own Two Hands*. New York: Schirmer Books, 1981. Pp.143–52.

Bilson, Malcolm. "The Soft Pedal Revisited." *The Piano Quarterly* 30 (Spring 1982):36–38.

Bodky, Erwin. *The Interpretation of Bach's Keyboard Works*. Cambridge: Harvard University Press, 1960. Pp.93, 97.

Booth, Victor. *We Piano Teachers*. London: Skeffington and Son, Ltd., 1946. Pp.71–83.

Bowen, York. *Pedaling the Modern Pianoforte*. London: Oxford University Press, 1936.

Breckenridge, W. K. *Hints for Piano Normal Studies*. New York: Vantage Press, Inc., 1955. Pp.18–20.

Brée, Malevine. *The Groundwork of the Leschetizky Method*. New York: G. Schirmer, Inc., 1902. Pp.61–64, 84.

Brendel, Alfred. *Musical Thoughts and Afterthoughts*. Princeton: Princeton University Press, 1976. Pp.34, 133–35.

Brower, Harriette. "Poetic Pedaling." In *The Art of the Pianist*. New York: Carl Fischer, 1911. Pp.173–77.

———. *Piano Mastery: Talks with Master Pianists and Teachers*. New York: Frederick A. Stokes Co., 1915. Pp.203–204.

Busoni, Ferruccio, ed. *The Well-Tempered Clavichord* [sic] by J. S. Bach. New York: G. Schirmer, 1894. First Appendix to Volume I: "On the Transcription of Bach's Organ Works for the Pianoforte," pp.176–80.

Camp, Max. *Developing Piano Performance*. Chapel Hill: Hinshaw Music, 1981. Pp. 60–61.

Canin, Martin. "Pianist's Problems: The Soft Pedal." *The Piano Quarterly* 29 (Summer 1981): 42.

Carreño, Teresa. *Possibilities of Tone Color by Artistic Use of the Pedals*. Cincinnati: The John Church Co., 1919.

Chase, Gilbert. *The Music of Spain*, 2d ed. New York: Dover Publications, 1959.

Chase, Mary Wood. "The Pedals." In *Natural Laws in Piano Technic*. Boston: Oliver Ditson Co., 1910. Pp. 61–67.

Chenée, Ann. "Pedaling—The 'Stepchild' of Piano Study." *The Etude* 65 (June 1947): 323, 345, 348.

Ching, James. *Points on Pedaling*. London: Forsyth Brothers Ltd., 1930.

Chissell, Joan. *Schumann*. New York: Collier Books, 1962. P. 122.

Chittenden, L. W. "What Good Is the Middle Pedal?" *The Etude* 58 (June 1940): 378.

Collet, Robert. "Studies, Preludes and Impromptus." In *The Chopin Companion*, edited by Alan Walker. New York: W. W. Norton 1973. Pp. 125–27.

Cooke, James Francis. *Great Pianists on Piano Playing*. Philadelphia: Theodore Presser Co., 1917. Pp. 214, 319, 372–73.

Copland, George. "Debussy, the Man I Knew." *Atlantic Monthly* 195 (January 1955): 34–38.

Craxton, Harold, ed., with commentaries and notes by Donald Francis Tovey. *Ludwig van Beethoven Sonatas for Pianoforte*, 3 vols. London: The Associated Board of the Royal Schools of Music, 1931.

Crowder, Louis. "Still More on the Sostenuto Pedal." *Clavier* 6 (September 1967): 44–45.

Czerny, Carl. *Complete Theoretical and Practical Pianoforte School*, Op. 500. London: R. Cocks and Co., 1839. Pp. 57–65.

———. *On the Proper Performance of All Beethoven's Works for the Piano*, edited and with commentary by Paul Badura-Skoda. Vienna: Universal Edition, 1970.

D'Abreu, Gerald. *Playing the Piano with Confidence*. London: Faber and Faber, 1964. Pp. 85–88.

Dilson, L. "Pedal Pointers for Piano Teachers." *Music Journal* 26 (February 1968): 38ff.

Drake, Kenneth. *The Sonatas of Beethoven as He Played and Taught Them*. Bloomington: Indiana University Press, 1981. Pp. 141–63.

Dumesnil, Maurice. *How to Play and Teach Debussy*. New York: Schroeder and Gunther, Inc., 1932.

———. "Debussy's Principles in Pianoforte Playing." *The Etude* 56 (March 1938): 153–54.

———. "Debussy's Influence on Piano Writing and Playing," in *Proceedings of the Music Teachers National Association*, Series 39, Pittsburgh, 1945. Pp. 39–42.

———. "Pedaling." In *Handbook for Piano Teachers*. Evanston: Summy-Birchard Publishing Co., 1958. Pp. 56–64.

Ehrenfechter, C. A. "The Pedal." In *Technical Study in the Art of Pianoforte-Playing*, 4th ed. London: William Reeves, 189(?). Pp. 77–89.

Eisenberg, Jacob. "The Magnifying Pedal." In *Natural Technics in Piano Mastery*. London: William Reeves Bookseller, Limited, 1929. Pp. 195–229.

———. "Discovering the Soft Pedal." *The Etude* 61 (August 1943): 511–12.

Elder, Dean. *Pianists at Play.* Evanston: The Instrumentalist Co., 1982. Pp.24, 29, 40, 51, 69, 91, 120–21, 131, 192–93, 225–27, 235–36, 246, 248–55, 267.

Everhart, Powell. "The Pedal." In *The Pianist's Art.* Atlanta: Powell Everhart, 1958. Pp.225–50.

Fairchild, Leslie. "Artistic Pedaling." *The Etude* 42 (July 1924):453.

Farjeon, Harry. *The Art of Piano Pedaling,* 2 vols. London: Joseph Williams Limited, 1923.

———. "Points in Pedaling." *The Etude* 51 (October 1933):657–58.

Ferguson, Howard. *Keyboard Interpretation.* New York: Oxford University Press, 1975. Pp.161–68.

Fetsch, Wolfgang. "What's That Extra Pedal For (Sostenuto Pedal)?" *Clavier* 5 (December 1966):12–17.

Fischer, Edwin. *Beethoven's Pianoforte Sonatas: A Guide for Students and Amateurs,* translated by Stanley Godman, with collaboration of Paul Hamburger. London: Faber and Faber, 1959. Pp.24–25, 32–33, 47, 63, 73, 81, 87, 98, 116–17.

Foldes, Andor. *Keys to the Keyboard.* New York: E. P. Dutton and Co., 1948. Pp.90–91.

Foote, Arthur. *Some Practical Things in Piano Playing.* Boston: Arthur P. Schmidt Co., 1909. Pp.13–17.

Foreman, Lewis, ed. *The Percy Grainger Companion.* London: Thames Publishing, 1981. Pp.118–21, 181–82.

Formsma, R. K. "The Use of Pedal in Beethoven's Sonatas." *The Piano Quarterly* 24 (Spring, 1976):38, 40, 42–45.

Frampton, John Ross. "The Demands of the Pedal." *The Etude* 43 (November 1925):774.

Freeman, Thomas Frederick. "Hold the Pedal!" *The Etude* 49 (July 1931): 469–70.

Friedheim, Arthur. "Artistic Pedaling and How to Achieve It." *The Etude* 50 (August 1932):537, 588.

Gát, József. *The Technique of Piano Playing.* London: Collet's, 1974. P.275.

Gebhard, Heinrich. *The Art of Pedaling.* New York: Franco Colombo, Inc., 1963.

Gerig, Reginald. *Famous Pianists and Their Technique.* Washington: Robert B. Luce, 1974.

Gieseking, Walter. "Increasing the Resources of the Piano" *The Etude* 53 (July 1935):399, 434.

Grainger, Percy. "Grieg's 'Norwegian Bridal Procession,' a Masterlesson." *The Etude* 38 (November 1920):741–45.

———. *Guide to Virtuosity.* New York: G. Schirmer, Inc., 1927. Pp.vii–viii, 1, 4, 6, 8, 10, 12.

Green, Gordon, ed. *Liszt.* London: Oxford University Press, 1973. Pp.7–8, 61–63.

Grover, David S. *The Piano: Its Story, from Zither to Grand.* New York: Charles Scribner's Sons, 1978. Pp.67–68, 101, 124, 168, 196.

Gunn, Glenn Dillard. "New Pianistic Beauties through New Pedal Effects." Part 1, *The Etude* 38 (May 1920):303–304. Part 2, *The Etude* 38 (June 1920):373–74.

Hambourg, Mark. "On the Use of the Pedal." *The Etude* 31 (May 1913):331.

———. *How to Play the Piano.* Philadelphia: Theodore Presser Co., 1922. Pp.83–85.

Hamilton, Clarence. *Piano Teaching, Its Principles and Problems.* New York: Oliver Ditson Co., 1910. Pp.67, 80–81, 101–103.

Harding, Rosamond E. M. *The Piano-Forte, Its History Traced to the Great Exhibition of 1851,* 2d ed. 1933. Reprint, Surrey: Gresham Press, 1978.

Harrison, Sidney. "Pedaling." In *Piano Technique.* London: Sir Isaac Pitman and Sons, Ltd., 1953. Pp.53–56.

———. *The Young Person's Guide to Playing the Piano.* London: Faber and Faber, 1982. Pp.24–27.

Harrison, Viva. "The Use of the Pedals." *The Etude* 43 (July 1925):464.

Herman-Philipp, Lillie. *Piano Study: Application and Technique.* New York: MCA Music Co., 1969. Pp.57–60.

Higgins, Thomas. "The Damper Pedal." In "Chopin Interpretation: A Study of Performance Directions in Selected Autographs and Other Sources." Ph.D. diss. University of Iowa, 1966. Pp.59–75.

Hipkins, Edith J. *How Chopin Played.* London: J. M. Dent and Sons, 1937.

Hirt, Franz Josef. *Stringed Keyboard Instruments,* translated by M. Boehme-Brown from the original German of 1955. Zurich: Urs-Graf-Verlag, 1981.

Hofmann, Josef. "The Use of the Pedal." In *Piano Playing with Piano Questions Answered.* New York: The McClure Co., 1908. Reprint, New York: Dover Publications, Inc., 1976. Pp.41–48.

———. "The Pedals." In *Piano Questions.* Garden City: Doubleday, Page and Co., 1914. Pp.39–44.

———. "Practical Ideas on Artistic Pedaling." *The Etude* 39 (September 1921):563–64.

Holcman, Jan. *The Legacy of Chopin.* New York: Philosophical Library, 1954. Pp.16–17.

Holland, Jeanne. "Chopin's Teaching and His Pupils." Ph.D. diss., University of North Carolina at Chapel Hill, 1973.

Hopkins, Edwina Patricia. "The Use of Pedal in J. S. Bach's French Suites, English Suites, and Partitas: A General Guide to Pedaling in the Keyboard Music." D.M.A. diss., The Ohio State University, 1980.

Horowitz, Vladimir. "Technic the Outgrowth of Musical Thought." An educational conference secured by Florence Leonard. *The Etude* 50 (March 1932):163–64.

Howard, S. "Perfect Pedaling." *Music Teacher* 48 (August 1969):21.

Huneker, James. *Franz Liszt.* New York: Charles Scribner's Sons, 1927. Pp.99, 394.

Jacobson, Robert. *Reverberations: Interviews with the World's Leading Musicians.* New York: William Morrow and Co., Inc., 1974. Pp.45–52.

Jervis, Perlee. "What Every Piano Student Should Know About Pedaling." *The Etude* 38 (July 1920):441–42.

Johnstone, Charles. "The Why and How of Pedaling." *The Etude* 37 (July 1919):447.

Kentner, Louis. *Piano.* New York: Schirmer Books, 1976. Pp.26–28, 69–78.

Kleczynski, Jean. *Frederick Chopin: An Interpretation of His Works,* translated by W. Kirkbride. Palma de Mallorca: Mossèn Alcover, 1970. Pp.67–72.

Kochevitsky, G. A. "Controversial Pedaling in Beethoven's Piano Sonatas." *The Piano Quarterly* 40 (July 1962):24–28.

Kullak, Adolph. *The Aesthetics of Pianoforte-Playing.* New York: G. Schirmer, 1895. Pp.302–14.

Kullak, Franz. *Beethoven's Piano-Playing,* translated from the original German of
    1881 by Theodore Baker. New York: G. Schirmer, 1901. Reprint, New
    York: Da Capo Press, 1973.
Lamar, Richard. *College Piano Pedagogy.* Freeman, S.D.: Pine Hill Press, 1968.
    Pp.47–52.
Larrocha, Alicia de. "Granados, the Composer." *Clavier* 6 (October 1967):
    21–23.
———. "Goya of Music." *Opera News,* December 9, 1967. Pp.6–7.
Last, Joan. *Introduction to Pedaling.* New York: Galaxy Music Corp., 1963.
———. *Interpretation for the Piano Student.* London: Oxford University Press,
    1960. Pp.12, 14, 18, 31–32, 57, 92–113.
Leimer, Karl and Walter Gieseking. "The Pedal." In *Rhythmics, Dynamics, Pedal
    and Other Problems of Piano Playing,* translated by Frederick C. Rauser. New
    York: Theodore Presser Co., 1938. Pp.48–64.
Lhévinne, Josef. *Basic Principles in Pianoforte Playing.* 1924. Reprint, New York:
    Dover Publications, Inc., 1973. Pp. 46–48.
Lindquist, Orvil. "The 'Mysterious' Middle Pedal." *The Etude* 36 (December
    1918):759–60.
———. "The Proper Use of the 'Forte' Pedal." *The Etude* 37 (September
    1919):557–58.
———. "Pedaling: Using the Damper Pedal to Achieve Legato." *Clavier* 5
    (October 1966):48–50.
———. "Pedaling: Subtleties in the Use of the Damper Pedal; Watching for
    Clarity." *Clavier* 7 (April 1968):34–37.
Liszt, Franz. *Klavierwerke,* compiled by Zoltán Gárdonyi and István Szelényi.
    Budapest: Bärenreiter and Editio Budapest, 1970–. Preface.
———. *Frédéric Chopin.* Translated and with an introduction by Edward N.
    Waters. New York: Vienna House, 1973.
Lucas, Clarence. "Debussy and the Pedal Blur." *The Etude* 53 (March
    1935):145–46.
Ludden, Bennet. "Beethoven's Broadwood, a Present-Day Memoir." *The
    Juilliard Review* 8 (Spring 1961):9–11, 15.
McGrigor, Albert. "The Catalan Piano School." Record jacket notes from *The
    Catalan Piano Tradition.* International Piano Archives recording no. 109.
    New York: Desmar, 1979.
Mach, Elyse. *Great Pianists Speak for Themselves.* New York: Dodd, Mead and
    Co., 1980. Pp.4, 40–41, 60, 71, 117.
Machnek, Elsie. "The Pedagogy of Franz Liszt." Ph.D. diss., Northwestern
    University, 1965. Pp.84–86, 152–53.
Mackinnon, Lilias. *Musical Secrets.* London: Oxford University Press, 1946.
    Pp.65–78.
MacNabb, George. "The Pedals—The Soul of the Pianoforte." *The Etude* 65
    (September 1947):503, 532–33.
———. "Techniques of Damper Pedaling." *The Etude* 65 (October 1947):553,
    588.
Maier, Guy. *The Piano Teacher's Companion.* New York: Belwin Mills Publishing
    Corp., 1963. P.22.
Marcus, Adele. *Great Pianists Speak with Adele Marcus.* Neptune City, N.J.:
    Paganiniana Publications, Inc., 1979. Pp.107–19.
Matthay, Tobias. *The Act of Touch in All Its Diversity.* London: Bosworth and
    Co., Ltd., 1903. Pp.56–60.

———. *Musical Interpretation, Its Laws and Principles and Their Application in Teaching and Performing.* London: Joseph Williams, Ltd., 1913. Pp. 89, 125–47.

———. "The Principles of Fingering and Laws of Pedaling." In *Muscular and Relaxation Studies.* London: Bosworth and Co., Ltd., 1911. Pp. 12–20.

Melville, Derek. "Beethoven's Pianos." In *The Beethoven Reader,* edited by Denis Arnold and Nigel Fortune. New York: W. W. Norton, 1971. P. 28.

———. *Chopin.* London: Clive Bingley, 1977.

Merrick, Frank. *Practicing the Piano.* London: Salisbury Square, 1958. Pp. 2, 17–26, 32, 65–66, 80, 85, 109.

Methuen-Campbell, James. *Chopin Playing from the Composer to the Present Day.* New York: Taplinger Publishing Co., 1981. Pp. 19–20, 79–80.

Moore, Wayne T. "Liszt's Monster Instrument: The Piano-Harmonium." *The Diapason* 61 (August 1970):14–15.

Neuhaus, Heinrich. *The Art of Piano Playing,* translated by K. A. Leibovitch. New York: Praeger Publishers, 1973. Pp. 156–68.

Newman, William S. "Beethoven's Pianos Versus His Piano Ideals." *Journal of the American Musicological Society* 23 (1970):484–504.

———. *Performance Practices in Beethoven's Piano Sonatas.* New York: W. W. Norton, 1971. Pp. 15, 33–35, 42–43, 61, 63–64.

———. "Do You Hear What You Pedal?" In *The Pianist's Problems.* New York: Harper and Row Publishers, 1974. Pp. 121–24.

———. "Beethoven's Fingerings as Interpretative Clues." *Journal of Musicology* I (1982):171–97.

Ohlsson, Garrick. "Pedaling Hints and Habits." *Keyboard Magazine* 8 (January 1982):66.

Oxford Piano Course: Teachers' Second Manual. New York: Oxford University Press, 1932. Articles by Charles J. Haake, Gail Martin Haake, Osbourne McConathy, and Ernest Schelling. Pp. 23–27, 126, 130, 136, 152.

Palmer, King. *The Piano.* London: The English Universities Press, Ltd., 1972. Pp. 13–14, 16, 67–70.

Pasquet, J. "The Pedals: Three or More." *The Piano Quarterly* 29 (Fall 1981):29ff.

Patterson, Annie. *Schumann.* London: J. M. Dent and Sons, Ltd., 1934. Pp. 131–34.

"Pianoforte Pedals." *Musical Opinion* 89 (March, 1966):385.

Pierce, E. H. "Syncopated Pedal." *The Etude* 42 (October 1924): 668.

Plaskin, Glenn. *Horowitz, a Biography.* New York: William Morrow and Co., 1983. P. 100.

Prentner, Marie. *The Modern Pianist, Being My Experiences in the Technic and Execution of Pianoforte Playing, According to the Principles of Prof. Theo. Leschetizky,* translated by M. de Kendler and A. Maddock. Philadelphia: Theodore Presser Co., 1903. Pp. 74–78.

Randett, Samuel. "More on the Sostenuto Pedal." *Clavier* 6 (February 1967):50–52.

Rathbun, James Ronald. "A Textual History and Analysis of Schumann's Sonatas Op. 11, Op. 14, and Op. 22: An Essay Together with a Comprehensive Project in Piano Performance." D.M.A. diss. University of Iowa, 1976.

Rezits, Joseph. "The Interrelationship of Quantitative and Qualitative Elements in Piano Playing." *American Music Teacher* 22 (July 1973): 29–31; 23 (September/October, 1973):25–29.

Riefling, Reimar. *Piano Pedalling,* translated by Kathleen Dale. London: Oxford University Press, 1962.

Rogers, James H. "The Difficult Art of Good Pedaling." *The Etude* 28 (December 1910):796.

Rosen, Charles, ed. *Bach.* London: Oxford University Press, 1975. Pp.3–4.

———. "The Romantic Pedal." In *The Book of the Piano,* edited by Dominic Gill. Ithaca: Cornell University Press, 1981.

Rosenthal, Moriz. "If Franz Liszt Should Come Back Again." *The Etude* 42 (April 1924):223–24.

Rubinstein, Beryl. "Pedaling." In *Outline of Piano Pedagogy,* rev. ed. New York: Carl Fischer, Inc., 1957. Pp.37–43.

Saint-Saëns, Camille. "A Chopin Ms." In *Outspoken Essays of Music,* translated by Fred Rothwell. London: Kegan Paul, Tranch, Truber and Co., Ltd., 1922.

Samaroff, Olga. "The Soft Pedal Problem." *The Etude* 59 (January 1941):16.

Sándor, György. "The Pedals." In *On Piano Playing.* New York: Schirmer Books, 1981. Pp.161–78.

Schick, Robert D. *The Vengerova System of Piano Playing.* University Park: Pennsylvania State University Press, 1982. Pp.87–98.

Schindler, Anton. *The Life of Beethoven,* 2 vols., translated and edited by Ignaz Moscheles. London: Henry Colburn, 1841.

Schmitt, Hans. *Pedals of the Piano-Forte,* translated by Frederick S. Law. Philadelphia: Theodore Presser Co., 1893.

Schmitz, Elie Robert. *The Piano Works of Claude Debussy.* New York: Duell, Sloan and Pearce Publishers, 1950. Pp.38–39, 132, 147, 158, 164, 186, 213.

Schnabel, Artur, ed. *Ludwig van Beethoven 32 Sonatas for the Pianoforte,* 2 vols. New York: Simon and Schuster, Inc., 1935.

Schnabel, Karl Ulrich. *Modern Technique of the Pedal.* Oakville, Ontario: Frederick Harris Music Co., 1950.

Schumann, Robert. *Pianoforte Sonata,* Op. 11. Leipzig: Friedrich Kistner, 1836. P.1.

Silber, Sidney. "The So-Called 'Soft' Pedal." *The Etude* 43 (January 1925): 9–10.

Slenczynska, Ruth. "About Pedaling." *The Piano Teacher* IV:5 (May–June 1962):15–16.

———. "Slenczynska's Practice Routine for Working Up a New Piece, with Special Reference to Pedaling." *Clavier* 8 (February 1969):18.

———. "Added Color from Special Pedal Techniques." *Clavier* 8 (February 1969):19–20.

Smith, Hannah L. "Helpful Pedal Exercise." *The Etude* 32 (June 1914):406.

———. "When to Use the Pedal." *The Etude* 33 (January 1915):10.

Taylor, Kendall. *Principles of Piano Technique and Interpretation.* Borough Green: Novello, 1981. Pp.24–27.

Tollefson, Arthur R. "Debussy's Pedaling." *Clavier* 9 (October 1970):22–33.

Tureck, Rosalyn. *An Introduction to the Performance of Bach,* 3 vols. London: Oxford University Press, 1960. Vol. 1, pp.6–7; vol. 2, p.10; vol. 3, p.10.

Walker, Alan. *Robert Schumann: The Man and His Music.* New York: Harper and Row Publishers, Inc., 1974. Pp.86, 97–99.

———. *Franz Liszt.* Vol. I: *The Virtuoso Years 1811–1847.* New York: Alfred A. Knopf, 1983. Pp.311–12.

————, ed. *Franz Liszt: The Man and His Music*. New York: Taplinger Publishing Co., 1970. Pp. 140, 149, 189–90, 196, 214–17.

Werder, R. "The Ups and Downs of Pedaling." *Clavier* 17 (January 1978):28–32.

Whiteside, Abby. *Indispensables of Piano Playing*. New York: Coleman, Ross, 1961. Pp. 63–64.

Williams, T. D. "The Sustaining Pedal and What It Does to Piano Music." *The Etude* 39 (August 1921):500.

Wolff, Konrad. *Schnabel's Interpretation of Piano Music*. New York: W. W. Norton, 1972. Pp. 157–59.

Wolfram, Victor. *The Sostenuto Pedal*. Stillwater: Oklahoma State University, 1965.

Wright, W. Ward. "The 'Forgotten' Pedal of the Piano." *The Etude* 54 (November 1936):689–90.

INDEX

Small roman numerals following the title or opus number of a composition refer to the number of the movement. Capital letters indicate major keys; lower-case letters minor keys.